1001 BEST
SLOW COOKER
RECIPES OF ALL TIME

EMMA KATIE

Check out more books by Emma Katie at:
www.amazon.com/author/emmakatie

$\mathcal{C}$ONTENTS

Oatmeal Recipes

Beef

Pork

Lamb

Poultry

Seafood

Soups and Stews

Casseroles and Pasta Dishes

Vegetables

Rice, Beans, and Grains

Sauces

Snacks and Appetizers

Cakes

Drinks

*I*NTRODUCTION

We all want to be able to enjoy delicious, health meals regularly, but who has time to do all that cooking? We lead busy lives, and the last thing we have time for is to spend hours creating amazing meals. Or, do we have time after all? If you have a slow cooker, you can create awesome meals for your family, without having to do a lot of work or spend hours slaving over a hot stove.

When you use a slow cooker, you can prepare everything you need to make a meal before going to bed. Then, when you wake up, simply put all of the ingredients in the slow cooker, and let it do the rest of the work for you. Your meal will be cooking while you are at work, running errands, playing with the kids, etc., and your family will think you spent hours cooking for them.

You can make just about anything in a slow cooker, from breakfast foods to main courses to soups and stews to appetizers to candies and even drinks. After a while, you may end up wanting to get a few different slow cookers, so you have various sizes for different types of meals. You might even find that your slow cooker is your go-to small appliance, because it is so convenient and easy to use.

In this book, you will find recipes for breakfasts, main courses, snacks, appetizers, and drinks. We encourage you to try all of the recipes, and then to play with them and make them your own.

BENEFITS OF USING A SLOW COOKER

We can't say enough about how great cooking with a slow cooker really is. Obviously, one of the main benefits of using one is how much time and effort you save. After all, you don't have to stand at a stove, and most, if not all of the ingredients are added all at once and then left alone after that until the meal is cooked. But, saving time is just one of many benefits to having at least one slow cooker in your kitchen. Here are some other awesome benefits of using a slow cooker.

- ➢ **Prepare Meals Ahead of Time** – You may not always have time to prepare meals, and you end up eating foods that are fast and unhealthy. When you are using a slow cooker, you can prepare meals before going to bed. Then, simply place the prepared ingredients in the fridge, and take them out in the morning and start the slow cooker. When you get home from work, your meal will be all ready to eat.

- ➢ **Save Money** – Many people don't realize just how much money they can save by using a slow cooker. For instance, because food cooks slowly, meat will be tender. This means that you can buy cheaper cuts of meat, but still have them cook up fork-tender. You can also cook large amounts of food and freeze meals for later, which will save money in the long run because you are not buying ingredients for a lot of smaller meals.

- ➢ **Save Money on Energy Bills** – When you use a slow cooker instead of an oven or stove top, you use a lot less energy. This means you are going to see a reduction in your home energy bills. Slow cookers use about as much energy as a regular light bulb, as opposed to the much higher amounts of energy that other appliances use.

- ➢ **Eat Healthier** – One of the greatest things about using a slow cooker is that you don't need a lot of fat or oil when you cook. In fact, you don't have to add any oil at all. As long as there is moisture inside, your food isn't going to stick to the inside of the cooker. You can also use lean cuts of meat, because unlike with frying, the fat isn't going to cook off and drain away. You will end up eating a lot healthier because you will be consuming a lot less fat.

- ➢ **Slow Cookers are Versatile** – When most people think about using slow cookers, the first thing that comes to mind are roasts or stews. Actually, there are many things you can cook in a slow cooker. You can make all kinds of delicious meals, desserts, snacks, drinks, and more. You can even make your own yogurt, and there are some awesome bread recipes that have been created specifically for slow cookers.

- ➢ **Easy Cleanup** – A slow cooker is a lot easier to clean than other appliances, pots, or pans. All you have to do is take out the crock, submerge it in water, let it soak for a half hour or so, and then wipe it clean. In addition to being easy to clean, you also only use one pot, so you don't have a lot of pots and pans to wash later.

- ➢ **No More Burnt Food** – Because a slow cooker uses lower temperatures, you don't have to worry about your meals being burned. There will be nothing scorched, and nothing to scrape off the bottom of the pan. Most meals cook in four to eight hours, so there is no way anything is going to burn.

*I*t's Easy to Create Your Own Slow Cooker Recipes

If you are the type who loves to experiment in the kitchen, you really need to get yourself a slow cooker. There are so many great meals you can make, and you can play with any recipe to make it your own. After a while, you will be so used to cooking with this awesome small appliance that you will be coming up with all kinds of your own awesome recipes.

The thing to keep in mind when creating your own recipes is to not go too crazy at first. It is best to start out by playing around with recipes you are already using. Once you are used to substituting ingredients, you can start coming up with your own great kitchen creations. Start out by substituting one or two ingredients, and go from there.

When creating your own recipes, make sure that you keep the people who will be eating the meals in mind. Choose ingredients that your whole family loves, and everyone will be asking for seconds. It won't be long before word gets around about your amazing kitchen skills, and how your creations are the best in the neighborhood.

Here are some more things to keep in mind for when you start experimenting with your own slow cooker recipes:

- ➢ **Use "Like" Ingredients** – When choosing ingredients for your meals, make sure that you use ingredients that are going to take about the same amount of time to cook. For instance, if you are making potatoes and want to add vegetables, use carrots or turnip, which take longer to cook than other veggies.
- ➢ **Go Light on Seasonings** – The longer foods take to cook, the longer the flavors have to set in. This means that you don't need to use as much in the way of seasonings as you would if you were using other cooking methods.
- ➢ **Study other Recipes** – Not all of your kitchen experiments are going to be successful. But, your chances of success will increase when you know what you are doing. Study other slow cooker recipes, including the ones in this e-book, and get to know how foods are cooked in a slow cooker.
- ➢ **Practice** – The best way to get good at anything, including mastering the slow cooker, is to practice, practice, and practice some more. You have to make meals anyway, so why not get a lot more use out of your slow cooker, and learn how to create your own kitchen masterpieces.

SLOW COOKER TIPS

Now that you have decided to start using your slow cooker more often, you may as well get the most out of it. While this is one of the easiest small appliances to use, there are still ways that you can mess up what could be a really great meal. With this in mind, we have compiled a list of cooking tips that will help you create masterpieces every time.

> **Keep the Lid Shut** – We are always tempted to lift the lid to see how things are coming along, and of course, to have a little sample. This is a habit you need to get out of when using a slow cooker. These appliances work by locking in heat so food cooks over long periods of time. Each time you lift the lid, heat is lost, and it will take that much longer to cook your food because the slow cooker has to heat up again.

> **Go Easy on the Liquor** – Liquor in food boils off and reduces in most cases. This is not really the case when you are using a slow cooker. Instead of subtle flavors, you may find that your meals have an overpowering taste of liquor. If you are using liquor, use it to deglaze pans after browning meat, allowing the high heat to burn off the alcohol. Then, transfer the meat and liquor to the slow cooker.

> **Add Dairy Products Later** – Because dairy products tend to curdle, many recipes will tell you to add them near the end of the cooking time. For instance, if the recipes says to cook for six hours, cook for five hours, and add the dairy products during the final hour. This is a good rule to follow for fresh herbs as well.

> **Boil Off Liquids** – You may find that with some recipes, there is too much liquid left over when the food is cooked, or that the liquid is not thick enough. This is simple to fix. All you have to do is take the lid off, put the slow cooker on high, and cook for an additional 30-45 minutes. This will boil off any excess liquid.

> **Times and Temperatures may Vary** – Not all slow cookers are the same, so you may find that the time and temperature for a recipe in one slow cooker may not quite work in a different model. Don't be afraid to play around with time and temperatures once you are used to using your slow cooker.

Oatmeal Recipes

All oatmeal recipes are overnight recipes. They can be cooked in half the time by cooking on high for 4 hours.

OATMEAL

Prep time: 5-10 minutes   Cook time: 8 hours

Ingredients
½ C rolled oats   ¾ C cold water
¼ tsp coarse sea salt   ¾ C milk
¼ tsp white sugar   1 tbsp butter

Directions
Combine all ingredients together in slow cooker. Cook on low for 8 hours.

MAPLE OATMEAL

Prep time: 5 minutes   Cook time: 8 hours

Ingredients
¼ C steel-cut oats   ½ tsp butter
¾ C water   1 tbsp pure maple syrup
¼ tsp salt

Directions
Combine all ingredients together in slow cooker. Cook on low for 8 hours.

STRAWBERRY OATMEAL

Prep time: 5 minutes   Cook time: 15-20 minutes

Ingredients
1/3 C rolled oats   ¼ tsp salt
2/3 C milk   ½ tsp sugar
2 tbsp dried or frozen strawberries

Directions
Combine all ingredients together in slow cooker. Cook on low for 8 hours.

BLUEBERRY OATMEAL

Prep time: 5 minutes   Cook time: 15-20 minutes

Ingredients
1/3 C rolled oats   ¼ tsp salt
2/3 C milk   ½ tsp sugar
2 tbsp dried or frozen blueberries

Directions
Combine all ingredients together in slow cooker. Cook on low for 8 hours.

PEACHES AND CREAM OATMEAL

Prep time: 5 minutes   Cook time: 8 hours

Ingredients
1/3 C rolled oats   ¼ tsp salt
2/3 C milk   ½ tsp sugar
2 tbsp chopped canned peaches

Directions
Combine all ingredients together in slow cooker. Cook on low for 8 hours.

HONEY OATMEAL

Prep time: 5 minutes   Cook time: 8 hours

Ingredients
1/3 C rolled oats   ¼ tsp salt
2/3 C milk   ½ tsp sugar
2 tbsp raw honey

Directions
Combine all ingredients together in slow cooker. Cook on low for 8 hours.

FUDGE OATMEAL

Prep time: 5 minutes   Cook time: 8 hours

Ingredients
1/3 C rolled oats   ½ tsp sugar
2/3 C milk   ½ C fudge sauce
¼ tsp salt

Directions
Combine all ingredients together in slow cooker. Cook on low for 8 hours.

CARROT CAKE OATMEAL

Prep time: 5 minutes   Cook time: 8 hours

Ingredients
4 C water   3 tbsp pure maple syrup
1 C grated carrots   1 tbsp butter
1 C steel cut oats   2 tsp cinnamon
½ C raisins   ¼ tsp salt

Directions
Combine all ingredients together in slow cooker. Cook on low for 8 hours.

ALMOND OATMEAL

Prep time: 5 minutes

Cook time: 8 hours

Ingredients
1 C steel cut oats
3 ½ C milk
¼ C toasted, shredded coconut

¼ C mini chocolate chips
¼ C sliced almonds
¼ tsp salt

Directions
Combine all ingredients together in slow cooker. Cook on low for 8 hours.

CINNAMON APPLE OATMEAL

Prep time: 5 minutes

Cook time: 8 hours

Ingredients
1 C steel cut oats
3 ½ C water
1 large apple (peeled, cored, and diced)

2 tbsp light brown sugar
1 tbsp ground cinnamon
¼ tsp salt

Directions
Combine all ingredients together in slow cooker. Cook on low for 8 hours.

BACON AND EGGS OATMEAL

Prep time: 10 minutes

Cook time: 8 hours

Ingredients
2 poached eggs (see poached eggs recipe)
½ pound bacon, chopped (weight before cooking)
1 C steel cut oats

3 C water
1 tbsp butter
¼ tsp salt
½ C grated sharp cheddar cheese

Directions
Cook bacon in a skillet, reserve 1 tbsp fat, set aside. Combine all ingredients, including bacon, together in slow cooker. Cook on low for 8 hours.

CINNAMON OATMEAL

Prep time: 10 minutes

Cook time: 8 hours

Ingredients
1 C steel cut oats
3 C water
½ C half & half

2 tbsp sugar
2 tsp ground cinnamon

Directions
Combine all ingredients together in slow cooker. Cook on low for 8 hours.

Brown Sugar Oatmeal

Prep time: 10 minutes

Cook time: 8 hours

Ingredients

1 C steel cut oats
3 C water
½ C light cream

4 tbsp brown sugar
¼ tsp salt

Directions

Combine all ingredients together in slow cooker. Cook on low for 8 hours.

Raspberry Oatmeal

Prep time: 10 minutes

Cook time: 8 hours

Ingredients

1 C steel cut oats
3 C water
½ C light cream

2 tbsp brown sugar
½ C fresh raspberries
¼ tsp salt

Directions

Combine all ingredients together in slow cooker. Cook on low for 8 hours.

Fruit and Nut Oatmeal

Prep time: 10 minutes

Cook time: 8 hours

Ingredients

1 C steel cut oats
3 C water
½ C half & half
2 tbsp brown sugar

¼ tsp salt
½ C chopped apples, peaches, pears, etc.
½ C chopped walnuts

Directions

Combine all ingredients together in slow cooker. Cook on low for 8 hours.

Cashew Oatmeal

Prep time: 10 minutes

Cook time: 8 hours

Ingredients

1 C steel cut oats
3 C water
½ C milk

2 tbsp brown sugar
¼ tsp salt
1 ½ C toasted, unsalted cashews

Directions

Combine all ingredients together in slow cooker. Cook on low for 8 hours.

PEANUT BUTTER OATMEAL

Prep time: 10 minutes

Cook time: 8 hours

Ingredients
1 C steel cut oats
3 C water

½ C peanut butter
2 tbsp brown sugar

Directions
Combine all ingredients together in slow cooker. Cook on low for 8 hours.

GRAPE JELLY OATMEAL

Prep time: 10 minutes

Cook time: 8 hours

Ingredients
1 C steel cut oats
3 C water
½ C milk

2 tbsp brown sugar
¼ tsp salt
½ C grape jelly

Directions
Combine all ingredients together in slow cooker. Cook on low for 8 hours.

PEACH OATMEAL

Prep time: 10 minutes

Cook time: 8 hours

Ingredients
1 C steel cut oats
3 C water
1 small can diced peaches in water or juice, not drained

2 tbsp brown sugar
¼ tsp salt

Directions
Saute butter in the pressure cooker. When butter is melted, add oats to toast them, stirring continuously until they give off a nutty odor. Add remaining ingredients and cook on high pressure for 10 minutes. Use the natural release for 10 minutes, followed by a quick pressure release. Let sit for 5-10 minutes.

FRUIT COCKTAIL OATMEAL

Prep time: 10 minutes

Cook time: 8 hours

Ingredients
1 C steel cut oats
3 C water
1 Can fruit cocktail in juice, not drained

2 tbsp Karo syrup
¼ tsp salt

Directions
Combine all ingredients together in slow cooker. Cook on low for 8 hours.

Oatmeal with Granola

Prep time: 10 minutes   Cook time: 8 hours

Ingredients
1 C steel cut oats
3 C water
½ C light cream

2 tbsp brown sugar
1 C granola cereal
¼ tsp salt

Directions
Combine all ingredients except granola together in slow cooker. Cook on low for 8 hours. Stir in granola before serving.

Oatmeal with Raisins

Prep time: 10 minutes   Cook time: 8 hours

Ingredients
1 C steel cut oats
3 C water
½ C light cream

½ C raisins
1 tbsp brown sugar
¼ tsp salt

Directions
Combine all ingredients together in slow cooker. Cook on low for 8 hours.

Chocolate Chip Oatmeal

Prep time: 10 minutes   Cook time: 8 hours

Ingredients
1 C steel cut oats
3 C water
½ C half & half

½ C chocolate chips
2 tsp brown sugar
¼ tsp salt

Directions
Combine all ingredients together in slow cooker. Cook on low for 8 hours.

S'mores Oatmeal

Prep time: 10 minutes   Cook time: 8 hours

Ingredients
1 C steel cut oats
3 C water
½ C half & half
¼ C chocolate chips

¼ C mini marshmallows
¼ C broken graham crackers
¼ tsp salt

Directions
Combine all ingredients together in slow cooker. Cook on low for 8 hours.

CAMP OATMEAL

Prep time: 10 minutes   Cook time: 8 hours

Ingredients
1 C steel cut oats   1 tbsp brown sugar
3 ½ C water   ¼ tsp salt
1 ½ C mixed frozen berries, thawed

Directions
Combine all ingredients except berries together in slow cooker. Cook on low for 8 hours. Stir in berries before serving.

FRUIT SNACK OATMEAL

Prep time: 10 minutes   Cook time: 8 hours

Ingredients
1 C steel cut oats   ½ C fruit snacks
3 C water   2 tsp brown sugar
½ C skim milk   ¼ tsp salt

Directions
Combine all ingredients together in slow cooker. Cook on low for 8 hours.

SAUSAGE OATMEAL

Prep time: 10 minutes   Cook time: 8 hours

Ingredients
1 C steel cut oats   ½ C half & half
3 C water   2 tbsp pure maple syrup
2-3 breakfast sausages, cooked and chopped   ¼ tsp salt

Directions
Combine all ingredients together in slow cooker. Cook on low for 8 hours.

WILD BERRY OATMEAL

Prep time: 10 minutes   Cook time: 8 hours

Ingredients
1 C steel cut oats   1 C mixed wild berries
3 C water   2 tbsp brown sugar
½ C whole milk   ¼ tsp salt

Directions
Combine all ingredients together in slow cooker. Cook on low for 8 hours.

LOADED OATMEAL

Prep time: 10 minutes   Cook time: 8 hours

Ingredients

1 ½ C steel cut oats   ½ C mixed, unsalted nuts
4 C water   ½ C chocolate chips
1 C mixed fruit   ¼ tsp salt

Directions

Combine all ingredients together in slow cooker. Cook on low for 8 hours.

OATMEAL WITH FRUIT AND WHIPPED CREAM

Prep time: 10 minutes   Cook time: 8 hours

Ingredients

1 C steel cut oats   1 tsp brown sugar
3 C water   ¼ tsp salt
½ C half & half   1 C whipped cream
½ C mixed chopped fruit

Directions

Combine all ingredients except whipped cream together in slow cooker. Cook on low for 8 hours. Top with whipped cream before serving.

CITRUS OATMEAL

Prep time: 10 minutes   Cook time: 8 hours

Ingredients

1 C steel cut oats   1 can pineapple, drained
2 ½ C water   ¼ tsp salt
1 C orange juice

Directions

Combine all ingredients together in slow cooker. Cook on low for 8 hours.

CRANBERRY OATMEAL

Prep time: 10 minutes   Cook time: 8 hours

Ingredients

1 C steel cut oats   1 C fresh cranberries
3 C water   1 tsp ground cinnamon
½ C orange juice

Directions

Combine all ingredients together in slow cooker. Cook on low for 8 hours.

Coconut Oatmeal

Prep time: 10 minutes

Cook time: 8 hours

Ingredients

1 C steel cut oats
3 C water
½ C coconut milk

1 C toasted coconut
¼ tsp salt

Directions

Combine all ingredients together in slow cooker. Cook on low for 8 hours.

Strawberry Jam Oatmeal

Prep time: 10 minutes

Cook time: 8 hours

Ingredients

1 C steel cut oats
3 ½ C water

3 tbsp strawberry jam

Directions

Combine all ingredients together in slow cooker. Cook on low for 8 hours.

Buttery Oatmeal

Prep time: 10 minutes

Cook time: 8 hours

Ingredients

1 C steel cut oats
3 C water

½ C butter
¼ tsp salt

Directions

Combine all ingredients together in slow cooker. Cook on low for 8 hours.

Corn Syrup Oatmeal

Prep time: 10 minutes

Cook time: 8 hours

Ingredients

1 C steel cut oats
3 C water

½ C corn syrup

Directions

Combine oats and water together in slow cooker. Cook on low for 8 hours. Add corn syrup before serving.

GUMMY BEAR OATMEAL

Prep time: 10 minutes

Cook time: 8 hours

Ingredients

1 C steel cut oats
3 C water
½ C orange juice
1 can pineapple, drained

1 can mandarin oranges, drained
½ C gummy bears
¼ tsp salt

Directions

Combine all ingredients except gummy bears together in slow cooker. Cook on low for 8 hours. Stir in gummy bears before serving.

WALNUT OATMEAL

Prep time: 10 minutes

Cook time: 8 hours

Ingredients

1 C steel cut oats
3 C water

½ C walnuts
¼ tsp salt

Directions

Combine all ingredients together in slow cooker. Cook on low for 8 hours.

PEANUT OATMEAL

Prep time: 10 minutes

Cook time: 8 hours

Ingredients

1 C steel cut oats
3 C water
½ C apple juice juice

1 can pineapple, drained
¼ tsp salt

Directions

Combine all ingredients together in slow cooker. Cook on low for 8 hours.

Chocolate Oatmeal

Prep time: 10 minutes

Cook time: 8 hours

Ingredients

1 C steel cut oats
3 C water

½ C chocolate syrup
¼ tsp salt

Directions

Combine all ingredients together in slow cooker. Cook on low for 8 hours.

COFFEE OATMEAL

Prep time: 10 minutes

Cook time: 8 hours

Ingredients

1 C steel cut oats
3 C water

½ C black coffee
1 tbsp white sugar

Directions

Combine all ingredients together in slow cooker. Cook on low for 8 hours.

PISTACHIO OATMEAL

Prep time: 10 minutes

Cook time: 8 hours

Ingredients

1 C steel cut oats
3 C water

½ C chopped pistachios
1 tbsp brown sugar

Directions

Combine all ingredients together in slow cooker. Cook on low for 8 hours.

CHEERIOS OATMEAL

Prep time: 10 minutes

Cook time: 8 hours

Ingredients

1 C steel cut oats
3 C water
½ C orange juice

1 C Cheerios
1 tbsp white sugar

Directions

Combine all ingredients except Cheerios together in slow cooker. Cook on low for 8 hours. Stir in Cheerios before serving.

GRANOLA OATMEAL

Prep time: 10 minutes

Cook time: 8 hours

Ingredients

1 C steel cut oats
3 C water
½ C orange juice
½ C raisins

½ C nuts
1 tbsp brown sugar
1 C granola cereal
¼ tsp salt

Directions

Combine all ingredients except granola together in slow cooker. Cook on low for 8 hours. Stir in granola before serving.

PUMPKIN OATMEAL

Prep time: 10 minutes

Cook time: 8 hours

Ingredients

1 C steel cut oats
3 C water
½ C pumpkin puree
1 tbsp brown sugar

½ tsp ground nutmeg
½ tsp ground cinnamon
¼ tsp salt

Directions

Combine all ingredients together in slow cooker. Cook on low for 8 hours.

DRIED FRUIT OATMEAL

Prep time: 10 minutes

Cook time: 8 hours

Ingredients

2 C steel cut oats
6 C water
1 C orange juice
¼ C dried pineapple

¼ C dried apples, chopped
¼ C dried cranberries
¼ tsp salt

Directions

Combine all ingredients together in slow cooker. Cook on low for 8 hours.

KIDS' OATMEAL

Prep time: 10 minutes

Cook time: 8 hours

Ingredients

1 C steel cut oats
3 C water
½ C orange juice

½ C dried apples, chopped
½ C mini chocolate chips
¼ tsp salt

Directions

Combine all ingredients together in slow cooker. Cook on low for 8 hours.

GINGERBREAD OATMEAL

Prep time: 10 minutes

Cook time: 8 hours

Ingredients

1 C steel cut oats
3 C water
½ C orange juice

1 tsp ground ginger
½ tsp ground cinnamon
2 tbsp brown sugar

Directions

Combine all ingredients together in slow cooker. Cook on low for 8 hours.

BROWNIE OATMEAL

Prep time: 10 minutes

Cook time: 8 hours

Ingredients

1 C steel cut oats
3 C water
½ C whole milk

1 tbsp white sugar
3-4 small brownies, chopped
¼ tsp salt

Directions

Combine all ingredients except brownies together in slow cooker. Cook on low for 8 hours. Stir brownies in before serving.

CRUNCHY OATMEAL

Prep time: 10 minutes

Cook time: 8 hours

Ingredients

1 C steel cut oats
3 C water
½ C orange juice

1 can pineapple, drained
1 C toasted Chinese noodles
¼ tsp salt

Directions

Combine all ingredients except Chinese noodles together in slow cooker. Cook on low for 8 hours. Stir in crunchy noodles before serving.

BASIC QUINOA

Prep time: 5 minutes

Cook time: 6-8 hours

Ingredients

1 ½ C raw quinoa, rinsed
2 ¼ C water
2 tbsp pure maple syrup

½ tsp vanilla extract
¼ tsp ground cinnamon
¼ tsp salt

Directions

Combine all ingredients in slow cooker. Cook on low for 6-8 hours.

QUINOA WITH BLUEBERRIES

Prep time: 5 minutes

Cook time: 6-8 hours

Ingredients

1 ½ C raw quinoa, rinsed
2 ¼ C water
2 tbsp pure maple syrup

½ tsp vanilla extract
½ tsp ground cinnamon
½ C blueberries

Directions

Combine all ingredients in slow cooker. Cook on low for 6-8 hours.

QUINOA WITH BROWN SUGAR

Prep time: 5 minutes

Cook time: 6-8 hours

Ingredients

1 ½ C raw quinoa, rinsed
2 ¼ C water
2 tbsp brown sugar

½ tsp vanilla extract
¼ tsp salt

Directions

Combine all ingredients in slow cooker. Cook on low for 6-8 hours.

QUINOA AND GRANOLA

Prep time: 5 minutes

Cook time: 6-8 hours

Ingredients

1 ½ C raw quinoa, rinsed
2 ¼ C water
2 tbsp pure maple syrup
½ tsp vanilla extract

¼ tsp ground cinnamon
¼ tsp salt
½ C granola

Directions

Combine all ingredients in slow cooker. Cook on low for 6-8 hours.

QUINOA WITH NUTS AND RAISINS

Prep time: 5 minutes

Cook time: 6-8 hours

Ingredients

1 ½ C raw quinoa, rinsed
2 ¼ C water
2 tbsp raw honey
½ C raisins
½ C mixed chopped nuts

½ tsp vanilla extract
¼ tsp ground cinnamon
¼ tsp salt
½ C granola

Directions

Combine all ingredients in slow cooker. Cook on low for 6-8 hours.

CRUNCHY QUINOA WITH RAISINS

Prep time: 5 minutes

Cook time: 6-8 hours

Ingredients

1 ½ C raw quinoa, rinsed
2 ¼ C water
2 tbsp raw honey

½ C crunchy granola cereal
½ C raisins

Directions

Combine all ingredients in slow cooker. Cook on low for 6-8 hours.

QUINOA WITH GRAPE JELLY

Prep time: 5 minutes

Cook time: 6-8 hours

Ingredients

1 ½ C raw quinoa, rinsed
2 ¼ C water
2 tbsp pure maple syrup
½ tsp vanilla extract

¼ tsp ground cinnamon
¼ tsp salt
½ C jelly (your choice)

Directions

Combine all ingredients except jelly in slow cooker. Cook on low for 6-8 hours. Stir in jelly before serving.

PEANUT BUTTER QUINOA

Prep time: 5 minutes

Cook time: 6-8 hours

Ingredients

1 ½ C raw quinoa, rinsed
2 ¼ C water
2 tbsp peanut butter

½ tsp vanilla extract
¼ tsp salt
½ C granola

Directions

Combine all ingredients except granola in slow cooker. Cook on low for 6-8 hours. Stir in granola and serve.

QUINOA WITH BERRIES

Prep time: 5 minutes

Cook time: 6-8 hours

Ingredients

1 ½ C raw quinoa, rinsed
2 ¼ C water
2 tbsp brown sugar
½ tsp vanilla extract

¼ tsp ground cinnamon
½ C mixed berries
¼ tsp salt

Directions

Combine all ingredients except berries in slow cooker. Cook on low for 6-8 hours. Stir in berries and serve.

QUINOA WITH JAM

Prep time: 5 minutes

Cook time: 6-8 hours

Ingredients

1 ½ C raw quinoa, rinsed
2 ¼ C water
2 tbsp brown sugar
½ tsp vanilla extract

¼ tsp ground cinnamon
2 tbsp jam
¼ tsp salt

Directions

Combine all ingredients except jam in slow cooker. Cook on low for 6-8 hours. Stir in jam and serve.

Peanut Butter and Jam Quinoa

Prep time: 5 minutes

Cook time: 6-8 hours

Ingredients

1 ½ C raw quinoa, rinsed
2 ¼ C water
2 tbsp brown sugar
½ tsp vanilla extract

¼ tsp ground cinnamon
2 tbsp peanut butter
2 tbsp jam
¼ tsp salt

Directions

Combine all ingredients except peanut butter jam in slow cooker. Cook on low for 6-8 hours. Stir in peanut butter and jam and serve.

Quinoa with Fruit

Prep time: 5 minutes

Cook time: 6-8 hours

Ingredients

1 ½ C raw quinoa, rinsed
2 ¼ C water
2 tbsp maple syrup
½ tsp vanilla extract

¼ tsp ground cinnamon
1 C chopped apples, peaches, bananas, etc.
¼ tsp salt

Directions

Combine all ingredients except fruit in slow cooker. Cook on low for 6-8 hours. Stir in fruit and serve.

Trail Mix Quinoa

Prep time: 5 minutes

Cook time: 6-8 hours

Ingredients

1 ½ C raw quinoa, rinsed
2 ¼ C water
2 tbsp brown sugar
½ tsp vanilla extract

¼ tsp ground cinnamon
½ mixed seeds and nuts
½ C raisins

Directions

Combine first 4 ingredients except jam in slow cooker. Cook on low for 6-8 hours. Stir in remaining ingredients and serve.

BROWN RICE CEREAL

Prep time: 5 minutes

Cook time: 6-8 hours

Ingredients

2 C brown rice (if you can get sweet brown rice, all the better)
1 C black or red quinoa
1 tsp sea salt

5 ½ C water
¼ C coconut oil
¼ C Xagave

Directions

Combine first 4 ingredients except jam in slow cooker. Cook on low for 6-8 hours. Add coconut oil and Xagave, stir, cover, and let sit for 5-10 minutes to thicken.

MAPLE BROWN RICE CEREAL

Prep time: 5 minutes

Cook time: 6-8 hours

Ingredients

2 C brown rice (if you can get sweet brown rice, all the better)
1 C black or red quinoa
1 tsp sea salt

5 ½ C water
¼ C coconut oil
¼ C maple syrup

Directions

Combine first 4 ingredients except jam in slow cooker. Cook on low for 6-8 hours. Add coconut oil and maple syrup, stir, cover, and let sit for 5-10 minutes to thicken.

GLUTEN-FREE CEREAL 1

Prep time: 5 minutes

Cook time: 6-8 hours

Ingredients

1 C black or red quinoa
5 ½ C water

1 tsp salt

Directions

Combine all ingredients in slow cooker. Cook on low for 6-8 hours.

GLUTEN-FREE CEREAL 2

Prep time: 5 minutes

Cook time: 6-8 hours

Directions

2 C sweet brown rice
1 C red quinoa
5 C water

½ tsp salt
1 tbsp brown sugar

Directions

Combine all ingredients in slow cooker. Cook on low for 6-8 hours.

GLUTE-FREE CEREAL 3

Prep time: 5 minutes

Cook time: 6-8 hours

Ingredients

3 tbsp rolled oats
3 tbsp millet
3 tbsp quinoa
1 C water
4 ½ tsp amaranth

1 C milk
2 tbsp yeast
½ tsp paprika
Salt and pepper to taste

Directions

Combine all ingredients in slow cooker. Cook on low for 6-8 hours.

FRUITY BREAKFAST RISOTTO

Prep time: 5 minutes

Cook time: 6-8 hours

Ingredients

1 ½ C Arborio rice
2 large apples, cored and diced
1/3 C brown sugar
1 C apple juice
3 C milk

½ C dried fruit (pineapples, cherries, strawberries, cranberries, etc.)
2 tsp ground cinnamon
¼ tsp salt

Directions

Combine all ingredients except fruit in slow cooker. Cook on low for 6-8 hours. Stir in fruit before serving.

KAMUT

Prep time: 5 minutes

Cook time: 6-8 hours

Ingredients

1 C uncooked kamut
3 C water

2 tbsp canola oil

Directions

Combine all ingredients in slow cooker. Cook on low for 6-8 hours.

Beef

Roast Beef 1

Prep time: 10 minutes

Cook time: 6-8 hours

Ingredients
2 pounds roast beef
2 C beef broth

Salt and pepper to taste

Directions
Place all ingredients together in slow cooker. Cook on low for 6-8 hours.

Roast Beef 2

Prep time: 10 minutes

Cook time: 6-8 hours

Ingredients
2 pounds roast beef
1 C beef broth
1 C tomato juice

1 large onion, sliced
1 garlic clove, minced
Salt and pepper to taste

Directions
Place all ingredients together in slow cooker. Cook on low for 6-8 hours.

Roast Beef 3

Prep time: 10 minutes

Cook time: 6-8 hours

Ingredients
2 pounds roast beef
1 large onion, sliced
1 packet taco seasoning

2 C beef broth
Salt and pepper to taste

Directions
Place all ingredients together in slow cooker. Cook on low for 6-8 hours.

Roast Beef 4

Prep time: 10 minutes

Cook time: 6-8 hours

Ingredients
2 pounds roast beef
2 C beef broth
1 can cream of mushroom soup

2 large carrots, cut into 1" pieces
Salt and pepper to taste

Directions
Place all ingredients except carrots together in slow cooker. Cook on low for 4-5 hours. Add carrots and cook another 2-3 hours.

ROAST BEEF 5

Prep time: 10 minutes

Cook time: 6-8 hours

Ingredients

2 pounds roast beef
2 C water
3 tbsp beef bouillon powder
1 tsp garlic powder

1 tsp onion powder
1 tbsp soya sauce
½ tsp ground black pepper

Directions

Place all ingredients together in slow cooker. Cook on low for 6-8 hours.

ROAST BEEF 6

Prep time: 10 minutes

Cook time: 6-8 hours

Ingredients

2 pounds roast beef
2 C beef broth

2 cans cream of beef soup
Salt and pepper to taste

Directions

Place all ingredients together in slow cooker. Cook on low for 6-8 hours.

ROAST BEEF 7

Prep time: 10 minutes

Cook time: 6-8 hours

Ingredients

2 pounds roast beef
1 C beef broth
2 C tomato sauce
1 tbsp beef bouillon powder

1 leek, chopped
1 garlic clove, minced
1 tbsp hot sauce
Salt and pepper to taste

Directions

Place all ingredients together in slow cooker. Cook on low for 6-8 hours.

ROAST BEEF 8

Prep time: 10 minutes

Cook time: 6-8 hours

Ingredients

2 pounds roast beef
1 C beef broth
1 C apple juice
1 C water

1 small onion, sliced
1 garlic clove, minced
Salt and pepper to taste

Directions

Place all ingredients together in slow cooker. Cook on low for 6-8 hours.

Roast Beef 9

Prep time: 10 minutes

Cook time: 6-8 hours

Ingredients
2 pounds roast beef
1 C beef broth
1 C water
1 can beef gravy

1 large onion, sliced
2 garlic cloves, minced
Salt and pepper to taste

Directions
Place all ingredients together in slow cooker. Cook on low for 6-8 hours.

Roast Beef 10

Prep time: 10 minutes

Cook time: 6-8 hours

Ingredients
2 pounds roast beef
1 C beef broth
2 C tomato sauce
3 tbsp raw honey
1 leek, chopped

1 celery stalk, chopped
1 garlic clove, minced
1 tbsp hot sauce
Salt and pepper to taste
2 C chopped broccoli

Directions
Place all ingredients except broccoli together in slow cooker. Cook on low for 6-8 hours. Stir in broccoli and heat for a few minutes.

Beef Stroganoff

Prep time: 15 minutes

Cook time: 3-4 hours

Ingredients
2 pounds beef stew meat, cut into 1" cubes and browned
1 C sour cream
1 C beef broth
2 tbsp flour
1 tbsp Worcestershire sauce

2 tbsp tomato paste
¼ pound fresh mushrooms, sliced
1 package cooked egg noodles
1 onion, chopped
1 tsp garlic powder
Salt and pepper to taste

Directions
Place all ingredients except noodles together in slow cooker. Cook on low for 3-4 hours. Stir in noodles and heat through.

HUNGARIAN GOULASH

Prep time: 20 minutes

Cook time: 3-4 hours

Ingredients

½ pound lean beef, cut into small chunks and browned
½ C finely diced bacon
1 ½ C chopped onion
2 potatoes, peeled and chopped

2 cloves garlic, minced
½ tsp paprika
Salt and pepper to taste
1 package cooked egg noodles

Directions

Place all ingredients except noodles together in slow cooker. Cook on low for 6-8 hours. Stir in noodles and heat through.

SHREDDED BEEF SLOPPY JOES

Prep time: 10 minutes

Cook time: 6-8 hours

Ingredients

2 pounds boneless chuck
1 C barbecue sauce
½ C red chili sauce

½ C water
1 chopped onion

Directions

Place all ingredients together in slow cooker. Cook on low for 6-8 hours. Shred meat and serve on toasted buns.

SKIRT STEAK WITH POTATOES

Prep time: 10 minutes

Cook time: 4-6 hours

Ingredients

1 pound skirt steak, browned
1 tbsp soya sauce
1 tsp onion powder
½ tsp garlic powder

½ tsp black pepper
3-4 medium potatoes, sliced
Water

Directions

Place all ingredients together in slow cooker. Cook on low for 4-6 hours.

BALSAMIC STEAK

Prep time: 15 minutes

Cook time: 8-10 hours

Ingredients

1 pound steak, browned
½ C balsamic vinegar, or you can use balsamic salad dressing for a tangy twist

2 tbsp. soya sauce
1 tsp ground black pepper
1 tsp salt

1 tsp onion powder
1 tsp garlic powder

¾ tsp cayenne
½ tsp paprika

Directions

Place all ingredients together in slow cooker. Cook on low for 8-10 hours.

HOT AND SWEET STEAK

Prep time: 10 minutes

Cook time: 4-6 hours

Ingredients

1 pound steak, browned
½ C Soya sauce
¼ C Lemon juice
¼ C Red wine vinegar
½ C Brown sugar

2 tbsp. Worcestershire sauce
½ tsp ground black pepper
1 tbsp. Yellow mustard
1 Garlic clove
1 Small onion

Directions

Place all ingredients together in slow cooker. Cook on low for 4-6 hours.

TERIYAKI STEAK 1

Prep time: 10 minutes

Cook time: 4-6 hours

Ingredients

2 pounds round steak, browned
¼ C teriyaki sauce
2 tbsp. Soya sauce
¼ C orange juice

½ C brown sugar
½ tsp garlic powder
½ tsp ground ginger
2 tsp yellow mustard

Directions

Place all ingredients together in slow cooker. Cook on low for 4-6 hours.

TERIYAKI STEAK 2

Prep time: 10 minutes

Cook time: 4-6 hours

Ingredients

1 pound steak, sliced
2 tbsp extra virgin olive oil
½ C Teriyaki sauce
¼ C Soya sauce

½ C Orange juice
1 C Brown sugar
1 tsp ground ginger
½ tsp garlic powder

Directions

Place all ingredients together in slow cooker. Cook on low for 4-6 hours.

Steak with Spice Rub

Prep time: 10 minutes + 12 hours

Cook time: 4-6 hours

Ingredients

1 pound steak
½ tsp salt
½ tsp ground black pepper
½ tsp garlic powder

½ tsp onion powder
½ tsp paprika
1 tbsp brown sugar
1 C water

Directions

Mix seasonings together and rub into meat. Refrigerate overnight, then brown before putting in slow cooker. Place all ingredients together in slow cooker. Cook on low for 4-6 hours.

Barbecue Skirt Steak

Prep time: 10 minutes

Cook time: 4-6 hours

Ingredients

1 pound skirt steak, browned
1 C ketchup
¼ C white vinegar
¼ C honey
½ C brown Sugar

1 tsp garlic powder
1 tsp chili powder
Salt and pepper to taste
1 tsp liquid smoke

Directions

Mix seasonings together and rub into meat. Refrigerate overnight and brown before placing in slow cooker. Place all ingredients together in slow cooker. Cook on low for 4-6 hours.

Pepper Steak

Prep time: 15 minutes

Cook time: 4-6 hours

Ingredients

2 pounds beef sirloin, cut into strips and browned
½ tsp garlic powder
1 beef bouillon cube
1 small onion, chopped
1 green pepper, chopped

1 large can stewed, diced tomatoes in liquid
3 tbsp soya sauce
1 tsp sugar
1 tsp salt
1 tbsp corn starch
¼ C hot water

Directions

Mix bouillon cube with water until it dissolves, and add the rest of the seasonings. Place all ingredients together in slow cooker. Cook on low for 4-6 hours.

STEAK WITH BABY POTATOES

Prep time: 10 minutes + 12 hours

Cook time: 4-6 hours

Ingredients

1 pound steak, browned
8-10 baby potatoes, washed and unpeeled
1 tbsp soya sauce
½ tsp black pepper

1 small onion, diced
1 garlic clove, minced
Water

Directions

Mix seasonings together and rub into meat. Refrigerate overnight and brown before placing in slow cooker. Place all ingredients together in slow cooker. Cook on low for 4-6 hours.

BEER MARINATED STEAK

Prep time: 10 minutes + 12 hours

Cook time: 4-6 hours

Directions

1 pound steak
1 can of beer
2 tbsp Olive oil
1 tbsp Soya sauce

1 tbsp. brown sugar
1 tsp minced garlic
½ tsp black pepper
1 small onion, chopped

Directions

Mix beer, soya sauce, brown sugar, and pepper, and marinate meat overnight. Brown before placing in slow cooker. Place all ingredients together in slow cooker. Cook on low for 4-6 hours.

SIMPLE FLANK STEAK

Prep time: 10 minutes

Cook time: 4-6 hours

Ingredients

1 pound flank steak, browned
1 cube beef bullion
1 C water

1 tbsp soya sauce
1 clove garlic, finely chopped
½ tsp black pepper

Directions

Place all ingredients together in slow cooker. Cook on low for 4-6 hours.

FILET MIGNON WITH LEMON AND GARLIC

Prep time: 10 minutes

Cook time: 4-6 hours

Ingredients

1 pound beef tenderloin, browned
½ C soya sauce
¼ C brown sugar

2 tbsp. lemon juice
3 cloves fresh minced garlic
½ tsp ground black pepper

Directions

Place all ingredients together in slow cooker. Cook on low for 4-6 hours.

SPICE RUBBED FILET MIGNON

Prep time: 10 minutes + 4 hours

Cook time: 4-6 hours

Ingredients

1 pound beef tenderloin, browned
Uncooked bacon
1 tsp salt
½ tsp ground black pepper

½ tsp garlic powder
½ tsp onion powder
½ tsp chili powder

Directions

Mix spices and rub into meat, and wrap meat with bacon (hold in place with toothpicks). Refrigerate for 4 hours. Brown before placing in slow cooker. Place all ingredients together in slow cooker. Cook on low for 4-6 hours.

MARINATED FILET MIGNON

Prep time: 10 minutes + 12 hours

Cook time: 4-6 hours

Ingredients

1 pound beef tenderloin, browned
½ C soya sauce
¼ C white vinegar

½ C packed brown sugar
¼ C water
1 tsp garlic powder

Directions

Mix soya sauce, vinegar, brown sugar, and garlic powder. Add beef and marinate overnight. Brown before placing in slow cooker. Place all ingredients together in slow cooker. Cook on low for 4-6 hours.

PORTERHOUSE STEAK

Prep time: 10 minutes

Cook time: 4-6 hours

Ingredients

1 pound porterhouse steak, browned
2 tbsp extra virgin olive oil
2 tsp sea salt

1 tsp black pepper
1 C water

Directions

Place all ingredients together in slow cooker. Cook on low for 4-6 hours.

Spicy Porterhouse Steak

Prep time: 10 minutes + 12 hours

Cook time: 4-6 hours

Ingredients

1 pound porterhouse steak
1 small onion, diced
½ C cooking sherry
½ C ketchup
¼ C molasses
¼ C brown sugar
1 tbsp. yellow mustard

1 tbsp. cider vinegar
1 tsp chili powder
1 tsp Salt
1 tsp paprika
1 tsp cayenne pepper
½ tsp black pepper
½ C water

Directions

Combine cooking sherry, ketchup, molasses, brown sugar, mustard, vinegar, seasonings, and water. Add meat and marinate overnight. Brown before placing in slow cooker. Place all ingredients, including marinade, together in slow cooker. Cook on low for 4-6 hours.

Tangy & Sweet Porterhouse Steak

Prep time: 15 minutes

Cook time: 4-6 hours

Ingredients

1 pound porterhouse steak, browned
1 small onion, diced
1 garlic clove, minced
1 C A-1 Steak sauce

1 tbsp soya sauce
½ C Italian dressing
½ C honey
½ C water

Directions

Place all ingredients together in slow cooker. Cook on low for 4-6 hours.

Seasoned Tenderloin Steak

Prep time: 10 minutes + 4 hours

Cook time: 4-6 hours

Ingredients

1 pound tenderloin steak, browned
½ tsp ground black pepper
½ tsp garlic powder
½ tsp onion powder
½ tsp paprika

½ tsp chili powder
½ tsp cayenne pepper
1 tbsp. brown sugar
1 tbsp soya sauce
1 C water

Directions

Mix seasonings and rub into meat. Refrigerate for at least 4 hours before browning. Place all ingredients together in slow cooker. Cook on low for 4-6 hours.

Seasoned Ribeye Steak

Prep time: 10 minutes + 4 hours

Cook time: 4-6 hours

Ingredients
1 pound ribeye steak, browned
½ tsp salt
½ tsp ground black pepper
½ tsp garlic powder

½ tsp onion powder
½ tsp Montreal steak spice
1 tbsp. brown sugar
1 C water

Directions
Mix seasonings and rub into meat. Refrigerate for at least 4 hours before browning. Place all ingredients together in slow cooker. Cook on low for 4-6 hours.

Flank Steak

Prep time: 10 minutes + 4 hours

Cook time: 4-6 hours

Ingredients
1 pound flank steak, browned
2 tbsp extra virgin olive oil
½ tsp salt
½ tsp ground black pepper

½ tsp garlic powder
½ tsp onion powder
1 tbsp. brown sugar
1 C water

Directions
Mix seasonings and rub into meat. Refrigerate for at least 4 hours before browning. Place all ingredients together in slow cooker. Cook on low for 4-6 hours.

Herbed Ribeye Steak

Prep time: 10 minutes + 4 hours

Cook time: 4-6 hours

Ingredients
1 pound ribeye steak, browned
½ tsp salt
½ tsp ground black pepper

½ tsp garlic powder
½ tsp onion powder
1 C water

Directions
Mix seasonings and rub into meat. Refrigerate for at least 4 hours before browning. Place all ingredients together in slow cooker. Cook on low for 4-6 hours.

HERBED PORTERHOUSE STEAK

Prep time: 10 minutes + 4 hours

Cook time: 4-6 hours

Ingredients

1 pound porterhouse steak, browned
½ tsp salt
½ tsp ground black pepper
½ tsp garlic powder
½ tsp cumin
½ tsp chili powder

½ tsp barbecue seasoning
¼ tsp celery salt
½ tsp onion powder
½ tsp paprika
1 tbsp. brown sugar
1 C water

Directions

Mix seasonings and rub into meat. Refrigerate for at least 4 hours before browning. Place all ingredients together in slow cooker. Cook on low for 4-6 hours.

HERBED TENDERLOIN STEAK

Prep time: 10 minutes + 4 hours

Cook time: 4-6 hours

Ingredients

1 pound tenderloin steak, browned
½ tsp salt
½ tsp ground black pepper
½ tsp garlic powder
½ tsp cumin
½ tsp dry mustard

¼ tsp ground cinnamon
½ tsp onion powder
½ tsp paprika
1 tbsp. brown sugar
1 C water

Directions

Mix seasonings and rub into meat. Refrigerate for at least 4 hours before browning. Place all ingredients together in slow cooker. Cook on low for 4-6 hours.

HERBED FLANK STEAK

Prep time: 10 minutes + 4 hours

Cook time: 4-6 hours

Ingredients

1 pound flank steak, browned
1 tsp salt
1 tsp ground black pepper
1 tsp garlic powder
1 tsp onion powder

½ tsp paprika
½ tsp cayenne pepper
1 tbsp. brown sugar
1 C water

Directions

Mix seasonings and rub into meat. Refrigerate for at least 4 hours before browning. Place all ingredients together in slow cooker. Cook on low for 4-6 hours.

Herbed New York Strip Steak

Prep time: 10 minutes + 4 hours

Cook time: 4-6 hours

Ingredients
1 pound New York strip steak, browned
1 tsp salt
½ tsp ground black pepper
1 tsp garlic powder

1 ½ tsp onion powder
1 tbsp. brown sugar
1 C water

Directions
Mix seasonings and rub into meat. Refrigerate for at least 4 hours before browning. Place all ingredients together in slow cooker. Cook on low for 4-6 hours.

Herbed Sirloin Steak

Prep time: 10 minutes + 4 hours

Cook time: 4-6 hours

Ingredients
1 pound flank steak, browned
½ tsp salt
½ tsp ground black pepper
½ tsp garlic powder
1 tsp onion powder

½ tsp Italian seasoning
½ tsp dry mustard
1 tbsp. brown sugar
1 C water

Directions
Mix seasonings and rub into meat. Refrigerate for at least 4 hours before browning. Place all ingredients together in slow cooker. Cook on low for 4-6 hours.

Easy Sirloin Steak

Prep time: 10 minutes

Cook time: 4-6 hours

Ingredients
1 pound sirloin steak
2 tbsp extra virgin olive oil
1 tsp salt
1 tsp ground black pepper

1 small onion, chopped
1 garlic clove, minced
1 C water

Directions
Place all ingredients together in slow cooker. Cook on low for 4-6 hours.

*E*ASY NEW YORK STRIP STEAK

Prep time: 10 minutes

Cook time: 4-6 hours

Ingredients

1 pound New York strip steak, browned
½ tsp ground black pepper
1 small onion, chopped

1 garlic clove, minced
2 tbsp soya sauce
1 C water

Directions

Place all ingredients together in slow cooker. Cook on low for 4-6 hours.

*E*ASY FLANK STEAK

Prep time: 10 minutes

Cook time: 4-6 hours

Ingredients

1 pound flank steak, browned
½ tsp salt
½ tsp ground black pepper
1 small onion, chopped

1 garlic clove, minced
1 tsp barbecue steak spice
1 C water

Directions

Place all ingredients together in slow cooker. Cook on low for 4-6 hours.

*E*ASY PORTERHOUSE STEAK

Prep time: 10 minutes

Cook time: 4-6 hours

Ingredients

1 pound porterhouse steak, browned
1 tsp salt
1 tsp ground black pepper

1 small onion, chopped
1 garlic clove, minced
1 C water

Directions

Place all ingredients together in slow cooker. Cook on low for 4-6 hours.

*E*ASY TENDERLOIN STEAK

Prep time: 10 minutes

Cook time: 4-6 hours

Ingredients

1 pound tenderloin steak, browned
1 tsp salt

1 tsp ground black pepper
1 C water

Directions

Place all ingredients together in slow cooker. Cook on low for 4-6 hours.

Bacon Wrapped Filet Mignon

Prep time: 10 minutes

Cook time: 4-6 hours

Ingredients
1 pound tenderloin steak
bacon
1 tsp salt
1 tsp ground black pepper

1 small onion, chopped
1 garlic clove, minced
1 C water

Directions
Wrap bacon around steak, and hold in place with toothpicks, and brown before placing in slow cooker. Place all ingredients together in slow cooker. Cook on low for 4-6 hours.

Barbecue Sirloin Steak

Prep time: 10 minutes

Cook time: 4-6 hours

Ingredients
1 pound sirloin steak, browned
1 tsp salt
1 tsp ground black pepper
1 small onion, chopped

1 garlic clove, minced
½ C barbecue sauce
½ C water

Directions
Place all ingredients together in slow cooker. Cook on low for 4-6 hours.

Orange Steak

Prep time: 10 minutes

Cook time: 4-6 hours

Ingredients
1 pound steak, browned
1 tsp salt
1 tsp ground black pepper
1 small onion, chopped

1 garlic clove, minced
1 C water
½ C orange juice

Directions
Place all ingredients together in slow cooker. Cook on low for 4-6 hours.

Lemon Pepper Steak

Prep time: 10 minutes

Cook time: 4-6 hours

Ingredients
1 pound steak, browned
1 tsp salt
1 tsp ground black pepper

1 tsp lemon pepper
1 small onion, chopped
1 garlic clove, minced

1 C water

Directions

Place all ingredients together in slow cooker. Cook on low for 4-6 hours.

STEAK WITH PEPPERS

Prep time: 10 minutes

Cook time: 4-6 hours

Ingredients

1 pound steak, browned
1 tsp salt
1 tsp ground black pepper
¼ C chopped green and red peppers

1 small onion, chopped
1 garlic clove, minced
1 C water

Directions

Place all ingredients together in slow cooker. Cook on low for 4-6 hours.

STEAK WITH APPLES AND GINGER

Prep time: 10 minutes

Cook time: 4-6 hours

Ingredients

1 pound steak, browned
1 tsp salt
1 tsp ground black pepper
1 C chopped apple

1 tbsp fresh ginger, grated
1 small onion, chopped
1 garlic clove, minced
1 C water

Directions

Place all ingredients together in slow cooker. Cook on low for 4-6 hours.

PORCUPINE BALLS

Prep time: 20 minutes

Cook time: 4-5 hours

Ingredients

1 ½ pounds lean ground beef
½ C long grain white rice, cooked
1 egg
1 Can tomato soup

2 tbsp minced onion
½ C water
Salt and pepper to taste

Directions

Combine meat, rice, salt, pepper, onion, and egg and form into 2" balls. Combine water and tomato soup and add to slow cooker. Cook on low for 4-5 hours.

Swedish Meatballs

Prep time: 20 minutes

Cook time: 3-4 hours

Ingredients
1 pound lean ground beef
1 C bread crumbs
3 C beef broth
1/3 C flour

¾ C sour cream
5 tbsp butter
1 egg
Salt and pepper to taste

Directions
Mix ground beef, crumbs, salt, pepper, and egg together and form 2" meatballs. Place meatballs and remaining ingredients together in slow cooker. Cook on low for 3-4 hours.

Asian Meatballs

Prep time: 20 minutes

Cook time: 3-4 hours

Ingredients
½ pound lean ground beef
½ pound lean ground pork
½ C panko crumbs
1 egg

1 tsp fresh ginger paste
1 tsp minced garlic
½ jar Pulo Cuisine Lemongrass Atsuete Marinade

Directions
Mix ground beef, crumbs, salt, pepper, and egg together and form 2" meatballs. Place meatballs and remaining ingredients together in slow cooker. Cook on low for 3-4 hours.

Kung Pao Meatballs

Prep time: 20 minutes

Cook time: 3-4 hours

Ingredients
1 pound lean ground beef
1 C bread crumbs
1 egg
Salt and pepper to taste
2 tbsp minced green onions
2 tbsp extra virgin olive oil
1 garlic clove, minced

5 tbsp soy sauce
1 tbsp Sriracha
2 tbsp raw honey
¼ C chicken broth
2 tbsp corn starch
2 tbsp water

Directions
Mix ground beef, crumbs, salt, pepper, and egg together and form 2" meatballs. Place meatballs and remaining ingredients together in slow cooker. Cook on low for 3-4 hours.

Sweet & Sour Meatballs

Prep time: 20 minutes

Cook time: 3-4 hours

Ingredients

1 pound lean ground beef
1 C bread crumbs
1 egg

Salt and pepper to taste
3 C sweet & sour sauce (recipes in the Sauce Recipes section of this e-book)

Directions

Mix ground beef, crumbs, salt, pepper, and egg together and form 2" meatballs. Place meatballs and remaining ingredients together in slow cooker. Cook on low for 3-4 hours.

Cocktail Meatballs

Prep time: 20 minutes

Cook time: 3-4 hours

Ingredients

1 pound lean ground beef
1 C bread crumbs
1 egg
Salt and pepper to taste
3 tbsp minced onion

1 can cranberry sauce
1 C chili sauce
1 tbsp brown sugar, packed
1 tbsp lemon juice

Directions

Mix ground beef, crumbs, salt, pepper, and egg together and form 2" meatballs. Place meatballs and remaining ingredients together in slow cooker. Cook on low for 3-4 hours.

Honey Garlic Meatballs

Prep time: 20 minutes

Cook time: 3-4 hours

Ingredients

1 pound lean ground beef
1 C bread crumbs
1 egg
Salt and pepper

½ C ketchup
2 tbsp soy sauce
4 garlic cloves, minced

Directions

Mix ground beef, crumbs, salt, pepper, and egg together and form 2" meatballs. Place meatballs and remaining ingredients together in slow cooker. Cook on low for 3-4 hours.

CHINESE MEATBALLS

Prep time: 20 minutes

Cook time: 3-4 hours

Ingredients

1 pound lean ground beef
1 C bread crumbs
1 egg
Salt and pepper
2 tbsp extra virgin olive oil

3 tbsp hoisin sauce
¼ C rice vinegar
2 tbsp soy sauce
2 tsp ground ginger

Directions

Mix ground beef, crumbs, salt, pepper, and egg together and form 2" meatballs. Place meatballs and remaining ingredients together in slow cooker. Cook on low for 3-4 hours.

SWEET & SPICY MEATBALLS

Prep time: 20 minutes

Cook time: 3-4 hours

Ingredients

1 pound lean ground beef
1 C bread crumbs
1 egg
Salt and pepper
2 C barbecue sauce (recipes in the Sauce Recipes section of this e-book)

½ C raw honey
½ tsp chili powder
½ tsp paprika
½ tsp cayenne pepper

Directions

Mix ground beef, crumbs, salt, pepper, and egg together and form 2" meatballs. Place meatballs and remaining ingredients together in slow cooker. Cook on low for 3-4 hours.

SWEET SRIRACHA MEATBALLS

Prep time: 20 minutes

Cook time: 3-4 hours

Ingredients

1 pound lean ground beef
1 C bread crumbs
1 egg
Salt and pepper

¼ C sriracha
1 can cranberry jelly
1 C brown sugar
1/3 C raw honey

Directions

Mix ground beef, crumbs, salt, pepper, and egg together and form 2" meatballs. Place meatballs and remaining ingredients together in slow cooker. Cook on low for 3-4 hours.

Teriyaki Meatballs

Prep time: 20 minutes

Cook time: 3-4 hours

Ingredients
1 pound lean ground beef
1 C bread crumbs
1 egg

Salt and pepper
Teriyaki sauce (in the Sauce Recipes section of this e-book)

Directions
Mix ground beef, crumbs, salt, pepper, and egg together and form 2" meatballs. Place meatballs and remaining ingredients together in slow cooker. Cook on low for 3-4 hours.

Laotian Meatballs

Prep time: 20 minutes

Cook time: 3-4 hours

Ingredients
1 pound lean ground beef
1 C bread crumbs
1 egg
Salt and pepper
10 lime leaves

10 dried chilies
2 inches galangal root
1 tbsp white sugar
6 tbsp fish sauce

Directions
Mix ground beef, crumbs, salt, pepper, and egg together and form 2" meatballs. Place meatballs and remaining ingredients together in slow cooker. Cook on low for 3-4 hours.

Stew Beef 1

Prep time: 10 minutes

Cook time: 4 hours

Ingredients
2 pounds stewing beef, cubed and browned
3 C beef gravy

1 C water

Directions
Combine ingredients together in slow cooker. Cook on low for 4 hours.

Stew Beef 2

Prep time: 10 minutes

Cook time: 4 hours

Ingredients
2 pounds stewing beef, cubed and browned
3 C beef broth
1 C cream of beef soup

1 C water
1 tsp salt
½ tsp ground black pepper

Directions
Combine ingredients together in slow cooker. Cook on low for 4 hours.

STEW BEEF 3

Prep time: 10 minutes   Cook time: 4 hours

Ingredients
2 pounds stewing beef, cubed and browned   1 C water
3 C sweet & sour sauce

Directions
Combine ingredients together in slow cooker. Cook on low for 4 hours.

STEW BEEF 4

Prep time: 10 minutes   Cook time: 4 hours

Ingredients
2 pounds stewing beef, cubed and browned   1 C water
3 C dry garlic sauce

Directions
Combine ingredients together in slow cooker. Cook on low for 4 hours.

STEW BEEF 5

Prep time: 10 minutes   Cook time: 4 hours

Ingredients
2 pounds stewing beef, cubed and browned   ½ tsp ground black pepper
3 C beef broth   ½ tsp chili powder
1 tsp salt   1 tbsp hot sauce

Directions
Combine ingredients together in slow cooker. Cook on low for 4 hours.

STEW BEEF 6

Prep time: 10 minutes   Cook time: 4 hours

Ingredients
2 pounds stewing beef, cubed and browned   1 small onion, minced
3 C teriyaki sauce   1 C water
1 clove garlic, minced

Directions
Combine ingredients together in slow cooker. Cook on low for 4 hours.

Stew Beef 7

Prep time: 10 minutes   Cook time: 4 hours

Ingredients

2 pounds stewing beef, cubed and browned
3 C beef broth
1 C water
1 C sliced carrots

1 tbsp soya sauce
½ tsp black pepper
1 small onion, sliced
2 garlic cloves, minced

Directions

Combine ingredients together in slow cooker. Cook on low for 4 hours.

Stew Beef 8

Prep time: 10 minutes   Cook time: 4 hours

Ingredients

2 pounds stewing beef, cubed and browned
2 C beef broth
1 can cream of beef soup

1 C water
1 tsp ground black pepper
1 tsp salt

Directions

Combine ingredients together in slow cooker. Cook on low for 4 hours.

Stew Beef 9

Prep time: 10 minutes   Cook time: 4 hours

Ingredients

2 pounds stewing beef, cubed and browned
3 C beef gravy
1 tbsp soya sauce
1 celery stalk, chopped

1 large onion, sliced
1 tsp garlic powder
1 tsp curry powder
1 C water

Directions

Combine ingredients together in slow cooker. Cook on low for 4 hours.

Stew Beef 10

Prep time: 10 minutes   Cook time: 4 hours

Ingredients

2 pounds stewing beef, cubed and browned
3 C beef broth

1 C tomato juice
1 C mixed frozen vegetables

1 tsp salt
½ tsp ground black pepper
1 tsp onion powder

1 tsp garlic powder
1 tsp paprika

Directions
Combine ingredients together in slow cooker. Cook on low for 4 hours.

BEEF STIR-FRY 1

Prep time: 15 minutes

Cook time: 4 hours

Ingredients
1 pound steak, cut into strips and browned
3 tbsp soya sauce
1 tbsp white sugar
1 tsp ground ginger
2 tsp garlic powder

1 C sliced carrot
1 C chopped broccoli
1 C snow peas
1 C sprouts
1 C shredded red cabbage

Directions
Combine first 6 ingredients in slow cooker. Cook on low for 4 hours. Add remaining vegetables and heat through.

BEEF STIR-FRY 2

Prep time: 15 minutes

Cook time: 4 hours

Ingredients
1 pound steak, cut into strips and browned
2 C stir-fry sauce
1 C sliced carrot
1 C chopped broccoli

1 C snow peas
1 C sprouts
1 C shredded red cabbage

Directions
Combine first 3 ingredients in slow cooker. Cook on low for 4 hours. Add remaining vegetables and heat through.

BEEF STIR-FRY 3

Prep time: 15 minutes

Cook time: 4 hours

Ingredients
1 pound steak, cut into strips and browned
3 tbsp soya sauce
1 tbsp brown sugar
2 tsp garlic powder
1 C sliced carrot

1 C chopped cauliflower
1 C chopped broccoli
1 C snow peas
1 C sprouts
1 C shredded red cabbage

Directions
Combine first 5 ingredients in slow cooker. Cook on low for 4 hours. Add remaining vegetables and heat through.

BEEF STIR-FRY 4

Prep time: 15 minutes   Cook time: 4 hours

Ingredients

1 pound steak, cut into strips and browned
2 C dry garlic sauce
1 C sliced carrot
1 C chopped broccoli

1 C snow peas
1 C sprouts
1 C shredded red cabbage

Directions

Combine first 6 ingredients in slow cooker. Cook on low for 4 hours. Add remaining vegetables and heat through.

BEEF STIR-FRY 5

Prep time: 15 minutes   Cook time: 4 hours

Ingredients

1 pound steak, cut into strips and browned
2 C sweet & sour sauce
2 tsp garlic powder
1 C sliced carrot

1 C chopped broccoli
1 C snow peas
1 C sprouts
1 C shredded red cabbage

Directions

Combine first 3 ingredients in slow cooker. Cook on low for 4 hours. Add remaining vegetables and heat through.

BEEF STIR-FRY 6

Prep time: 15 minutes   Cook time: 4 hours

Ingredients

1 pound steak, cut into strips and browned
1 C beef broth
1 C sliced carrot
1 C chopped broccoli

1 C snow peas
1 C sprouts
1 C shredded red cabbage

Directions

Combine first 3 ingredients in slow cooker. Cook on low for 4 hours. Add remaining vegetables and heat through.

BEEF STIR-FRY 7

Prep time: 15 minutes   Cook time: 4 hours

Ingredients

1 pound steak, cut into strips and browned
3 tbsp soya sauce

2 tbsp teriyaki sauce
1 tbsp Worcestershire sauce

1 tbsp white sugar
2 tsp garlic powder
1 C sliced carrot
1 C chopped broccoli

1 C snow peas
1 C sprouts
1 C shredded red cabbage

Directions

Combine first 7 ingredients in slow cooker. Cook on low for 4 hours. Add remaining vegetables and heat through.

Beef Stir-Fry 8

Prep time: 15 minutes

Cook time: 4 hours

Ingredients

1 pound steak, cut into strips and browned
1 C beef gravy
1 C sliced carrot
1 C chopped broccoli

1 C snow peas
1 C sprouts
1 C shredded red cabbage

Directions

Combine first 3 ingredients in slow cooker. Cook on low for 4 hours. Add remaining vegetables and heat through.

Beef Stir-Fry 9

Prep time: 15 minutes

Cook time: 4 hours

Ingredients

1 pound steak, cut into strips and browned
3 tbsp soya sauce
1 C water
2 tsp garlic powder
1 large onion, sliced

1 C sliced carrot
1 C chopped broccoli
1 C snow peas
1 C sprouts
1 C shredded red cabbage

Directions

Combine first 6 ingredients in slow cooker. Cook on low for 4 hours. Add remaining vegetables and heat through.

Beef Stir-Fry 10

Prep time: 15 minutes

Cook time: 4 hours

Ingredients

1 pound steak, cut into strips and browned
2 C General Tau sauce
1 C sliced carrot
1 C chopped broccoli

1 C snow peas
1 C sprouts
1 C shredded red cabbage

Directions

Combine first 6 ingredients in slow cooker. Cook on low for 4 hours. Add remaining vegetables and heat through.

LOOSE BEEF 1

Prep time: 10 minutes   Cook time: 3-4 hour

Ingredients
1 pound lean ground beef, browned   1 C beef gravy

Directions
Combine ingredients in slow cooker. Cook on low for 3-4 hours.

LOOSE BEEF 2

Prep time: 10 minutes   Cook time: 3-4 hour

Ingredients
1 pound lean ground beef, browned   1 tbsp hot sauce
1 C beef broth

Directions
Combine ingredients in slow cooker. Cook on low for 3-4 hours.

LOOSE BEEF 3

Prep time: 10 minutes   Cook time: 3-4 hour

Ingredients
1 pound lean ground beef, browned   1 small onion, diced
1 C beef gravy   1 garlic clove, minced

Directions
Combine ingredients in slow cooker. Cook on low for 3-4 hours.

LOOSE BEEF 4

Prep time: 10 minutes   Cook time: 3-4 hour

Ingredients
1 pound lean ground beef, browned   Salt and pepper to taste
1 C sweet & sour sauce

Directions
Combine ingredients in slow cooker. Cook on low for 3-4 hours.

LOOSE BEEF 5

Prep time: 10 minutes

Cook time: 3-4 hour

Ingredients
1 pound lean ground beef, browned
1 C dry garlic sauce

Salt and pepper to taste

Directions
Combine ingredients in slow cooker. Cook on low for 3-4 hours.

LOOSE BEEF 6

Prep time: 10 minutes

Cook time: 3-4 hour

Ingredients
1 pound lean ground beef, browned
1 C spaghetti sauce
1 tsp garlic powder

1 tsp onion powder
Salt and pepper to taste

Directions
Combine ingredients in slow cooker. Cook on low for 3-4 hours.

LOOSE BEEF 7

Prep time: 10 minutes

Cook time: 3-4 hour

Ingredients
1 pound lean ground beef, browned
1 C beef broth
1 small onion, minced

2 garlic cloves, minced
Salt and pepper to taste

Directions
Combine ingredients in slow cooker. Cook on low for 3-4 hours.

LOOSE BEEF 8

Prep time: 10 minutes

Cook time: 3-4 hour

Ingredients
1 pound lean ground beef, browned
1 tbsp soya sauce
1 tbsp Worcestershire sauce

1 C water
½ C tomato sauce

Directions
Combine ingredients in slow cooker. Cook on low for 3-4 hours.

LOOSE BEEF 9

Prep time: 10 minutes   Cook time: 3-4 hour

Ingredients

1 pound lean ground beef, browned   1 large onion, minced
1 large can stewed diced tomatoes, not drained Salt and pepper to taste

Directions

Combine ingredients in slow cooker. Cook on low for 3-4 hours.

LOOSE BEEF 10

Prep time: 10 minutes   Cook time: 3-4 hour

Ingredients

1 pound lean ground beef, browned   1 can sliced mushrooms, not drained
1 can cream of mushroom soup   Salt and pepper to taste

Directions

Combine ingredients in slow cooker. Cook on low for 3-4 hours.

Pork

PORK ROAST 1

Prep time: 15 minutes

Cook time: 6-8hours

Ingredients

1 ½ pounds boneless pork loin
2 C chicken stock
1 small onion, thinly sliced

1 clove garlic, peeled and crushed
½ tsp ground black pepper

Directions

Combine all ingredients together in slow cooker. Cook on low for 6-8 hours.

PORK ROAST 2

Prep time: 15 minutes

Cook time: 6-8 hours

Ingredients

1 ½ pounds boneless pork loin
2 C chicken stock
1 small onion, thinly sliced

½ tsp ground cinnamon
½ tsp ground black pepper

Directions

Combine all ingredients together in slow cooker. Cook on low for 6-8 hours.

PORK ROAST 3

Prep time: 15 minutes

Cook time: 6-8 hours

Ingredients

1 ½ pounds boneless pork loin
2 C chicken stock

½ tsp ground black pepper

Directions

Combine all ingredients together in slow cooker. Cook on low for 6-8 hours.

PORK ROAST 4

Prep time: 15 minutes

Cook time: 6-8 hours

Ingredients

1 ½ pounds boneless pork loin
1 ¼ C chicken stock
¾ C orange juice

1 clove garlic, peeled and crushed
½ tsp ground black pepper
1 tbsp soya sauce

Directions

Combine all ingredients together in slow cooker. Cook on low for 6-8 hours.

$\mathcal{P}$ORK ROAST 5

Prep time: 15 minutes

Cook time: 6-8 hours

Ingredients

1 ½ pounds boneless pork loin
3 C beef stock
1 small onion, sliced
2 cloves garlic, minced

1 C pearl onions
1 celery stalk, chopped
½ tsp ground black pepper

Directions

Combine all ingredients together in slow cooker. Cook on low for 6-8 hours.

$\mathcal{P}$ORK ROAST 6

Prep time: 15 minutes

Cook time: 6-8 hours

Ingredients

1 ½ pounds boneless pork loin
3 C water
1 large onion, thinly sliced

3 garlic cloves, peeled and crushed
½ C raw honey
½ tsp ground black pepper

Directions

Combine all ingredients together in slow cooker. Cook on low for 6-8 hours.

$\mathcal{P}$ORK ROAST 7

Prep time: 15 minutes

Cook time: 6-8 hours

Ingredients

1 ½ pounds boneless pork loin
3 C chicken stock
1 large onion, thinly sliced

½ tsp curry powder
½ tsp garlic powder
½ tsp ground black pepper

Directions

Combine all ingredients together in slow cooker. Cook on low for 6-8 hours.

$\mathcal{P}$ORK ROAST 8

Prep time: 15 minutes

Cook time: 6-8 hours

Ingredients

1 ½ pounds boneless pork loin
3 C water

1 small onion, thinly sliced
½ tsp ground black pepper

Directions

Combine all ingredients together in slow cooker. Cook on low for 6-8 hours.

Pork Roast 9

Prep time: 15 minutes

Cook time: 6-8 hours

Ingredients

1 ½ pounds boneless pork loin
3 C chicken stock
¼ C lemon juice

1 small onion, thinly sliced
1 clove garlic, minced
½ tsp ground black pepper

Directions

Combine all ingredients together in slow cooker. Cook on low for 6-8 hours.

Pork Roast 10

Prep time: 15 minutes

Cook time: 6-8 hours

Ingredients

1 ½ pounds boneless pork loin
3 C chicken stock
1 small onion, thinly sliced

1 clove garlic, peeled and crushed
½ C orange marmalade
½ tsp ground black pepper

Directions

Combine all ingredients together in slow cooker. Cook on low for 6-8 hours.

Pork Roast 11

Prep time: 15 minutes

Cook time: 6-8 hours

Ingredients

1 ½ pounds boneless pork loin
2 C chicken stock
1 can cream of celery soup

1 small onion, thinly sliced
1 celery stalk, chopped
½ tsp ground black pepper

Directions

Combine all ingredients together in slow cooker. Cook on low for 6-8 hours.

Pork Roast 12

Prep time: 15 minutes

Cook time: 6-8 hours

Ingredients

1 ½ pounds boneless pork loin
3 C vegetable stock

1 small onion, thinly sliced
½ tsp ground black pepper

Directions

Combine all ingredients together in slow cooker. Cook on low for 6-8 hours.

PORK ROAST 13

Prep time: 15 minutes

Cook time: 6-8 hours

Ingredients

1 ½ pounds boneless pork loin
½ C water
1 small onion, thinly sliced

1 clove garlic, peeled and crushed
2 tbsp chicken bouillon powder
½ tsp ground black pepper

Directions

Combine all ingredients together in slow cooker. Cook on low for 6-8 hours.

PORK ROAST 14

Prep time: 15 minutes

Cook time: 6-8 hours

Ingredients

1 ½ pounds boneless pork loin
2 C chicken stock
½ C apple juice

1 C pearl onions
½ tsp ground black pepper

Directions

Combine all ingredients together in slow cooker. Cook on low for 6-8 hours.

PORK ROAST 15

Prep time: 15 minutes

Cook time: 6-8 hours

Ingredients

1 ½ pounds boneless pork loin
3 C chicken stock
1 leek, chopped

1 clove garlic, peeled and crushed
½ C pure maple syrup
½ tsp ground black pepper

Directions

Combine all ingredients together in slow cooker. Cook on low for 6-8 hours.

PORK ROAST 16

Prep time: 15 minutes

Cook time: 6-8 hours

Ingredients

1 ½ pounds boneless pork loin
3 C chicken stock
1 small onion, thinly sliced

1 clove garlic, peeled and crushed
Juice from 1 can mandarin oranges
½ tsp ground black pepper

Directions

Combine all ingredients together in slow cooker. Cook on low for 6-8 hours.

Pork Roast 17

Prep time: 15 minutes

Cook time: 6-8 hours

Ingredients
1 ½ pounds boneless pork loin
½ C water
1 packet French onion soup mix

1 small onion, thinly sliced
1 clove garlic, peeled and crushed
½ tsp ground black pepper

Directions
Combine all ingredients together in slow cooker. Cook on low for 6-8 hours.

Pork Roast 18

Prep time: 15 minutes

Cook time: 6-8 hours

Ingredients
1 ½ pounds boneless pork loin
3 C water
1 packet pork gravy mix

1 small onion, thinly sliced
1 clove garlic, peeled and crushed

Directions
Combine all ingredients together in slow cooker. Cook on low for 6-8 hours.

Pork Roast 19

Prep time: 15 minutes

Cook time: 6-8 hours

Ingredients
1 ½ pounds boneless pork loin
3 C chicken stock
1 small onion, thinly sliced
1 clove garlic, peeled and crushed

1 tbsp soya sauce
½ tsp ground ginger
½ tsp ground black pepper

Directions
Combine all ingredients together in slow cooker. Cook on low for 6-8 hours.

Pork Roast 20

Prep time: 15 minutes

Cook time: 6-8 hours

Ingredients
1 ½ pounds boneless pork loin
2 C chicken stock
1 can cream of mushroom soup
1 small onion, thinly sliced

1 clove garlic, peeled and crushed
1 C chopped mushrooms
½ tsp ground black pepper

Directions
Combine all ingredients together in slow cooker. Cook on low for 6-8 hours.

PORK CHOPS 1

Prep time: 10 minutes

Cook time: 6-8 hours

Ingredients

1 pound pork chops, browned
1 small onion, diced
1 garlic clove, minced

1 tsp soya sauce
1 C water

Directions

Combine all ingredients together in slow cooker. Cook on low for 6-8 hours.

PORK CHOPS 2

Prep time: 10 minutes

Cook time: 6-8 hours

Ingredients

1 pound pork chops, browned
1 small onion, diced
1 garlic clove, diced
1 tsp fresh grated ginger

1 C chopped apples
1 tbsp raw honey
1 tbsp soya sauce
1 C water

Directions

Combine all ingredients together in slow cooker. Cook on low for 6-8 hours.

PORK CHOPS 3

Prep time: 10 minutes

Cook time: 6-8 hours

Ingredients

1 pound pork chops, browned
1 C chicken stock
1 C water
1 small onion, diced

2 tbsp ketchup
2 tbsp brown sugar
1 can crushed pineapple

Directions

Combine all ingredients together in slow cooker. Cook on low for 6-8 hours.

PORK CHOPS 4

Prep time: 10 minutes

Cook time: 6-8 hours

Ingredients

1 pound pork chops, browned
1 small onion, thinly sliced

1 bottle dry garlic sauce
1 C water

Directions

Combine all ingredients together in slow cooker. Cook on low for 6-8 hours.

Pork Chops 5

Prep time: 10 minutes   Cook time: 6-8 hours

Ingredients
1 pound pork chops, browned   1 C tomato sauce
1 small onion, diced   1 tbsp soya sauce
1 16-ounce can diced tomatoes

Directions
Combine all ingredients together in slow cooker. Cook on low for 6-8 hours.

Pork Chops 6

Prep time: 10 minutes   Cook time: 6-8 hours

Ingredients
1 pound pork chops, browned   2 C apple juice
1 small onion, diced   1 C water
1 tbsp soya sauce   3 tbsp pure maple syrup

Directions
Combine all ingredients together in slow cooker. Cook on low for 6-8 hours.

Pork Chops 7

Prep time: 10 minutes   Cook time: 6-8 hours

Ingredients
1 pound pork chops, browned   1 can cream of mushroom soup
1 small onion, diced   1C chopped mushrooms
2 C water   1 tbsp soya sauce

Directions
Combine all ingredients together in slow cooker. Cook on low for 6-8 hours.

Pork Chops 8

Prep time: 10 minutes   Cook time: 6-8 hours

Ingredients
1 pound pork chops, browned   2 C vegetable broth
1 small onion, diced   1 tbsp soya sauce
1 garlic clove, minced   ½ tsp ground black pepper

Directions
Combine all ingredients together in slow cooker. Cook on low for 6-8 hours.

PORK CHOPS 9

Prep time: 10 minutes

Cook time: 6-8 hours

Ingredients
1 pound pork chops, browned
1 small onion, diced

2 jars dry garlic sauce

Directions
Combine all ingredients together in slow cooker. Cook on low for 6-8 hours.

PORK CHOPS 10

Prep time: 10 minutes

Cook time: 6-8 hours

Ingredients
1 pound pork chops, browned
1 C molasses
1 C water

½ C soya sauce
2 garlic cloves, minced
1 tbsp soya sauce

Directions
Combine all ingredients together in slow cooker. Cook on low for 6-8 hours.

PORK CHOPS 11

Prep time: 10 minutes

Cook time: 6-8 hours

Ingredients
1 pound pork chops, browned
1 small onion, diced
1 garlic clove, minced

1 can cream of chicken soup
1 C water
½ tsp black pepper

Directions
Combine all ingredients together in slow cooker. Cook on low for 6-8 hours.

PORK CHOPS 12

Prep time: 10 minutes

Cook time: 6-8 hours

Ingredients
1 pound pork chops, browned
1 small onion, diced
2 C vegetable broth

1 tbsp soya sauce
½ tsp Italian seasoning
½ tsp ground black pepper

Directions
Combine all ingredients together in slow cooker. Cook on low for 6-8 hours.

PORK CHOPS 13

Prep time: 10 minutes

Cook time: 6-8 hours

Ingredients

1 pound pork chops, browned
1 small onion, diced
1 garlic clove, minced
½ tsp ground black pepper

1 tsp ground cloves
2 tbsp white sugar
2 C tomato sauce
1 tbsp soya sauce

Directions

Combine all ingredients together in slow cooker. Cook on low for 6-8 hours.

PORK CHOPS 14

Prep time: 10 minutes

Cook time: 6-8 hours

Ingredients

1 pound pork chops, browned
1 small onion, diced
1 celery stalk, diced
½ C sliced mushrooms, chopped
1 can cream of mushroom soup

1 can cream of celery soup
1 C water
1 tbsp soya sauce
½ tsp ground black pepper

Directions

Combine all ingredients together in slow cooker. Cook on low for 6-8 hours.

PORK CHOPS 15

Prep time: 10 minutes

Cook time: 6-8 hours

Ingredients

1 pound pork chops, browned
1 small onion, diced
1 C pure maple syrup

1 C water
½ tsp ground black pepper

Directions

Combine all ingredients together in slow cooker. Cook on low for 6-8 hours.

PORK CHOPS 16

Prep time: 10 minutes

Cook time: 6-8 hours

Ingredients

1 pound pork chops, browned
1 small onion, diced

1 large can pineapple chunks in juice
½ C white vinegar

½ C ketchup
½ C white sugar

1 tbsp soya sauce

Directions

Combine all ingredients together in slow cooker. Cook on low for 6-8 hours.

PORK CHOPS 17

Prep time: 10 minutes

Cook time: 6-8 hours

Ingredients

1 pound pork chops, browned
1 tsp onion powder
1 tsp garlic powder
½ tsp ground ginger

½ C apple juice
1 ½ C water
1 tbsp chicken bouillon powder
½ tsp curry powder

Directions

Combine all ingredients together in slow cooker. Cook on low for 6-8 hours.

PORK CHOPS 18

Prep time: 10 minutes

Cook time: 6-8 hours

Ingredients

1 pound pork chops, browned
1 small onion, diced
2 C water

1 packet dry Chinese soup mix
1 tbsp soya sauce

Directions

Combine all ingredients together in slow cooker. Cook on low for 6-8 hours.

PORK CHOPS 19

Prep time: 10 minutes

Cook time: 6-8 hours

Ingredients

1 pound pork chops, browned
1 small onion, diced
1 16-ounce can diced tomatoes
1 C water
1 garlic clove, minced

½ tsp cayenne pepper
1 tbsp ground cloves
3 tbsp white sugar
1 tbsp soya sauce

Directions

Combine all ingredients together in slow cooker. Cook on low for 6-8 hours.

PORK CHOPS 20

Prep time: 10 minutes

Cook time: 6-8 hours

Ingredients

1 pound pork chops, browned
1 small onion, diced
1 large can pineapple chunks in juice
½ C apple juice

½ C water
2 garlic cloves, minced
½ tsp ground cinnamon
1 tbsp soya sauce

Directions

Combine all ingredients together in slow cooker. Cook on low for 6-8 hours.

BAKED HAM 1

Prep time: 10 minutes

Cook time: 6-8 hours

Ingredients

1 bone-in ham

2 C water

Directions

Trim excess fat off ham. Combine all ingredients together in slow cooker. Cook on low for 6-8 hours.

BAKED HAM 2

Prep time: 10 minutes

Cook time: 6-8 hours

Ingredients

1 bone-in ham
1 C water

1 C pineapple juice
½ tsp ground cloves

Directions

Trim excess fat off ham. Combine all ingredients together in slow cooker. Cook on low for 6-8 hours.

BAKED HAM 3

Prep time: 10 minutes

Cook time: 6-8 hours

Ingredients

1 bone-in ham
1 C water
½ C pure maple syrup

½ C apple juice
1 tsp ground cloves

Directions

Trim excess fat off ham. Combine all ingredients together in slow cooker. Cook on low for 6-8 hours.

BAKED HAM 4

Prep time: 10 minutes

Cook time: 6-8 hours

Ingredients
1 bone-in ham
1 C water

1 can cream of celery soup
1 tbsp soya sauce

Directions
Trim excess fat off ham. Combine all ingredients together in slow cooker. Cook on low for 6-8 hours.

BAKED HAM 5

Prep time: 10 minutes

Cook time: 6-8 hours

Ingredients
1 bone-in ham
1 C water
½ C raw honey
1 tsp ground cloves

½ tsp ground cinnamon
½ C brown sugar
½ C white vinegar

Directions
Trim excess fat off ham. Combine all ingredients together in slow cooker. Cook on low for 6-8 hours.

BAKED HAM 6

Prep time: 10 minutes

Cook time: 6-8 hours

Ingredients
1 bone-in ham
1 C water

1 C orange juice
1 tbsp soya sauce

Directions
Trim excess fat off ham. Combine all ingredients together in slow cooker. Cook on low for 6-8 hours.

BAKED HAM 7

Prep time: 10 minutes

Cook time: 6-8 hours

Ingredients
1 bone-in ham
2 C water
1 tsp ground cloves

2 tbsp brown sugar
1 C pineapple juice
1 tbsp yellow mustard

Directions
Trim excess fat off ham. Combine all ingredients together in slow cooker. Cook on low for 6-8 hours.

BAKED HAM 8

Prep time: 10 minutes

Cook time: 6-8 hours

Ingredients
1 bone-in ham
1 C water
1 C apple cider

¼ C sugar
2 tsp soya sauce

Directions
Trim excess fat off ham. Combine all ingredients together in slow cooker. Cook on low for 6-8 hours.

BAKED HAM 9

Prep time: 10 minutes

Cook time: 6-8 hours

Ingredients
1 bone-in ham
1 C water
1 can cream of mushroom soup

1 can sliced mushrooms, not drained
½ tsp ground black pepper

Directions
Trim excess fat off ham. Combine all ingredients together in slow cooker. Cook on low for 6-8 hours.

BAKED HAM 10

Prep time: 10 minutes

Cook time: 6-8 hours

Ingredients
1 bone-in ham
1 C water
½ C pineapple juice
½ C orange juice

1 can mandarin oranges
¼ C apple cider vinegar
¼ C white sugar

Directions
Trim excess fat off ham. Combine all ingredients together in slow cooker. Cook on low for 6-8 hours.

GLAZED HAM 1

Prep time: 15 minutes   Cook time: 6-8 hours

Ingredients
1 bone-in ham   ½ tsp ground cloves
1 C water   ¼ C white vinegar
1 C brown sugar

Directions
Slice excess fat off ham. Place water and ham in slow cooker. Cook on low for 6-8 hours. Mix brown sugar, cloves, and vinegar, and pour over ham. Preheat oven to broil. Place in oven and broil for 5-10 minutes, or until glaze begins to brown.

GLAZED HAM 2

Prep time: 15 minutes   Cook time: 6-8 hours

Ingredients
1 bone-in ham   ½ C crushed pineapple
1 C water   ¼ C raw honey
1 C brown sugar   ½ C white vinegar
½ tsp ground cloves

Directions
Slice excess fat off ham. Place water and ham in slow cooker. Cook on low for 6-8 hours. Mix brown sugar, cloves, and vinegar, and pour over ham. Preheat oven to broil. Place in oven and broil for 5-10 minutes, or until glaze begins to brown.

GLAZED HAM 3

Prep time: 15 minutes   Cook time: 6-8 hours

Ingredients
1 bone-in ham   ¼ C white vinegar
1 C water   ½ tsp ground cinnamon
1 C brown sugar   Whole cloves
½ tsp ground cloves

Directions
Slice excess fat off ham. Place water and ham in slow cooker. Cook on low for 6-8 hours. Mix brown sugar, cloves, and vinegar, and pour over ham. Preheat oven to broil. Place in oven and broil for 5-10 minutes, or until glaze begins to brown.

GLAZED HAM 4

Prep time: 15 minutes

Cook time: 6-8 hours

Ingredients

1 bone-in ham
1 C water
1 C brown sugar
½ tsp ground cloves

¼ C white vinegar
Whole cloves
½ C orange or three-fruit marmalade

Directions

Slice excess fat off ham. Place water and ham in slow cooker. Cook on low for 6-8 hours. Mix brown sugar, cloves, and vinegar, and pour over ham. Preheat oven to broil. Place in oven and broil for 5-10 minutes, or until glaze begins to brown.

GLAZED HAM 5

Prep time: 15 minutes

Cook time: 6-8 hours

Ingredients

1 bone-in ham
1 C water
1 C brown sugar
½ tsp ground cloves

¼ C white vinegar
Whole cloves
½ C orange or three-fruit marmalade

Directions

Slice excess fat off ham. Place water and ham in slow cooker. Cook on low for 6-8 hours. Mix brown sugar, cloves, and vinegar, and pour over ham. Preheat oven to broil. Place in oven and broil for 5-10 minutes, or until glaze begins to brown.

GLAZED HAM 6

Prep time: 15 minutes

Cook time: 6-8 hours

Ingredients

1 bone-in ham
1 C water
1 C brown sugar
½ tsp ground cloves
¼ C white vinegar

Whole cloves
½ C raw honey
½ C orange juice
½ C pineapple juice

Directions

Slice excess fat off ham. Place water and ham in slow cooker. Cook on low for 6-8 hours. Mix brown sugar, cloves, and vinegar, and pour over ham. Preheat oven to broil. Place in oven and broil for 5-10 minutes, or until glaze begins to brown.

GLAZED HAM 7

Prep time: 15 minutes

Cook time: 6-8 hours

Ingredients

1 bone-in ham
1 C water
1 C brown sugar
½ tsp ground cloves
¼ C white vinegar

Whole cloves
½ C orange or three-fruit marmalade
1 can mandarin oranges
½ C raw honey

Directions

Slice excess fat off ham. Place water and ham in slow cooker. Cook on low for 6-8 hours. Mix brown sugar, cloves, and vinegar, and pour over ham. Preheat oven to broil. Place in oven and broil for 5-10 minutes, or until glaze begins to brown.

GLAZED HAM 8

Prep time: 15 minutes

Cook time: 6-8 hours

Ingredients

1 bone-in ham
1 C water
1 C brown sugar
½ tsp ground cloves
¼ C white vinegar

Whole cloves
3 tbsp honey mustard
½ C pineapple juice
1 can crushed pineapple

Directions

Slice excess fat off ham. Place water and ham in slow cooker. Cook on low for 6-8 hours. Mix brown sugar, cloves, and vinegar, and pour over ham. Preheat oven to broil. Place in oven and broil for 5-10 minutes, or until glaze begins to brown.

GLAZED HAM 9

Prep time: 15 minutes

Cook time: 6-8 hours

Ingredients

1 bone-in ham
1 C water
1 C brown sugar
½ tsp ground cloves

¼ C white vinegar
Whole cloves
½ C orange or three-fruit marmalade

Directions

Slice excess fat off ham. Place water and ham in slow cooker. Cook on low for 6-8 hours. Mix brown sugar, cloves, and vinegar, and pour over ham. Preheat oven to broil. Place in oven and broil for 5-10 minutes, or until glaze begins to brown.

GLAZED HAM 10

Prep time: 15 minutes

Cook time: 6-8 hours

Ingredients

1 bone-in ham
½ C raw honey
½ C pure maple syrup
¼ C brown sugar

2 tbsp orange juice
1 tsp ground cinnamon
1 tsp nutmeg

Directions

Slice excess fat off ham. Place water and ham in slow cooker. Cook on low for 6-8 hours. Mix brown sugar, cloves, and vinegar, and pour over ham. Preheat oven to broil. Place in oven and broil for 5-10 minutes, or until glaze begins to brown.

PORK CHOPS AND RICE

Prep time: 5 minutes

Cook time: 6-8 hours

Ingredients

4 pork chops, ½" thick, browned
2 C uncooked rice
4 C canned tomatoes
6 tbsp chopped green pepper
4 tbsp chopped onion

2 C water
2 tsp salt
½ tsp pepper
½ tsp chili powder

Directions

Combine ingredients together in slow cooker. Cook on low for 6-8 hours.

HAWAIIAN PORK

Prep time: 15 minutes

Cook time: 5-6 hours

Ingredients

2 ½ pounds pork, cubed (1 inch cubes"), browned
1 ½ C pineapple juice
½ C water
½ C white vinegar
½ C brown sugar

2 large cans pineapple chunks
5 tbsp corn starch
2 tbsp soy sauce
1 onion, sliced
1 C diced green pepper
2 tsp salt

Directions

Combine pork, water, vinegar, pineapple juice, brown sugar, and salt. Cook on low for 5-6 hours. Add the green pepper, pineapple, and soy sauce. Mix the corn starch with water, and stir into the pork mixture until it is thick.

Pork in Beer with Onions

Prep time: 15 minutes

Cook time: 1 hour

Ingredients

2 pounds picnic pork shoulder, skin and fat removed
2 ½ C beer
6 C sliced onions
2 tbsp garlic, finely minced

2 tbsp brown sugar, tightly packed
2 tbsp corn starch dissolved in 3 tbsp water
1 tbsp soy sauce
½ tsp cayenne pepper
Salt and pepper to taste

Directions

Make a paste of garlic, soy sauce, sugar, cayenne pepper, salt, and pepper, and rub the paste into the pork. Add beer to the slow cooker, and then add the bay leaves. Combine ingredients together in slow cooker. Cook on low for 6-8 hours.

Herbed Pork Roast

Prep time: 15 minutes

Cook time: 6-8 hours

Ingredients

1 ½ pounds boneless pork loin
½ C chicken stock
1 tsp flaked rosemary
1 tsp thyme

½ tsp basil
1 clove garlic, peeled and crushed
Salt and pepper to taste

Directions

Combine ingredients together in slow cooker. Cook on low for 6-8 hours.

Pork Chop Casserole

Prep time: 15 minutes

Cook time: 6-8 hours

Ingredients

4 pork chops, browned
¼ C chicken stock
3 potatoes, not peeled and cut into large chunks
1 onion, sliced

½ C dry white wine
2 tbsp extra virgin olive oil
2 bay leaves
Salt and pepper to taste

Directions

Combine ingredients together in slow cooker. Cook on low for 6-8 hours.

Sweet Pork

Prep time: 15 minutes

Cook time: 6-8 hours

Ingredients
2 pound pork roast
½ C flour
1 ½ C raw honey
1 10-ounce can red enchilada sauce
1 C Worcestershire sauce

2 tsp chili powder
1 tsp garlic powder
1 tsp onion powder
Salt and pepper to taste

Directions
Combine ingredients together in slow cooker. Cook on low for 6-8 hours.

Seasoned Pork Roast

Prep time: 15 minutes

Cook time: 6-8 hours

Ingredients
1 ½ pounds boneless pork loin
½ C chicken stock
1 tsp flaked rosemary

1 clove garlic, peeled and crushed
1 onion, diced
Salt and pepper to taste

Directions
Combine ingredients together in slow cooker. Cook on low for 6-8 hours.

Asian Pork and Apples

Prep time: 10 minutes

Cook time: 5-6 hours

Ingredients
1 pound pork tenderloin, cut into 1" cubes
2 tbsp Oishi sauce
3 Granny Smith apples, chopped

2 garlic cloves, minced
1 tbsp fresh ginger, grated

Directions
Combine ingredients together in slow cooker. Cook on low for 5-6 hours.

Pork Stir-Fry

Prep time: 10 minutes

Cook time: 4-5 hours

Ingredients
1 pound pork tenderloin, cut into strips and browned
1 small onion, sliced
2 garlic cloves, minced
2 tbsp soya sauce

1 tbsp teriyaki sauce
1 tsp ground ginger
1 tbsp corn starch
2 tbsp white sugar
1 tbsp raw honey

1 C sliced carrots
1 C chopped broccoli
1 C snow peas

1 C green beans, chopped
1 C sprouts

Directions

Combine first 9 ingredients in slow cooker. Cook on low for 3 hours. Add vegetables and cook for 1-2 hours longer.

Pork and Applesauce

Prep time: 10 minutes

Cook time: 6-8 hours

Ingredients

1 pound pork tenderloin
1 tbsp extra virgin olive oil
1 small onion, thinly sliced

1 C water
2 C applesauce

Directions

Combine ingredients together in slow cooker. Cook on low for 5-6 hours.

Pork Stir-Fry 1

Prep time: 15 minutes

Cook time: 4 hours

Ingredients

1 pound pork tenderloin, cut into strips and browned
3 tbsp soya sauce
1 tbsp white sugar
1 tsp ground ginger
2 tsp garlic powder

1 C sliced carrot
1 C chopped broccoli
1 C snow peas
1 C sprouts
1 C shredded red cabbage

Directions

Combine first 6 ingredients in slow cooker. Cook on low for 4 hours. Add remaining vegetables and heat through.

Pork Stir-Fry 2

Prep time: 15 minutes

Cook time: 4 hours

Ingredients

1 pound pork tenderloin, cut into strips and browned
2 C stir-fry sauce
1 C sliced carrot

1 C chopped broccoli
1 C snow peas
1 C sprouts
1 C shredded red cabbage

Directions

Combine first 3 ingredients in slow cooker. Cook on low for 4 hours. Add remaining vegetables and heat through.

PORK STIR-FRY 3

Prep time: 15 minutes

Cook time: 4 hours

Ingredients

1 pound pork tenderloin, cut into strips and browned
3 tbsp soya sauce
1 tbsp brown sugar
2 tsp garlic powder
1 C sliced carrot

1 C chopped cauliflower
1 C chopped broccoli
1 C snow peas
1 C sprouts
1 C shredded red cabbage

Directions

Combine first 5 ingredients in slow cooker. Cook on low for 4 hours. Add remaining vegetables and heat through.

PORK STIR-FRY 4

Prep time: 15 minutes

Cook time: 4 hours

Ingredients

1 pound pork tenderloin, cut into strips and browned
2 C dry garlic sauce
1 C sliced carrot

1 C chopped broccoli
1 C snow peas
1 C sprouts
1 C shredded red cabbage

Directions

Combine first 6 ingredients in slow cooker. Cook on low for 4 hours. Add remaining vegetables and heat through.

PORK STIR-FRY 5

Prep time: 15 minutes

Cook time: 4 hours

Ingredients

1 pound pork tenderloin, cut into strips and browned
2 C sweet & sour sauce
2 tsp garlic powder
1 C sliced carrot

1 C chopped broccoli
1 C snow peas
1 C sprouts
1 C shredded red cabbage

Directions

Combine first 3 ingredients in slow cooker. Cook on low for 4 hours. Add remaining vegetables and heat through.

PORK STIR-FRY 6

Prep time: 15 minutes

Cook time: 4 hours

Ingredients

1 pound pork tenderloin, cut into strips and browned
1 C beef broth
1 C sliced carrot

1 C chopped broccoli
1 C snow peas
1 C sprouts
1 C shredded red cabbage

Directions

Combine first 3 ingredients in slow cooker. Cook on low for 4 hours. Add remaining vegetables and heat through.

PORK STIR-FRY 7

Prep time: 15 minutes

Cook time: 4 hours

Ingredients

1 pound pork tenderloin, cut into strips and browned
3 tbsp soya sauce
2 tbsp teriyaki sauce
1 tbsp Worcestershire sauce
1 tbsp white sugar

2 tsp garlic powder
1 C sliced carrot
1 C chopped broccoli
1 C snow peas
1 C sprouts
1 C shredded red cabbage

Directions

Combine first 7 ingredients in slow cooker. Cook on low for 4 hours. Add remaining vegetables and heat through.

PORK STIR-FRY 8

Prep time: 15 minutes

Cook time: 4 hours

Ingredients

1 pound pork tenderloin, cut into strips and browned
1 C beef gravy
1 C sliced carrot

1 C chopped broccoli
1 C snow peas
1 C sprouts
1 C shredded red cabbage

Directions

Combine first 3 ingredients in slow cooker. Cook on low for 4 hours. Add remaining vegetables and heat through.

PORK STIR-FRY 9

Prep time: 15 minutes

Cook time: 4 hours

Ingredients

1 pound pork tenderloin, cut into strips and browned
3 tbsp soya sauce
1 C water
2 tsp garlic powder
1 large onion, sliced

1 C sliced carrot
1 C chopped broccoli
1 C snow peas
1 C sprouts
1 C shredded red cabbage

Directions

Combine first 6 ingredients in slow cooker. Cook on low for 4 hours. Add remaining vegetables and heat through.

PORK STIR-FRY 10

Prep time: 15 minutes

Cook time: 4 hours

Ingredients

1 pound pork tenderloin, cut into strips and browned
2 C General Tau sauce
1 C sliced carrot

1 C chopped broccoli
1 C snow peas
1 C sprouts
1 C shredded red cabbage

Directions

Combine first 6 ingredients in slow cooker. Cook on low for 4 hours. Add remaining vegetables and heat through.

LOOSE PORK 1

Prep time: 10 minutes

Cook time: 3-4 hour

Ingredients

1 pound ground pork, browned
1 C beef gravy

Salt and pepper to taste

Directions

Combine ingredients in slow cooker. Cook on low for 3-4 hours.

LOOSE PORK 2

Prep time: 10 minutes

Cook time: 3-4 hour

Ingredients

1 pound ground pork, browned
1 C vegetable broth

1 tbsp hot sauce

Directions

Combine ingredients in slow cooker. Cook on low for 3-4 hours.

Loose Pork 3

Prep time: 10 minutes

Cook time: 3-4 hour

Ingredients
1 pound ground pork, browned
1 C beef gravy

1 small onion, diced
1 garlic clove, minced

Directions
Combine ingredients in slow cooker. Cook on low for 3-4 hours.

Loose Pork 4

Prep time: 10 minutes

Cook time: 3-4 hour

Ingredients
1 pound lean ground beef, browned
1 C sweet & sour sauce

Salt and pepper to taste

Directions
Combine ingredients in slow cooker. Cook on low for 3-4 hours.

Loose Pork 5

Prep time: 10 minutes

Cook time: 3-4 hour

Ingredients
1 pound ground pork, browned
1 C dry garlic sauce

Salt and pepper to taste

Directions
Combine ingredients in slow cooker. Cook on low for 3-4 hours.

Loose Pork 6

Prep time: 10 minutes

Cook time: 3-4 hour

Ingredients
1 pound ground pork, browned
1 C spaghetti sauce
1 tsp garlic powder

1 tsp onion powder
Salt and pepper to taste

Directions
Combine ingredients in slow cooker. Cook on low for 3-4 hours.

LOOSE PORK 7

Prep time: 10 minutes   Cook time: 3-4 hour

Ingredients

1 pound ground pork, browned   2 garlic cloves, minced
1 C beef broth   Salt and pepper to taste
1 small onion, minced

Directions

Combine ingredients in slow cooker. Cook on low for 3-4 hours.

LOOSE PORK 8

Prep time: 10 minutes   Cook time: 3-4 hour

Ingredients

1 pound ground pork, browned   1 C water
1 tbsp soya sauce   ½ C tomato sauce
1 tbsp Worcestershire sauce

Directions

Combine ingredients in slow cooker. Cook on low for 3-4 hours.

LOOSE BEEF 9

Prep time: 10 minutes   Cook time: 3-4 hour

Ingredients

1 pound lean ground beef, browned   1 large onion, minced
1 large can stewed diced tomatoes, not drained Salt and pepper to taste

Directions

Combine ingredients in slow cooker. Cook on low for 3-4 hours.

LOOSE PORK 10

Prep time: 10 minutes   Cook time: 3-4 hour

Ingredients

1 pound ground pork, browned   1 can sliced mushrooms, not drained
1 can cream of mushroom soup   Salt and pepper to taste

Directions

Combine ingredients in slow cooker. Cook on low for 3-4 hours.

Lamb

BRAISED LAMB SHANK 1

Prep time: 10 minutes

Cook time: 6 hours

Ingredients

2 pounds lamb shanks, browned
3 C beef stock
2 C canned tomatoes
5 garlic cloves, sliced
1 onion
2 carrots, sliced

½ tsp dry oregano
½ tsp thyme
½ tsp rosemary
Flour
Salt and pepper to taste

Directions

Combine all ingredients in slow cooker. Cook on high for 6 hours.

BRAISED LAMB SHANK 2

Prep time: 10 minutes

Cook time: 6 hours

Ingredients

2 pounds lamb shanks, browned
3 C beef stock
1 can stewed diced tomatoes
1 C tomato sauce

3 garlic cloves, sliced
1 onion
½ tsp dry oregano
Salt and pepper to taste

Directions

Combine all ingredients in slow cooker. Cook on high for 6 hours.

BRAISED LAMB SHANK 3

Prep time: 10 minutes

Cook time: 6 hours

Ingredients

2 pounds lamb shanks, browned
2 C beef stock
2 C chicken stock
2 C tomato sauce

4 garlic cloves, sliced
1 large onion, sliced
Salt and pepper to taste

Directions

Combine all ingredients in slow cooker. Cook on high for 6 hours.

BRAISED LAMB SHANK 4

Prep time: 10 minutes

Cook time: 6 hours

Ingredients

2 pounds lamb shanks, browned
4 C beef stock
1 cans stewed diced tomatoes
5 garlic cloves, minced

1 large onion, sliced
2 C chopped raw potato
2 carrots, sliced
Salt and pepper to taste

Directions

Combine all ingredients in slow cooker. Cook on high for 6 hours.

BRAISED LAMB SHANK 5

Prep time: 10 minutes

Cook time: 6 hours

Ingredients

2 pounds lamb shanks, browned
2 C beef stock
1 C chicken stock
4 garlic cloves, minced

5 tbsp extra virgin olive oil
1 small onion, diced
1 C whole kernel corn
Salt and pepper to taste

Directions

Combine all ingredients in slow cooker. Cook on high for 6 hours.

BRAISED LAMB SHANK 6

Prep time: 10 minutes

Cook time: 6 hours

Ingredients

2 pounds lamb shanks, browned
3 C beef stock
2 C stewed diced tomatoes
3 garlic cloves, sliced

2 tsp onion powder
1 tsp oregano
½ tsp Italian seasoning
Salt and pepper to taste

Directions

Combine all ingredients in slow cooker. Cook on high for 6 hours.

BRAISED LAMB SHANK 7

Prep time: 10 minutes

Cook time: 6 hours

Ingredients

2 pounds lamb shanks, browned
3 C beef stock

1 C tomato juice
6 garlic cloves, minced

1 large onion, sliced
½ C barbecue sauce

Salt and pepper to taste

Directions

Combine all ingredients in slow cooker. Cook on high for 6 hours.

BRAISED LAMB SHANK 8

Prep time: 10 minutes

Cook time: 6 hours

Ingredients

2 pounds lamb shanks, browned
2 C beef stock
1 C water
2 tsp garlic powder

2 tsp onion powder
1 tsp paprika
1 tsp curry powder
Salt and pepper to taste

Directions

Combine all ingredients in slow cooker. Cook on high for 6 hours.

BRAISED LAMB SHANK 9

Prep time: 10 minutes

Cook time: 6 hours

Ingredients

2 pounds lamb shanks, browned
3 C beef stock
1 C water
½ C sugar
½ C white vinegar

½ C ketchup
5 garlic cloves, sliced
6 tbsp extra virgin olive oil
Salt and pepper to taste

Directions

Combine all ingredients in slow cooker. Cook on high for 6 hours.

BRAISED LAMB SHANK 10

Prep time: 10 minutes

Cook time: 6 hours

Ingredients

2 pounds lamb shanks, browned
3 C beef stock
1 C water
6 garlic cloves, chopped

6 tbsp extra virgin olive oil
1 large onion, sliced
1 pound baby carrots
Salt and pepper to taste

Directions

Combine all ingredients in slow cooker. Cook on high for 6 hours.

LEG OF LAMB 1

Prep time: 10 minutes

Cook time: 6-8 hours

Ingredients

1 leg of lamb
5 garlic cloves, minced
1 tsp coarse sea salt

1 tsp ground black pepper
½ C chicken stock

Directions

Combine all ingredients together in slow cooker. Cook on low for 6-8 hours.

LEG OF LAMB 2

Prep time: 10 minutes

Cook time: 6-8 hours

Ingredients

1 leg of lamb
5 garlic cloves, minced
2 tbsp lemon juice

1 tsp ground black pepper
1 C chicken stock
1 tbsp soya sauce

Directions

Combine all ingredients together in slow cooker. Cook on low for 6-8 hours.

LEG OF LAMB 3

Prep time: 10 minutes

Cook time: 6-8 hours

Ingredients

1 leg of lamb
1 large onion, sliced
5 garlic cloves, minced
1 tsp salt

1 tsp ground black pepper
½ C beef stock
½ C water

Directions

Combine all ingredients together in slow cooker. Cook on low for 6-8 hours.

LEG OF LAMB 4

Prep time: 10 minutes

Cook time: 6-8 hours

Ingredients

1 leg of lamb
5 garlic cloves, minced
1 tsp ground black pepper

½ C tomato sauce
1 large can stewed diced tomatoes, not drained
1 tbsp soya sauce

Directions

Combine all ingredients together in slow cooker. Cook on low for 6-8 hours.

LEG OF LAMB 5

Prep time: 10 minutes   Cook time: 6-8 hours

Ingredients

1 leg of lamb
5 garlic cloves, minced
1 tsp coarse sea salt

1 tsp ground black pepper
½ C apple juice
½ C water

Directions

Combine all ingredients together in slow cooker. Cook on low for 6-8 hours.

LEG OF LAMB 6

Prep time: 10 minutes   Cook time: 6-8 hours

Ingredients

1 leg of lamb
1 large onion, sliced
5 garlic cloves, minced
1 tsp salt

½ tsp ground black pepper
½ C chicken stock
1 can crushed pineapple

Directions

Combine all ingredients together in slow cooker. Cook on low for 6-8 hours.

LEG OF LAMB 7

Prep time: 10 minutes   Cook time: 6-8 hours

Ingredients

1 leg of lamb
5 garlic cloves, minced
1 tsp onion powder
1 tsp paprika

½ tsp curry powder
1 tsp salt
½ tsp ground black pepper
½ C chicken stock

Directions

Combine all ingredients together in slow cooker. Cook on low for 6-8 hours.

LEG OF LAMB 8

Prep time: 10 minutes   Cook time: 6-8 hours

Ingredients

1 leg of lamb
5 garlic cloves, minced
1 tsp salt
½ tsp ground black pepper

½ C beef stock
½ C tomato juice
1 tsp onion powder

Directions

Combine all ingredients together in slow cooker. Cook on low for 6-8 hours.

Leg of Lamb 9

Prep time: 10 minutes

Cook time: 6-8 hours

Ingredients

1 leg of lamb
5 garlic cloves, minced
1 tbsp soya sauce
1 tbsp teriyaki sauce

1 tsp ground ginger
1 tsp ground black pepper
1 C chicken stock

Directions

Combine all ingredients together in slow cooker. Cook on low for 6-8 hours.

Leg of Lamb 10

Prep time: 10 minutes

Cook time: 6-8 hours

Ingredients

1 leg of lamb
5 garlic cloves, minced
1 tsp salt
½ tsp ground black pepper

1 C tomato sauce
1 tbsp white sugar
1 tsp ground cloves

Directions

Combine all ingredients together in slow cooker. Cook on low for 6-8 hours.

Lamb Chops 1

Prep time: 15 minutes

Cook time: 4-6 hours

Ingredients

2 lamb chops, browned
1 can stewed tomatoes
1 C chicken stock
1 C sliced carrots

1 sliced onion
1 crushed garlic clove
2 tbsp corn starch
Salt and pepper to taste

Directions

Combine all ingredients together in slow cooker. Cook on low for 4-6 hours.

Lamb Chops 2

Prep time: 15 minutes

Cook time: 4-6 hours

Ingredients

2 lamb chops, browned
1 C beef stock
1 C chicken stock
1 sliced onion

1 garlic clove, minced
2 tbsp corn starch
Salt and pepper to taste

Directions
Combine all ingredients together in slow cooker. Cook on low for 4-6 hours.

LAMB CHOPS 3

Prep time: 15 minutes

Cook time: 4-6 hours

Ingredients
2 lamb chops, browned
1 C spaghetti sauce
1 C chicken stock

1 sliced onion
Salt and pepper to taste

Directions
Combine all ingredients together in slow cooker. Cook on low for 4-6 hours.

LAMB CHOPS 4

Prep time: 15 minutes

Cook time: 4-6 hours

Ingredients
2 lamb chops, browned
1 C beef stock
1 C chicken stock
2 garlic cloves, minced

1 tsp onion powder
½ tsp chili powder
Salt and pepper to taste

Directions
Combine all ingredients together in slow cooker. Cook on low for 4-6 hours.

LAMB CHOPS 5

Prep time: 15 minutes

Cook time: 4-6 hours

Ingredients
2 lamb chops
1 C sweet & sour sauce
1 C chicken stock
1 C sliced carrots

1 sliced onion
1 crushed garlic clove
Salt and pepper to taste

Directions
Combine all ingredients together in slow cooker. Cook on low for 4-6 hours.

LAMB CHOPS 6

Prep time: 15 minutes

Cook time: 4-6 hours

Ingredients
2 lamb chops, browned
2 C chicken stock

1 C dry garlic sauce
1 C mixed frozen vegetables, thawed

1 small onion, sliced
2 garlic cloves, minced

Salt and pepper to taste

Directions

Combine all ingredients except mixed frozen vegetables together in slow cooker. Cook on low for 4-6 hours. Stir in vegetables and heat through for a few minutes.

LAMB CHOPS 7

Prep time: 15 minutes

Cook time: 4-6 hours

Ingredients

2 lamb chops, browned
1 can stewed tomatoes
1 C chicken stock
1 tsp garlic powder

1 tsp onion powder
½ tsp Italian seasoning
½ tsp oregano
Salt and pepper to taste

Directions

Combine all ingredients together in slow cooker. Cook on low for 4-6 hours.

LAMB CHOPS 8

Prep time: 15 minutes

Cook time: 4-6 hours

Ingredients

2 lamb chops, browned
½ C pure maple syrup
1 C chicken stock

1 sliced onion
1 crushed garlic clove
Salt and pepper to taste

Directions

Combine all ingredients together in slow cooker. Cook on low for 4-6 hours.

LAMB CHOPS 9

Prep time: 15 minutes

Cook time: 4-6 hours

Ingredients

2 lamb chops
2 C chicken stock

1 C whole kernel corn
Salt and pepper to taste

Directions

Combine all ingredients together in slow cooker. Cook on low for 4-6 hours.

LAMB CHOPS 10

Prep time: 15 minutes

Cook time: 4-6 hours

Ingredients

2 lamb chops
1 C chicken stock
1 C beef stock
1 C sliced mushrooms

½ C chopped green pepper
1 sliced onion
Salt and pepper to taste

Directions

Combine all ingredients together in slow cooker. Cook on low for 4-6 hours.

MEATBALLS

MEATBALLS 1

Prep time: 10 minutes

Cook time: 3-4 hours

Ingredients

1 pound ground turkey
1 C bread crumbs
2 eggs
1 tsp garlic powder
1 tsp onion powder

1 tsp salt
½ tsp ground black pepper
1 can cranberry jelly
1 C barbecue sauce

Directions

Combine first 7 ingredients and form into small meatballs. Combine cranberry jelly and barbecue sauce, and place in slow cooker. Add meatballs and stir. Cook on low for 3-4 hours.

MEATBALLS 2

Prep time: 10 minutes

Cook time: 3-4 hours

Ingredients

1 pound ground turkey
1 C bread crumbs
2 eggs
1 tsp garlic powder
1 tsp onion powder

1 tsp salt
½ tsp ground black pepper
1 can grape jelly
1 C barbecue sauce

Directions

Combine first 7 ingredients and form into small meatballs. Combine jelly and barbecue sauce, and place in slow cooker. Add meatballs and stir. Cook on low for 3-4 hours.

MEATBALLS 3

Prep time: 10 minutes

Cook time: 3-4 hours

Ingredients

1 pound lean ground beef
1 C bread crumbs
2 eggs
1 small onion, minced

1 tsp garlic powder
1 tsp salt
½ tsp ground black pepper
2 jars spaghetti sauce

Directions

Combine first 7 ingredients and form into small meatballs. Place meatballs and sauce in slow cooker. Cook on low for 3-4 hours.

MEATBALLS 4

Prep time: 10 minutes

Cook time: 3-4 hours

Ingredients

1 pound lean ground beef
1 C Italian bread crumbs
1 egg
½ C spaghetti sauce
1 tsp garlic powder

1 tsp onion powder
1 tsp salt
½ tsp ground black pepper
1 jar spaghetti sauce
1 large can stewed diced tomatoes

Directions

Combine first 8 ingredients and form into small meatballs. Combine spaghetti sauce and diced tomatoes, and place in slow cooker. Add meatballs and stir. Cook on low for 3-4 hours.

MEATBALLS 5

Prep time: 10 minutes

Cook time: 3-4 hours

Ingredients

1 pound ground pork
1 C bread crumbs
2 eggs
1 tsp garlic powder

1 tsp onion powder
1 tsp salt
½ tsp ground black pepper
2 jars sweet & sour sauce

Directions

Combine first 7 ingredients and form into small meatballs. Place meatballs and sauce in slow cooker. Cook on low for 3-4 hours.

MEATBALLS 6

Prep time: 10 minutes

Cook time: 3-4 hours

Ingredients

1 pound lean ground beef
1 C bread crumbs
2 eggs
1 garlic clove, minced

1 small onion, minced
1 tsp salt
½ tsp ground black pepper
5 C beef broth

Directions

Combine first 7 ingredients and form into small meatballs. Place meatballs and broth in slow cooker. Cook on low for 3-4 hours.

MEATBALLS 7

Prep time: 10 minutes

Cook time: 3-4 hours

Ingredients

1 pound ground turkey
1 C bread crumbs
2 eggs
1 tsp garlic powder
1 tsp onion powder
1 tsp paprika

1 tsp chili powder
½ tsp cayenne pepper
1 tsp salt
½ tsp ground black pepper
4 C tomato sauce
½ C hot sauce

Directions

Combine first 10 ingredients and form into small meatballs. Combine tomato sauce and hot sauce, and place in slow cooker. Add meatballs and stir. Cook on low for 3-4 hours.

MEATBALLS 8

Prep time: 10 minutes

Cook time: 3-4 hours

Ingredients

1 pound ground chicken
1 C Italian bread crumbs
1 egg
½ C spaghetti sauce
1 tsp garlic powder

1 tsp onion powder
1 tsp salt
½ tsp ground black pepper
4 C spaghetti sauce

Directions

Combine first 8 ingredients and form into small meatballs. Place meatballs and sauce in slow cooker. Cook on low for 3-4 hours.

MEATBALLS 9

Prep time: 10 minutes

Cook time: 3-4 hours

Ingredients

1 pound ground sausage
1 C bread crumbs
2 eggs
1 tsp garlic powder

1 tsp onion powder
1 tsp salt
½ tsp ground black pepper
5 C pork gravy

Directions

Combine first 6 ingredients and form into small meatballs. Place meatballs and gravy in slow cooker. Cook on low for 3-4 hours.

MEATBALLS 10

Prep time: 10 minutes

Cook time: 3-4 hours

Ingredients

1 pound lean ground beef
1 C bread crumbs
2 eggs
1 tsp garlic powder

1 tsp onion powder
1 tsp salt
4 C dry garlic sauce

Directions

Combine first 6 ingredients and form into small meatballs. Place meatballs and sauce in slow cooker. Cook on low for 3-4 hours.

MEATBALLS 11

Prep time: 10 minutes

Cook time: 3-4 hours

Ingredients

1 pound lean ground beef and pork mixture
1 C bread crumbs
2 eggs
1 tsp garlic powder
1 tsp onion powder

1 tsp chili powder
1 tsp paprika
1 tsp salt
½ tsp ground black pepper
4 C pork gravy

Directions

Combine first 9 ingredients and form into small meatballs. Place meatballs and sauce in slow cooker. Cook on low for 3-4 hours.

MEATBALLS 12

Prep time: 10 minutes

Cook time: 3-4 hours

Ingredients

1 pound lean ground beef and pork mixture
1 C Panko crumbs
2 eggs
1 tsp garlic powder

1 small onion, minced
1 tsp salt
½ tsp ground black pepper
4 C beef gravy

Directions

Combine first 9 ingredients and form into small meatballs. Place meatballs and sauce in slow cooker. Cook on low for 3-4 hours.

MEATBALLS 13

Prep time: 10 minutes

Cook time: 3-4 hours

Ingredients

1 pound ground chicken
1 C Panko crumbs
1 egg
½ C sweet & sour sauce
1 tsp garlic powder
1 tsp onion powder

1 tsp chili powder
1 tsp paprika
1 tsp salt
½ tsp ground black pepper
4 C sweet & sour sauce

Directions

Combine first 10 ingredients and form into small meatballs. Place meatballs and sauce in slow cooker. Cook on low for 3-4 hours.

MEATBALLS 14

Prep time: 10 minutes

Cook time: 3-4 hours

Ingredients

1 pound lean ground beef
1 C bread crumbs
2 eggs
1 garlic clove, minced

1 small onion, minced
1 tsp salt
½ tsp ground black pepper
4 C beef broth

Directions

Combine first 7 ingredients and form into small meatballs. Place meatballs and broth in slow cooker. Cook on low for 3-4 hours.

MEATBALLS 15

Prep time: 10 minutes

Cook time: 3-4 hours

Ingredients

1 pound lean ground beef
1 C bread crumbs
2 eggs
1 small onion, minced
1 tsp chili powder

½ tsp cayenne pepper
1 tsp salt
½ tsp ground black pepper
4 C mushroom gravy

Directions

Combine first 8 ingredients and form into small meatballs. Place meatballs and gravy in slow cooker. Cook on low for 3-4 hours.

MEATBALLS 16

Prep time: 10 minutes

Cook time: 3-4 hours

Ingredients

1 pound lean ground beef and pork mixture
1 C bread crumbs
2 eggs
1 tsp garlic powder
1 tsp onion powder

1 tsp chili powder
1 tsp paprika
1 tsp salt
½ tsp ground black pepper
4 C pork gravy

Directions

Combine first 9 ingredients and form into small meatballs. Place meatballs and sauce in slow cooker. Cook on low for 3-4 hours.

MEATBALLS 17

Prep time: 10 minutes

Cook time: 3-4 hours

Ingredients

1 pound lean ground beef
1 C bread crumbs
2 eggs

1 tsp salt
½ tsp ground black pepper
4 C spaghetti sauce

Directions

Combine first 5 ingredients and form into small meatballs. Place meatballs and sauce in slow cooker. Cook on low for 3-4 hours.

MEATBALLS 18

Prep time: 10 minutes

Cook time: 3-4 hours

Ingredients

1 pound lean ground beef
1 C bread crumbs
2 eggs

1 tsp salt
½ tsp ground black pepper
4 C dry garlic sauce

Directions

Combine first 5 ingredients and form into small meatballs. Place meatballs and sauce in slow cooker. Cook on low for 3-4 hours.

MEATBALLS 19

Prep time: 10 minutes

Cook time: 3-4 hours

Ingredients

1 pound lean ground beef
1 C bread crumbs
1 egg
½ C sweet & sour sauce

1 tsp salt
½ tsp ground black pepper
4 C sweet & sour sauce

Directions

Combine first 6 ingredients and form into small meatballs. Place meatballs and sauce in slow cooker. Cook on low for 3-4 hours.

MEATBALLS 20

Prep time: 10 minutes

Cook time: 3-4 hours

Ingredients

1 pound lean ground beef
1 C bread crumbs
2 eggs
1 tsp salt
½ tsp ground black pepper

½ tsp chili powder
½ tsp cayenne pepper
1 tbsp beef bouillon powder
4 C beef gravy

Directions

Combine first 8 ingredients and form into small meatballs. Place meatballs and gravy in slow cooker. Cook on low for 3-4 hours.

Meatballs 21

Prep time: 10 minutes

Cook time: 3-4 hours

Ingredients

1 package frozen meatballs, thawed and browned

4 C spaghetti sauce

Directions

Place ingredients in slow cooker. Cook on low for 3-4 hours.

Meatballs 22

Prep time: 10 minutes

Cook time: 3-4 hours

Ingredients

1 package frozen meatballs, thawed and browned

4 C dry garlic sauce

Directions

Place ingredients in slow cooker. Cook on low for 3-4 hours.

Meatballs 23

Prep time: 10 minutes

Cook time: 3-4 hours

Ingredients

1 package frozen meatballs, thawed and browned
3 C tomato sauce
1 small onion, diced
2 garlic cloves, minced

1 large can stewed, diced tomatoes
1 C water
1 tsp Italian seasoning
½ tsp oregano
1 C shredded mozzarella cheese

Directions

Place ingredients except cheese in slow cooker. Cook on low for 3-4 hours. Stir in cheese before serving.

Meatballs 24

Prep time: 10 minutes

Cook time: 3-4 hours

Ingredients

1 package frozen meatballs, thawed and browned
2 cans cream of mushroom soup
1 can cream of celery soup
2 C water

1 small onion, diced
2 garlic cloves, minced
1 tsp salt
½ tsp ground black pepper

Directions

Place ingredients in slow cooker. Cook on low for 3-4 hours.

MEATBALLS 25

Prep time: 10 minutes

Cook time: 3-4 hours

Ingredients

1 package frozen meatballs, thawed and browned
3 cans tomato soup
2 C water
1 large onion, chopped

1 celery stalk, chopped
1 tbsp beef bouillon powder
1 tsp salt
½ tsp ground black pepper

Directions

Place ingredients in slow cooker. Cook on low for 3-4 hours.

MEATLOAF

All meatloaf recipes can be cooked in half the time by cooking on high.

MEATLOAF 1

Prep time: 10 minutes

Cook time: 6 hours

Ingredients

2 pounds lean ground beef
2 eggs, lightly beaten
1 C milk

1 package onion soup mix
1 C bread crumbs

Directions

Combine all ingredients and mix thoroughly. Shape into a loaf that is small enough to not touch the sides of the slow cooker. Place in slow cooker and cook on low for 6 hours.

MEATLOAF 2

Prep time: 10 minutes

Cook time: 6 hours

Ingredients

2 pounds lean ground beef
2 eggs, lightly beaten
½ C ketchup + 3 tbsp
¼ C brown sugar

1 C bread crumbs
1 tsp salt
½ tsp ground black pepper

Directions

Combine ground beef, eggs, bread crumbs, salt, and pepper, and mix thoroughly. Shape into a loaf that is small enough to not touch the sides of the slow cooker. In a separate bowl, combine brown sugar and 3 tbsp ketchup. Place meatloaf in slow cooker and cook on low for 5 hours. Spread ketchup mixture on top of meatloaf, and cook on low for an additional hour.

MEATLOAF 3

Prep time: 10 minutes

Cook time: 6 hours

Ingredients

2 pounds lean ground beef
2 eggs, lightly beaten
½ C minced onion
1 C bread crumbs
1 tsp salt

½ tsp ground black pepper
½ C ketchup + 3 tbsp
¼ C brown sugar
½ tsp garlic powder

Directions

Combine ground beef, eggs, bread crumbs, salt, and pepper, and mix thoroughly. Shape into a loaf that is small enough to not touch the sides of the slow cooker. In a separate bowl, combine brown sugar, garlic powder, and 3 tbsp ketchup. Place meatloaf in slow cooker and cook on low for 5 hours. Spread ketchup mixture on top of meatloaf, and cook on low for an additional hour.

MEATLOAF 4

Prep time: 10 minutes

Cook time: 6 hours

Ingredients

2 pounds lean ground beef
2 eggs, lightly beaten
½ C minced onion
1 C Italian bread crumbs
1 tsp salt

½ tsp ground black pepper
½ C spaghetti sauce + 3 tbsp
¼ C brown sugar
½ tsp garlic powder

Directions

Combine ground beef, eggs, bread crumbs, salt, and pepper, and mix thoroughly. Shape into a loaf that is small enough to not touch the sides of the slow cooker. In a separate bowl, combine brown sugar, garlic powder, and 3 tbsp spaghetti sauce. Place meatloaf in slow cooker and cook on low for 5 hours. Spread ketchup mixture on top of meatloaf, and cook on low for an additional hour.

MEATLOAF 5

Prep time: 10 minutes

Cook time: 6 hours

Ingredients

2 pounds lean ground beef
1 egg, lightly beaten
½ C honey garlic sauce
½ C minced onion

1 C Italian bread crumbs
1 tsp salt
½ tsp ground black pepper
4-5 tbsp honey garlic sauce

Directions

Combine ground beef, egg, honey garlic sauce, bread crumbs, salt, and pepper, and mix thoroughly. Shape into a loaf that is small enough to not touch the sides of the slow cooker. Place meatloaf in slow cooker and cook on low for 5 hours. Spread 4-5 tbsp honey garlic sauce on top of meatloaf, and cook on low for an additional hour.

MEATLOAF 6

Prep time: 10 minutes

Cook time: 6 hours

Ingredients

2 pounds lean ground beef
1 egg, lightly beaten
½ C sweet and sour sauce
½ C minced onion

1 C bread crumbs
1 tsp salt
½ tsp ground black pepper
4 tbsp sweet and sour sauce

Directions

Combine ground beef, egg, ½ C sweet and sour sauce, bread crumbs, salt, and pepper, and mix thoroughly. Shape into a loaf that is small enough to not touch the sides of the slow cooker. Place meatloaf in slow cooker and cook on low for 5 hours. Spread 4 tbsp sweet and sour sauce on top of meatloaf, and cook on low for an additional hour.

MEATLOAF 7

Prep time: 10 minutes

Cook time: 6 hours

Ingredients

2 pounds lean ground beef
2 eggs, lightly beaten
½ C minced onion
1 tsp garlic powder

1 C bread crumbs
1 tsp salt
½ tsp ground black pepper

Directions

Combine ground beef, eggs, bread crumbs, salt, and pepper, and mix thoroughly. Shape into a loaf that is small enough to not touch the sides of the slow cooker. Place meatloaf in slow cooker and cook on low for 6 hours.

MEATLOAF 8

Prep time: 10 minutes

Cook time: 6 hours

Ingredients

2 pounds lean ground beef
2 eggs, lightly beaten
½ C minced onion
1 C bread crumbs
1 tsp salt

½ tsp ground black pepper
3 tbsp ketchup
¼ C brown sugar
½ tsp garlic powder
½ C Panko crumbs

Directions

Combine ground beef, eggs, bread crumbs, salt, and pepper, and mix thoroughly. Shape into a loaf that is small enough to not touch the sides of the slow cooker. In a separate bowl, combine brown sugar, garlic powder, and 3 tbsp spaghetti sauce. Place meatloaf in slow cooker and cook on low for 5 hours. Spread ketchup mixture and Panko crumbs on top of meatloaf, and cook on low for an additional hour.

MEATLOAF 9

Prep time: 10 minutes   Cook time: 6 hours

Ingredients

1 pounds lean ground beef
1 pound ground pork
2 eggs, lightly beaten
1 tsp onion powder
1 C bread crumbs

1 tsp salt
½ tsp ground black pepper
1 tsp garlic powder
2 tbsp ketchup
1 tbsp raw honey

Directions

Combine ground beef, eggs, bread crumbs, salt, and pepper, and mix thoroughly. Shape into a loaf that is small enough to not touch the sides of the slow cooker. In a separate bowl, combine ketchup and honey. Place meatloaf in slow cooker and cook on low for 5 hours. Spread ketchup mixture on top of meatloaf, and cook on low for an additional hour.

MEATLOAF 10

Prep time: 10 minutes   Cook time: 6 hours

Ingredients

2 pounds ground turkey
1 egg, lightly beaten
½ C spaghetti sauce
½ C minced onion
1 C Italian bread crumbs
1 tsp salt

½ tsp ground black pepper
1 tsp garlic powder
3 tbsp spaghetti sauce
¼ C brown sugar
½ tsp garlic powder

Directions

Combine ground beef, egg, spaghetti sauce, garlic, bread crumbs, salt, and pepper, and mix thoroughly. Shape into a loaf that is small enough to not touch the sides of the slow cooker. In a separate bowl, combine brown sugar, garlic powder, and 3 tbsp spaghetti sauce. Place meatloaf in slow cooker and cook on low for 5 hours. Spread ketchup mixture on top of meatloaf, and cook on low for an additional hour.

MEATLOAF 11

Prep time: 10 minutes   Cook time: 6 hours

Ingredients

1 pound lean ground beef
1 pound lean ground sausage
2 eggs, lightly beaten
½ C minced onion

1 C bread crumbs
1 tsp salt
½ tsp ground black pepper
4 tbsp pure maple syrup

Directions

Combine ground beef, eggs, bread crumbs, salt, and pepper, and mix thoroughly. Shape into a loaf that is small enough to not touch the sides of the slow cooker. Place meatloaf in slow cooker and cook on low for 5 hours. Spread maple syrup on top of meatloaf, and cook on low for an additional hour.

MEATLOAF 12

Prep time: 10 minutes

Cook time: 6 hours

Ingredients

2 pounds ground turkey
1 egg, lightly beaten
1 C bread crumbs
½ C dry garlic sauce

1 tsp salt
½ tsp ground black pepper
½ C spaghetti sauce + 3 tbsp
4 tbsp dry garlic sauce

Directions

Combine ground beef, eggs, bread crumbs, salt, and pepper, and mix thoroughly. Shape into a loaf that is small enough to not touch the sides of the slow cooker. Place meatloaf in slow cooker and cook on low for 5 hours. Spread 4 tbsp dry garlic sauce on top of meatloaf, and cook on low for an additional hour.

MEATLOAF 13

Prep time: 10 minutes

Cook time: 6 hours

Ingredients

2 pounds lean ground beef
2 eggs, lightly beaten
½ C minced onion
1 C Italian bread crumbs
1 tsp salt

½ tsp ground black pepper
½ C spaghetti sauce + 3 tbsp
¼ C brown sugar
½ tsp garlic powder

Directions

Combine ground beef, eggs, bread crumbs, salt, and pepper, and mix thoroughly. Shape into a loaf that is small enough to not touch the sides of the slow cooker. In a separate bowl, combine brown sugar, garlic powder, and 3 tbsp spaghetti sauce. Place meatloaf in slow cooker and cook on low for 5 hours. Spread ketchup mixture on top of meatloaf, and cook on low for an additional hour.

MEATLOAF 14

Prep time: 10 minutes

Cook time: 6 hours

Ingredients

2 pounds lean ground beef
2 eggs, lightly beaten
½ C minced onion
½ C Italian bread crumbs
½ C Panko crumbs
1 tsp salt

½ tsp ground black pepper
1 tbsp raw honey
1 tbsp pure maple syrup
1 tbsp white vinegar
¼ C brown sugar
½ tsp garlic powder

Directions

Combine first 7 and mix thoroughly. Shape into a loaf that is small enough to not touch the sides of the slow cooker. In a separate bowl, combine remaining ingredients. Place meatloaf in slow cooker and cook on low for 5 hours. Spread honey mixture on top of meatloaf, and cook on low for an additional hour.

MEATLOAF 15

Prep time: 10 minutes

Cook time: 6 hours

Ingredients
2 pounds lean ground beef
2 eggs, lightly beaten
½ C minced onion
1 C Italian bread crumbs
1 tsp salt

½ tsp ground black pepper
½ C spaghetti sauce + 3 tbsp
¼ C brown sugar
½ tsp garlic powder

Directions
Combine ground beef, eggs, bread crumbs, salt, and pepper, and mix thoroughly. Shape into a loaf that is small enough to not touch the sides of the slow cooker. In a separate bowl, combine brown sugar, garlic powder, and 3 tbsp spaghetti sauce. Place meatloaf in slow cooker and cook on low for 5 hours. Spread ketchup mixture on top of meatloaf, and cook on low for an additional hour.

BROWN SUGAR GLAZED MEATLOAF

Prep time: 20 minutes

Cook time: 6 hours

Ingredients
2 pound mix of ground beef, pork, and veal (lean)
3 slices bread, shredded
1/3 C brown sugar, packed
¼ C onion, diced

1 beaten egg
1 tbsp beef bouillon powder
4 tbsp lemon juice
1 tsp dry mustard

Directions
Mix meat, egg, bread, onion, 1 tbsp lemon juice, and bouillon powder in a bowl, and shape into a loaf that is small enough to not touch the sides of the slow cooker. In a separate bowl, combine remaining ingredients. Place meatloaf in slow cooker and cook on low for 5 hours. Spread ketchup mixture on top of meatloaf, and cook on low for an additional hour.

SWEET & SOUR MEATLOAF 1

Prep time: 20 minutes

Cook time: 6 hours

Ingredients
1 pound ground beef
1 C bread crumbs
1 egg
2 tbsp sweet & sour sauce

1 tsp salt
½ tsp ground pepper
1 tsp onion powder
1 bottle sweet & sour sauce

Directions
Combine first 7 ingredients and mix thoroughly. Shape into a loaf that is small enough to not touch the sides of the slow cooker. In a separate bowl, combine brown sugar, garlic powder, and 3 tbsp spaghetti sauce. Place meatloaf in slow cooker and cook on low for 5 hours. Spread sweet & sour sauce on top of meatloaf, and cook on low for an additional hour.

SWEET & SOUR MEATLOAF 2

Prep time: 20 minutes

Cook time: 6 hours

Ingredients
2 pounds ground beef
1 C bread crumbs
2 eggs
1 tsp salt
½ tsp ground pepper
1 tsp onion powder

1 15-ounce can tomato sauce
2 tbsp brown sugar
2 tbsp cider vinegar
½ C white sugar
2 tsp prepared mustard

Directions
Combine first 6 ingredients and mix thoroughly. Shape into a loaf that is small enough to not touch the sides of the slow cooker. In a separate bowl, combine remaining ingredients. Place meatloaf in slow cooker and cook on low for 5 hours. Spread sweet & sour mixture on top of meatloaf, and cook on low for an additional hour.

SWEET & SOUR MEATLOAF 3

Prep time: 20 minutes

Cook time: 6 hours

Ingredients
2 pounds ground beef
1 C bread crumbs
2 eggs
1 tsp salt

½ tsp ground pepper
1 tsp onion powder
1 can pineapple tidbits, drained
1 jar sweet & sour sauce

Directions
Combine first 7 ingredients and mix thoroughly. Shape into a loaf that is small enough to not touch the sides of the slow cooker. In a separate bowl, combine remaining ingredients. Place meatloaf in slow cooker and cook on low for 5 hours. Spread sweet & sour mixture on top of meatloaf, and cook on low for an additional hour.

SWEET & SOUR MEATLOAF 4

Prep time: 20 minutes

Cook time: 6 hours

Ingredients
2 pounds ground beef
1 C bread crumbs
2 eggs
1 tsp salt
½ tsp ground pepper

1 tsp onion powder
1 can pineapple tidbits, drained
1 C brown sugar
½ C vinegar
2 tbsp ketchup

Directions
Combine first 7 ingredients and mix thoroughly. Shape into a loaf that is small enough to not touch the sides of the slow cooker. In a separate bowl, combine remaining ingredients. Place meatloaf in slow cooker and cook on low for 5 hours. Spread sweet & sour mixture on top of meatloaf, and cook on low for an additional hour.

Sweet & Sour Meatloaf 5

Prep time: 20 minutes

Cook time: 6 hours

Ingredients

2 pounds ground beef
1 C bread crumbs
2 eggs
1 tsp salt
½ tsp ground pepper

1 tsp onion powder
1 can crushed pineapple
¼ C white vinegar
3 tbsp brown sugar

Directions

Combine first 6 ingredients and mix thoroughly. Shape into a loaf that is small enough to not touch the sides of the slow cooker. In a separate bowl, combine remaining ingredients. Place meatloaf in slow cooker and cook on low for 5 hours. Spread sweet & sour mixture on top of meatloaf, and cook on low for an additional hour.

Mexican Meatloaf

Prep time: 20 minutes

Cook time: 6 hours

Ingredients

1 pound ground beef
1 ½ C medium salsa
1/3 C grated parmesan cheese

¼ C shredded Monterey Jack cheese
1 egg
1 C crushed salted crackers

Directions

Combine all ingredients and mix thoroughly. Shape into a loaf that is small enough to not touch the sides of the slow cooker. Place in slow cooker and cook on low for 6 hours.

Dill Pickle Meatloaf

Prep time: 20 minutes

Cook time: 6 hours

Ingredients

1 pound lean ground beef
½ C dill pickle juice
¼ C chopped dill pickles
¼ C ketchup
1 egg
1 onion, finely chopped

1 slice bread, shredded
2 tbsp water
1 tsp salt
½ tsp ground black pepper
1 tbsp brown sugar
½ tsp Worcestershire sauce

Directions

Combine beef, pickle juice, egg, onion, bread, salt, and pepper, and shape into a loaf that is small enough to not touch the sides of the slow cooker. Mix remaining ingredients in a separate bowl and spread on top of meatloaf. Place in slow cooker and cook on low for 6 hours.

*B*ACON MUSHROOM & SWISS MEATLOAF

Prep time: 20 minutes

Cook time: 6 hours

Ingredients

1 pounds lean ground beef
¼ C evaporated milk
6 ounces shredded Swiss cheese
½ C corn flakes, crushed into crumbs to make ½ C

1 egg
1 onion, finely chopped
5 button mushrooms
12 ounces chopped bacon, cooked

Directions

Combine all ingredients and mix thoroughly. Shape into a loaf that is small enough to not touch the sides of the slow cooker. Place in slow cooker and cook on low for 6 hours.

*C*HILI MEATLOAF

Prep time: 20 minutes

Cook time: 6 hours

Ingredients

1 pound lean ground beef
½ C bread crumbs
1 tsp salt
1 egg
½ tsp black pepper

1 tsp chili powder
½ tsp cayenne pepper
½ tsp paprika
¼ C chopped green pepper
¼ C chopped red pepper

Directions

Combine all ingredients and mix thoroughly. Shape into a loaf that is small enough to not touch the sides of the slow cooker. Place in slow cooker and cook on low for 6 hours.

*T*HAI MEATLOAF

Prep time: 20 minutes

Cook time: 15 minutes

Ingredients

1 pound lean ground beef
½ C bread crumbs
1 tsp salt
1 egg
½ tsp black pepper

½ tsp cayenne pepper
½ tsp paprika
¼ C chopped green pepper
¼ C chopped red pepper
1 tbsp peanut butter

Directions

Combine all ingredients and mix thoroughly. Shape into a loaf that is small enough to not touch the sides of the slow cooker. Place in slow cooker and cook on low for 6 hours.

Garlic Meatloaf

Prep time: 20 minutes

Cook time: 6 hours

Ingredients

1 pound lean ground beef
½ C bread crumbs
1 tsp salt
1 egg

½ tsp black pepper
2-3 cloves garlic, minced
½ C ketchup
2 tbsp brown sugar

Directions

Combine all ingredients except ketchup and brown sugar, and mix thoroughly. Shape into a loaf that is small enough to not touch the sides of the slow cooker. Place in slow cooker and cook on low for 5 hours. Mix remaining ingredients in a separate bowl, and pour on top of meatloaf, and cook for an additional hour.

Onion Meatloaf.

Prep time: 20 minutes

Cook time: 6 hours

Ingredients

1 pound lean ground beef
½ C bread crumbs
1 large onion, chopped
1 tsp salt

1 egg
½ tsp black pepper
½ tsp paprika
1 package onion soup mix

Directions

Combine all ingredients and mix thoroughly. Shape into a loaf that is small enough to not touch the sides of the slow cooker. Place in slow cooker and cook on low for 6 hours.

Cashew Meatloaf

Prep time: 20 minutes

Cook time: 6 hours

Ingredients

1 pound lean ground beef
½ C bread crumbs
1 large onion, chopped
1 tsp salt

1 egg
½ tsp black pepper
½ C chopped, unsalted cashews

Directions

Combine all ingredients and mix thoroughly. Shape into a loaf that is small enough to not touch the sides of the slow cooker. Place in slow cooker and cook on low for 6 hours.

Meatloaf with Green Onions

Prep time: 20 minutes

Cook time: 6 hours

Ingredients

1 pound lean ground beef
1 egg
½ C bread crumbs
1 small onion, chopped

½ C chopped green onions + ¼ C green onions
1 tsp salt
½ tsp black pepper
1 package onion soup mix

Directions

Combine all ingredients and mix thoroughly. Shape into a loaf that is small enough to not touch the sides of the slow cooker. Sprinkle remaining green onion on top of meatloaf. Place in slow cooker and cook on low for 6 hours.

Macaroni Meatloaf

Prep time: 20 minutes

Cook time: 6 hours

Ingredients

1 pound lean ground beef
½ C bread crumbs
1 large onion, chopped
1 tsp salt
1 egg

½ tsp black pepper
½ tsp paprika
1 package onion soup mix
1 C elbow macaroni, cooked

Directions

Combine all ingredients and mix thoroughly. Shape into a loaf that is small enough to not touch the sides of the slow cooker. Place in slow cooker and cook on low for 6 hours.

Macaroni & Cheese Meatloaf

Prep time: 20 minutes

Cook time: 6 hours

Ingredients

1 pound lean ground beef
½ C bread crumbs
1 large onion, chopped
1 tsp salt
1 egg

½ tsp black pepper
½ tsp paprika
1 C elbow macaroni, cooked
½ C shredded cheddar cheese

Directions

Combine all ingredients and mix thoroughly. Shape into a loaf that is small enough to not touch the sides of the slow cooker. Place in slow cooker and cook on low for 6 hours.

Meatloaf Italiana

Prep time: 20 minutes

Cook time: 6 hours

Ingredients

1 pound lean ground beef
½ C bread crumbs
1 large onion, chopped
2 cloves garlic, minced
1 tsp salt

½ C spaghetti sauce
½ tsp black pepper
½ tsp paprika
½ C shredded mozzarella cheese

Directions

Combine all ingredients and mix thoroughly. Shape into a loaf that is small enough to not touch the sides of the slow cooker. Place in slow cooker and cook on low for 6 hours. Sprinkle cheese on top and let sit for a couple of minutes to melt.

Meatloaf with Potatoes

Prep time: 20 minutes

Cook time: 6 hours

Ingredients

1 pound lean ground beef
½ C bread crumbs
1 large onion, chopped
1 tsp salt
1 egg

½ tsp black pepper
½ tsp paprika
1 package onion soup mix
2 C instant potatoes, cooked

Directions

Combine all ingredients except potatoes and mix thoroughly. Shape into a loaf that is small enough to not touch the sides of the slow cooker. Place in slow cooker and cook on low for 6 hours. Cover with potatoes and serve.

Holiday Meatloaf

Prep time: 20 minutes

Cook time: 6 hours

Ingredients

1 pound lean ground beef
½ C bread crumbs
1 large onion, chopped
1 tsp salt

1 C cranberry jelly, divided
½ tsp black pepper
½ tsp paprika

Directions

Combine all ingredients and mix thoroughly. Shape into a loaf that is small enough to not touch the sides of the slow cooker. Place in slow cooker and cook on low for 6 hours.

CRUSTED MEATLOAF

Prep time: 20 minutes

Cook time: 6 hours

Ingredients
1 pound lean ground beef
½ C bread crumbs
1 large onion, chopped
1 tsp salt

1 egg
½ tsp black pepper
½ tsp paprika

CRUST

1 C bread crumbs
¼ C ketchup
1 tsp salt

½ tsp black pepper
½ tsp garlic powder
½ tsp onion powder

Directions
Combine all ingredients and mix thoroughly. Shape into a loaf that is small enough to not touch the sides of the slow cooker. Mix crust ingredients, and spread on top of meat loaf. Place in slow cooker and cook on low for 6 hours.

STUFFED MEATLOAF

Prep time: 20 minutes

Cook time: 6 hours

Ingredients
1 pound lean ground beef
½ C bread crumbs
1 large onion, chopped
1 tsp salt
1 egg
½ tsp black pepper

½ tsp paprika
1 package onion soup mix
½ C canned mushrooms, drained
½ C chopped peppers (green and red)
½ C cream cheese

Directions
Combine first 8 ingredients, and mix well. Flatten out beef mixture to about 1 inch thick. In a separate bowl, mix mushrooms, peppers, and cream cheese. Spread into the middle of the beef mixture, and fold edges over to create a sealed pocket. Place in slow cooker and cook on low for 6 hours.

ALPHABET SOUP MEATLOAF

Prep time: 20 minutes

Cook time: 15 minutes

Ingredients
1 pound lean ground beef
1 C bread crumbs
1 can alphabet soup
1 large onion, chopped

1 tsp salt
½ tsp black pepper
½ tsp paprika

Directions

Combine all ingredients and mix thoroughly. Shape into a loaf that is small enough to not touch the sides of the slow cooker. Mix crust ingredients, and spread on top of meat loaf. Place in slow cooker and cook on low for 6 hours.

Meatloaf with Peppers

Prep time: 20 minutes   Cook time: 6 hours

Ingredients

1 pound lean ground beef
1 C bread crumbs
1 egg
1 large onion, chopped

1 green pepper, chopped
1 red pepper, chopped
1 tsp salt
1 tsp black pepper

Directions

Combine all ingredients and mix thoroughly. Shape into a loaf that is small enough to not touch the sides of the slow cooker. Mix crust ingredients, and spread on top of meat loaf. Place in slow cooker and cook on low for 6 hours.

Taco Meatloaf

Prep time: 20 minutes   Cook time: 6 hours

Ingredients

1 pound lean ground beef
1 C bread crumbs
1 egg
1 large onion, chopped
1 green pepper, chopped
1 C stewed diced tomatoes, drained

1 tsp salt
1 tsp black pepper
1 C broken taco shells
½ C taco sauce
1 C stewed diced tomatoes, drained

Directions

Combine first 8 ingredients and mix thoroughly. Shape into a loaf that is small enough to not touch the sides of the slow cooker. Mix crust ingredients, and spread on top of meat loaf. Place in slow cooker and cook on low for 6 hours. broken taco shells on top of sauce. Place pan in basket, and lower into the cooker. Close and lock the lid, bring pressure to high, lower heat, and cook for 15 minutes. Use a quick release.

Honey Garlic Meatloaf

Prep time: 20 minutes   Cook time: 6 hours

Ingredients

1 pound lean ground beef
1 C bread crumbs
1 egg
½ C honey garlic sauce

1 tsp salt
1 tsp black pepper
1 tsp garlic powder
1 C honey garlic sauce

Directions
Combine first 7 ingredients and mix thoroughly. Shape into a loaf that is small enough to not touch the sides of the slow cooker. Spread honey garlic sauce on top of meatloaf. Place in slow cooker and cook on low for 6 hours.

Meatloaf with Potato Chips

Prep time: 20 minutes   Cook time: 6 hours

Ingredients
1 pound lean ground beef
1 C crushed potato chips
1 egg
1 clove garlic, minced

1 tsp salt
1 tsp black pepper
1 C crushed potato chips

Directions
Combine first 6 ingredients and mix thoroughly. Shape into a loaf that is small enough to not touch the sides of the slow cooker. Sprinkle crushed potato chips on top of meatloaf. Place in slow cooker and cook on low for 6 hours.

Ranch Dressing Meatloaf

Prep time: 20 minutes   Cook time: 6 hours

Ingredients
1 pound lean ground beef
1 C bread crumbs
1 egg
2 tbsp ranch dressing
½ C chopped green onion

1 clove garlic, minced
1 tsp salt
1 tsp black pepper
½ C ranch dressing
½ C shredded cheddar cheese

Directions
Combine first 6 ingredients and mix thoroughly. Shape into a loaf that is small enough to not touch the sides of the slow cooker. Spread dressing and cheese on top of meatloaf. Cook on low for 6 hours.

Mixed Meatloaf 1

Prep time: 20 minutes   Cook time: 6 hours

Ingredients
1 pound mixture of lean ground beef, ground sausage, and ground pork
1 C bread crumbs
1 egg
1 large onion, chopped
1 tsp salt

½ tsp black pepper
½ tsp paprika
½ tsp chili powder
½ tsp cayenne pepper
1 tbsp powdered beef bouillon

Directions
Combine all ingredients and mix thoroughly. Shape into a loaf that is small enough to not touch the sides of the slow cooker. Place in slow cooker and cook on low for 6 hours.

Mixed Meatloaf 2

Prep time: 20 minutes

Cook time: 6 hours

Ingredients

1 pound mixture of lean ground beef and ground pork
1 C bread crumbs
1 egg

1 large onion, chopped
1 tsp salt
½ tsp black pepper
1 tbsp powdered beef bouillon

Directions

Combine all ingredients and mix thoroughly. Shape into a loaf that is small enough to not touch the sides of the slow cooker. Place in slow cooker and cook on low for 6 hours.

Mixed Meatloaf 3

Prep time: 20 minutes

Cook time: 6 hours

Ingredients

1 pound mixture of lean ground beef and ground sausage
1 C bread crumbs
¼ C barbecue sauce

1 small onion, chopped
1 tsp salt
½ tsp black pepper

Directions

Combine all ingredients and mix thoroughly. Shape into a loaf that is small enough to not touch the sides of the slow cooker. Place in slow cooker and cook on low for 6 hours.

Mixed Meatloaf 4

Prep time: 20 minutes

Cook time: 6 hours

Ingredients

1 pound mixture of lean ground beef, ground sausage, and ground pork
1 C bread crumbs
1 egg

1 large onion, chopped
1 tsp salt
½ tsp black pepper

Directions

Combine all ingredients and mix thoroughly. Shape into a loaf that is small enough to not touch the sides of the slow cooker. Place in slow cooker and cook on low for 6 hours.

MIXED MEATLOAF 5

Prep time: 20 minutes

Cook time: 6 hours

Ingredients

1 pound mixture of lean ground beef, ground sausage, and ground pork
1 C bread crumbs
1 egg
1 large onion, chopped
½ tsp black pepper

1 tbsp powdered beef bouillon
½ C ketchup
2 tbsp brown sugar
1 tsp garlic powder
½ tsp onion powder
½ tsp black pepper

Directions

Combine first 6 ingredients and mix thoroughly. Shape into a loaf that is small enough to not touch the sides of the slow cooker. In a separate bowl, combine remaining ingredients. Spread ketchup mixture on top of meatloaf. Place in slow cooker and cook on low for 6 hours.

MIXED MEATLOAF 6

Prep time: 20 minutes

Cook time: 6 hours

Ingredients

1 pound mixture of lean ground sausage, ground turkey, and ground pork
1 C bread crumbs
1 egg
1 large onion, chopped

1 tsp salt
½ tsp black pepper
½ tsp paprika
½ tsp chili powder
½ tsp curry powder

Directions

Combine all ingredients and mix thoroughly. Shape into a loaf that is small enough to not touch the sides of the slow cooker. Place in slow cooker and cook on low for 6 hours.

MIXED MEATLOAF 7

Prep time: 20 minutes

Cook time: 6 hours

Ingredients

1 pound mixture of lean ground beef, ground sausage, and ground pork
1 C Panko crumbs
1 egg
1 large onion, chopped
1 tsp salt
½ tsp black pepper

½ C Panko crumbs
¼ C barbecue sauce
½ tsp paprika
½ tsp chili powder
½ tsp cayenne pepper
1 tbsp powdered beef bouillon

Directions

Combine first 6 ingredients and mix thoroughly. Shape into a loaf that is small enough to not touch the sides of the slow cooker. Combine remaining ingredients in a separate bowl, and spread mixture on top of meatloaf. Place in slow cooker and cook on low for 6 hours.

MIXED MEATLOAF 8

Prep time: 20 minutes

Cook time: 6 hours

Ingredients

1 pound mixture of lean ground beef and ground pork
1 C bread crumbs
¼ C honey garlic sauce

1 large onion, chopped
1 tsp salt
½ tsp black pepper
½ C honey garlic sauce

Directions

Combine first 6 ingredients and mix thoroughly. Shape into a loaf that is small enough to not touch the sides of the slow cooker. Spread honey garlic sauce on top of meatloaf. Place in slow cooker and cook on low for 6 hours.

MIXED MEATLOAF 9

Prep time: 20 minutes

Cook time: 15 minutes

Ingredients

1 pound mixture of lean ground beef, ground sausage, ground turkey, and ground pork
1 C bread crumbs
1 egg

1 large onion, chopped
1 tsp salt
½ tsp black pepper
1 can tomato soup

Directions

Combine first 6 ingredients, mix well, form into a loaf, and place in a prepared pan. Spread tomato soup on top of meatloaf. Place pan in basket, and lower into the cooker. Close and lock the lid, bring pressure to high, lower heat, and cook for 15 minutes. Use a quick release.

MIXED MEATLOAF 10

Prep time: 20 minutes

Cook time: 6 hours

Ingredients

1 pound mixture of lean ground beef, ground sausage, and ground pork
1 C garlic bread crumbs
1 egg

1 large onion, chopped
1 tsp salt
½ tsp black pepper
2 garlic cloves, minced

Directions

Combine all ingredients and mix thoroughly. Shape into a loaf that is small enough to not touch the sides of the slow cooker. Place in slow cooker and cook on low for 6 hours.

TURKEY MEATLOAF 1

Prep time: 20 minutes

Cook time: 6 hours

Ingredients

1 pound ground turkey
½ C bread crumbs
1 large onion, chopped
1 tsp salt
1 egg

1 tbsp powdered chicken bouillon
½ tsp black pepper
½ tsp poultry seasoning
½ tsp thyme
½ tsp sage

Directions

Combine all ingredients and mix thoroughly. Shape into a loaf that is small enough to not touch the sides of the slow cooker. Place in slow cooker and cook on low for 6 hours.

TURKEY MEATLOAF 2

Prep time: 20 minutes

Cook time: 6 hours

Ingredients

1 pound ground turkey
½ C bread crumbs
¼ C cranberry jelly
1 large onion, chopped
1 tsp salt

½ tsp black pepper
½ tsp poultry seasoning
½ tsp thyme
½ tsp sage

Directions

Combine all ingredients and mix thoroughly. Shape into a loaf that is small enough to not touch the sides of the slow cooker. Place in slow cooker and cook on low for 6 hours.

TURKEY MEATLOAF 3

Prep time: 20 minutes

Cook time: 6 hours

Ingredients

1 pound ground turkey
½ C Panko crumbs
1 egg
1 large onion, chopped

1 tbsp chicken bouillon powder
1 tsp salt
½ tsp black pepper
½ tsp poultry seasoning

Directions

Combine all ingredients and mix thoroughly. Shape into a loaf that is small enough to not touch the sides of the slow cooker. Place in slow cooker and cook on low for 6 hours.

TURKEY MEATLOAF 4

Prep time: 20 minutes

Cook time: 6 hours

Ingredients

1 pound ground turkey
½ C bread crumbs
¼ C barbecue sauce
1 large onion, chopped
1 tsp salt
½ tsp black pepper

½ tsp poultry seasoning
½ tsp thyme
½ tsp sage
½ C barbecue sauce
2 tbsp brown sugar
1 tsp garlic powder

Directions

Combine first 9 ingredients and mix thoroughly. Mix remaining ingredients in a separate bowl. Shape into a loaf that is small enough to not touch the sides of the slow cooker. Spread sauce mixture on top of meatloaf. Place in slow cooker and cook on low for 6 hours.

TURKEY MEATLOAF 5

Prep time: 20 minutes

Cook time: 6 hours

Ingredients

1 pound ground turkey
½ C Italian bread crumbs
1 egg
1 large onion, chopped

1 tsp salt
½ tsp black pepper
½ C spaghetti sauce

Directions

Combine first 6 ingredients and mix thoroughly. Shape into a loaf that is small enough to not touch the sides of the slow cooker. Combine remaining ingredients in a separate bowl and spread on top of meatloaf. Place in slow cooker and cook on low for 6 hours.

TURKEY MEATLOAF 6

Prep time: 20 minutes

Cook time: 6 hours

Ingredients

1 pound ground turkey
½ C bread crumbs
¼ C dry garlic sauce

1 large onion, chopped
1 tsp salt
½ tsp black pepper

Directions

Combine all ingredients and mix thoroughly. Shape into a loaf that is small enough to not touch the sides of the slow cooker. Place in slow cooker and cook on low for 6 hours.

TURKEY MEATLOAF 7

Prep time: 20 minutes

Cook time: 6 hours

Ingredients
1 pound ground turkey
½ C bread crumbs
¼ C turkey gravy
1 egg

1 large onion, chopped
1 tsp salt
½ tsp black pepper

Directions
Combine all ingredients and mix thoroughly. Shape into a loaf that is small enough to not touch the sides of the slow cooker. Place in slow cooker and cook on low for 6 hours.

TURKEY MEATLOAF 8

Prep time: 20 minutes

Cook time: 6 hours

Ingredients
1 pound ground turkey
½ C bread crumbs
¼ C tomato sauce

1 large onion, chopped
1 tsp salt
½ tsp black pepper

Directions
Combine all ingredients and mix thoroughly. Shape into a loaf that is small enough to not touch the sides of the slow cooker. Place in slow cooker and cook on low for 6 hours.

TURKEY MEATLOAF 9

Prep time: 20 minutes

Cook time: 6 hours

Ingredients
1 pound ground turkey
½ C bread crumbs
¼ C ketchup

1 large onion, chopped
1 tsp salt
½ tsp black pepper

Directions
Combine all ingredients and mix thoroughly. Shape into a loaf that is small enough to not touch the sides of the slow cooker. Place in slow cooker and cook on low for 6 hours.

Turkey Meatloaf 10

Prep time: 20 minutes

Cook time: 6 hours

Ingredients

1 pound ground turkey
½ C Italian bread crumbs
¼ C spaghetti sauce
1 tsp garlic powder

1 large onion, chopped
1 tsp salt
½ tsp black pepper

Directions

Combine all ingredients and mix thoroughly. Shape into a loaf that is small enough to not touch the sides of the slow cooker. Place in slow cooker and cook on low for 6 hours.

Chicken Meatloaf 1

Prep time: 20 minutes

Cook time: 6 hours

Ingredients

1 pound ground chicken
½ C Panko crumbs
1 egg

1 small onion, chopped
1 tsp salt
½ tsp black pepper

Directions

Combine all ingredients and mix thoroughly. Shape into a loaf that is small enough to not touch the sides of the slow cooker. Place in slow cooker and cook on low for 6 hours.

Chicken Meatloaf 2

Prep time: 20 minutes

Cook time: 6 hours

Ingredients

1 pound ground chicken
½ C bread crumbs
1 egg
1 small onion, chopped
1 tbsp chicken bouillon powder
1 tsp salt

½ tsp black pepper
½ tsp poultry seasoning
½ C ketchup
3 tbsp brown sugar
2 garlic cloves, minced

Directions

Combine first 7 ingredients and mix thoroughly. Shape into a loaf that is small enough to not touch the sides of the slow cooker. Combine remaining ingredients in a separate bowl, and spread on top of meatloaf. Place in slow cooker and cook on low for 6 hours.

CHICKEN MEATLOAF 3

Prep time: 20 minutes

Cook time: 6 hours

Ingredients

1 pound ground turkey
½ C bread crumbs
¼ C spaghetti sauce
1 large onion, chopped
2 cloves garlic, minced
1 tsp Italian seasoning

1 tsp salt
½ tsp black pepper
½ tsp poultry seasoning
½ C spaghetti sauce
½ C shredded mozzarella cheese

Directions

Combine first 9 ingredients and mix thoroughly. Shape into a loaf that is small enough to not touch the sides of the slow cooker. Spread spaghetti sauce and cheese on top of meatloaf. Place in slow cooker and cook on low for 6 hours.

CHICKEN MEATLOAF 4

Prep time: 20 minutes

Cook time: 6 hours

Ingredients

1 pound ground chicken
½ C bread crumbs
¼ C sweet & sour sauce
1 large onion, chopped
1 tbsp chicken bouillon powder

1 tsp salt
½ tsp black pepper
½ tsp poultry seasoning
½ C sweet & sour sauce
¼ C chopped green onion

Directions

Combine first 8 ingredients and mix thoroughly. Shape into a loaf that is small enough to not touch the sides of the slow cooker. Spread sweet & sour sauce and green onion on top of meatloaf. Place in slow cooker and cook on low for 6 hours.

CHICKEN MEATLOAF 5

Prep time: 20 minutes

Cook time: 6 hours

Ingredients

1 pound ground chicken
½ C bread crumbs
¼ C tomato soup

1 small onion, chopped
1 tsp salt
½ tsp black pepper

Directions

Combine all ingredients and mix thoroughly. Shape into a loaf that is small enough to not touch the sides of the slow cooker. Place in slow cooker and cook on low for 6 hours.

CHICKEN MEATLOAF 6

Prep time: 20 minutes

Cook time: 6 hours

Ingredients

1 pound ground chicken
½ C Italian bread crumbs
¼ C tomato sauce
½ C stewed diced tomatoes, drained

1 small onion, chopped
1 tsp salt
½ tsp black pepper

Directions

Combine all ingredients and mix thoroughly. Shape into a loaf that is small enough to not touch the sides of the slow cooker. Place in slow cooker and cook on low for 6 hours.

CHICKEN MEATLOAF 7

Prep time: 20 minutes

Cook time: 6 hours

Ingredients

1 pound ground chicken
½ C bread crumbs
¼ C sweet & sour sauce

1 small onion, chopped
1 tsp salt
½ tsp black pepper

Directions

Combine all ingredients and mix thoroughly. Shape into a loaf that is small enough to not touch the sides of the slow cooker. Place in slow cooker and cook on low for 6 hours.

CHICKEN MEATLOAF 8

Prep time: 20 minutes

Cook time: 6 hours

Ingredients

1 pound ground chicken
½ C bread crumbs
¼ C teriyaki dipping sauce

1 tbsp soya sauce
1 small onion, chopped
½ tsp black pepper

Directions

Combine all ingredients and mix thoroughly. Shape into a loaf that is small enough to not touch the sides of the slow cooker. Place in slow cooker and cook on low for 6 hours.

CHICKEN MEATLOAF 9

Prep time: 20 minutes

Cook time: 6 hours

Ingredients

1 pound ground chicken
½ C bread crumbs
2 small eggs

1 small onion, chopped
1 tsp salt
½ tsp black pepper

Directions

Combine all ingredients and mix thoroughly. Shape into a loaf that is small enough to not touch the sides of the slow cooker. Place in slow cooker and cook on low for 6 hours.

CHICKEN MEATLOAF 10

Prep time: 20 minutes

Cook time: 6 hours

Ingredients

1 pound ground chicken
½ C bread crumbs
2 small eggs
1 small onion, chopped
1 tsp garlic powder

1 tsp paprika
1 tsp curry powder
1 tsp salt
½ tsp black pepper

Directions

Combine all ingredients and mix thoroughly. Shape into a loaf that is small enough to not touch the sides of the slow cooker. Place in slow cooker and cook on low for 6 hours.

PORK MEATLOAF 1

Prep time: 20 minutes

Cook time: 6 hours

Ingredients

1 pound lean ground pork
1 C bread crumbs
1 egg

1 small onion, chopped
½ tsp black pepper

Directions

Combine all ingredients and mix thoroughly. Shape into a loaf that is small enough to not touch the sides of the slow cooker. Place in slow cooker and cook on low for 6 hours.

PORK MEATLOAF 2

Prep time: 20 minutes   Cook time: 6 hours

Ingredients
1 pound lean ground pork
1 C bread crumbs
1 egg

1 small onion, chopped
½ tsp black pepper

Directions
Combine all ingredients and mix thoroughly. Shape into a loaf that is small enough to not touch the sides of the slow cooker. Place in slow cooker and cook on low for 6 hours.

PORK MEATLOAF 3

Prep time: 20 minutes   Cook time: 6 hours

Ingredients
1 pound lean ground pork
1 C bread crumbs
1 egg
1 small onion, chopped
½ tsp black pepper
2 tbsp chicken bouillon powder

1 tsp soya sauce
1 tsp curry powder
½ C ketchup
2 tbsp brown sugar
1 tsp garlic powder
1 tsp soya sauce

Directions
Combine first 8 ingredients and mix thoroughly. Shape into a loaf that is small enough to not touch the sides of the slow cooker. Combine remaining ingredients in a separate bowl, and spread on top of meatloaf. Place in slow cooker and cook on low for 6 hours.

PORK MEATLOAF 4

Prep time: 20 minutes   Cook time: 6 hours

Ingredients
1 pound lean ground pork
1 C bread crumbs
1 egg
1 small onion, chopped

½ tsp black pepper
1 C pork gravy
1 C mixed frozen vegetables, thawed

Directions
Combine first 5 ingredients and mix thoroughly. Shape into a loaf that is small enough to not touch the sides of the slow cooker. Spread gravy and vegetables on top of meatloaf. Place in slow cooker and cook on low for 6 hours.

PORK MEATLOAF 5

Prep time: 20 minutes

Cook time: 6 hours

Ingredients

1 pound lean ground pork
1 C bread crumbs
1 egg
1 small onion, chopped

½ tsp black pepper
½ tsp garlic powder
1 C applesauce

Directions

Combine all ingredients except applesauce and mix thoroughly. Shape into a loaf that is small enough to not touch the sides of the slow cooker. Spread applesauce on top of meatloaf. Place in slow cooker and cook on low for 6 hours.

PORK MEATLOAF 6

Prep time: 20 minutes

Cook time: 6 hours

Ingredients

1 pound lean ground pork
1 C Panko crumbs
1 egg
¼ C ketchup

1 small onion, chopped
½ tsp black pepper
½ tsp garlic powder
1 C applesauce

Directions

Combine all ingredients except applesauce and mix thoroughly. Shape into a loaf that is small enough to not touch the sides of the slow cooker. Spread applesauce on top of meatloaf. Place in slow cooker and cook on low for 6 hours.

PORK MEATLOAF 7

Prep time: 20 minutes

Cook time: 6 hours

Ingredients

1 pound lean ground pork
1 C Italian bread crumbs
1 egg
¼ C spaghetti sauce

1 small onion, chopped
½ tsp black pepper
½ tsp garlic powder
1 C applesauce

Directions

Combine all ingredients except applesauce and mix thoroughly. Shape into a loaf that is small enough to not touch the sides of the slow cooker. Spread applesauce on top of meatloaf. Place in slow cooker and cook on low for 6 hours.

PORK MEATLOAF 8

Prep time: 20 minutes

Cook time: 6 hours

Ingredients
1 pound lean ground pork
1 C bread crumbs
1 egg
1 small onion, chopped

1 tsp ground ginger
1 tsp soya sauce
½ tsp black pepper
½ tsp garlic powder

Directions
Combine all ingredients except applesauce and mix thoroughly. Shape into a loaf that is small enough to not touch the sides of the slow cooker. Spread applesauce on top of meatloaf. Place in slow cooker and cook on low for 6 hours.

PORK MEATLOAF 9

Prep time: 20 minutes

Cook time: 6 hours

Ingredients
1 pound lean ground pork
1 C seasoned bread crumbs
1 egg

½ tsp black pepper
½ tsp garlic powder

Directions
Combine all ingredients except applesauce and mix thoroughly. Shape into a loaf that is small enough to not touch the sides of the slow cooker. Spread applesauce on top of meatloaf. Place in slow cooker and cook on low for 6 hours.

PORK MEATLOAF 10

Prep time: 20 minutes

Cook time: 6 hours

Ingredients
1 pound lean ground pork
1 C Panko crumbs
½ C ketchup

½ tsp black pepper
1 tsp salt

Directions
Combine all ingredients except applesauce and mix thoroughly. Shape into a loaf that is small enough to not touch the sides of the slow cooker. Spread applesauce on top of meatloaf. Place in slow cooker and cook on low for 6 hours.

Sausage Meatloaf 1

Prep time: 20 minutes

Cook time: 6 hours

Ingredients

1 pound ground sausage
1 C bread crumbs
1 egg
1 small onion, chopped

½ tsp black pepper
½ tsp chili powder
½ tsp cayenne pepper

Directions

Combine all ingredients and mix thoroughly. Shape into a loaf that is small enough to not touch the sides of the slow cooker. Place in slow cooker and cook on low for 6 hours.

Sausage Meatloaf 2

Prep time: 20 minutes

Cook time: 6 hours

Ingredients

1 pound ground Italian sausage
1 C bread crumbs
1 egg
1 small onion, chopped
½ tsp black pepper

2 tsp garlic powder
1 tsp Italian seasoning
1 C spaghetti sauce
1 C shredded mozzarella cheese

Directions

Combine first 7 ingredients and mix thoroughly. Shape into a loaf that is small enough to not touch the sides of the slow cooker. Spread sauce and cheese on top of meatloaf. Place in slow cooker and cook on low for 6 hours.

Sausage Meatloaf 3

Prep time: 20 minutes

Cook time: 6 hours

Ingredients

1 pound ground honey garlic sausage
1 C bread crumbs
¼ C honey garlic sauce
1 small onion, chopped

½ tsp black pepper
1 tsp garlic powder
½ C honey garlic sauce

Directions

Combine first 6 ingredients and mix thoroughly. Shape into a loaf that is small enough to not touch the sides of the slow cooker. Spread sauce on top of meatloaf. Place in slow cooker and cook on low for 6 hours.

SAUSAGE MEATLOAF 4

Prep time: 20 minutes

Cook time: 6 hours

Ingredients

1 pound ground sausage
½ pound Kielbasa sausage, cooked and chopped
1 C bread crumbs

1 egg
1 tbsp soya sauce
1 small onion, chopped
½ tsp black pepper

Directions

Combine all ingredients and mix thoroughly. Shape into a loaf that is small enough to not touch the sides of the slow cooker. Place in slow cooker and cook on low for 6 hours.

SAUSAGE MEATLOAF 5

Prep time: 20 minutes

Cook time: 6 hours

Ingredients

1 pound ground sausage
1 C bread crumbs
1 egg
1 C canned mushrooms, drained

1 small onion, chopped
½ tsp black pepper
1 C canned mushrooms, drained
1 C shredded cheese (your choice)

Directions

Combine first 6 ingredients and mix thoroughly. Shape into a loaf that is small enough to not touch the sides of the slow cooker. Spread cheese and mushrooms on top of meatloaf. Place in slow cooker and cook on low for 6 hours.

SAUSAGE MEATLOAF 6

Prep time: 20 minutes

Cook time: 6 hours

Ingredients

1 pound ground sausage
1 C bread crumbs
1 egg
1 C mixed frozen vegetables, thawed

1 small onion, chopped
½ tsp black pepper
1 C shredded cheese (your choice)

Directions

Combine first 6 ingredients and mix thoroughly. Shape into a loaf that is small enough to not touch the sides of the slow cooker. Spread cheese and mushrooms on top of meatloaf. Place in slow cooker and cook on low for 6 hours.

$\mathcal{S}$AUSAGE MEATLOAF 7

Prep time: 20 minutes   Cook time: 6 hours

Ingredients

1 pound ground sausage
1 C bread crumbs
1 egg
1 C sliced mushrooms

1 C chopped green pepper
1 small onion, chopped
½ tsp black pepper
1 tsp salt

Directions

Combine first 6 ingredients and mix thoroughly. Shape into a loaf that is small enough to not touch the sides of the slow cooker. Spread cheese and mushrooms on top of meatloaf. Place in slow cooker and cook on low for 6 hours.

$\mathcal{S}$AUSAGE MEATLOAF 8

Prep time: 20 minutes   Cook time: 6 hours

Ingredients

1 pound ground sausage
1 C bread crumbs
1 egg
½ C chopped bacon, cooked

1 tbsp soya sauce
1 tbsp teriyaki sauce
1 small onion, chopped
½ tsp black pepper

Directions

Combine first 6 ingredients and mix thoroughly. Shape into a loaf that is small enough to not touch the sides of the slow cooker. Spread cheese and mushrooms on top of meatloaf. Place in slow cooker and cook on low for 6 hours.

$\mathcal{S}$AUSAGE MEATLOAF 9

Prep time: 20 minutes   Cook time: 6 hours

Ingredients

1 pound ground sausage
1 C bread crumbs
1 egg
¼ C spaghetti sauce

1 tbsp hot sauce
1 tbsp Worcestershire sauce
1 small onion, chopped
½ tsp black pepper

Directions

Combine first 6 ingredients and mix thoroughly. Shape into a loaf that is small enough to not touch the sides of the slow cooker. Spread cheese and mushrooms on top of meatloaf. Place in slow cooker and cook on low for 6 hours.

SAUSAGE MEATLOAF 10

Prep time: 20 minutes   Cook time: 6 hours

Ingredients
1 pound ground sausage
1 C seasoned bread crumbs

2 small eggs
Salt and pepper to taste

Directions
Combine first 6 ingredients and mix thoroughly. Shape into a loaf that is small enough to not touch the sides of the slow cooker. Spread cheese and mushrooms on top of meatloaf. Place in slow cooker and cook on low for 6 hours.

Poultry

ROAST CHICKEN 1

Prep time: 15 minutes

Cook time: 6-8 hours

Ingredients

1 whole chicken, cleaned
2 C chicken broth
½ tsp poultry seasoning
Salt and pepper to taste

½ tsp thyme
½ tsp rosemary
½ tsp sage

Directions

Combine ingredients together in slow cooker. Cook on low for 6-8 hours.

ROAST CHICKEN 2

Prep time: 15 minutes

Cook time: 6-8 hours

Ingredients

1 whole chicken
2 C chicken broth
1 large onion, sliced
1 garlic clove, minced

½ tsp poultry seasoning
¼ tsp curry powder
Salt and pepper to taste

Directions

Combine ingredients together in slow cooker. Cook on low for 6-8 hours.

ROAST CHICKEN 3

Prep time: 15 minutes

Cook time: 6-8 hours

Ingredients

1 whole chicken
1 C chicken broth
1 can cream of chicken soup

1 small onion, diced
½ tsp poultry seasoning
Salt and pepper to taste

Directions

Combine ingredients together in slow cooker. Cook on low for 6-8 hours.

Roast Chicken 4

Prep time: 15 minutes

Cook time: 6-8 hours

Ingredients

1 whole chicken
2 C chicken broth
1 large onion, sliced
1 garlic clove, minced

½ tsp poultry seasoning
½ tsp Italian seasoning
1 tbsp ground parsley
Salt and pepper to taste

Directions

Combine ingredients together in slow cooker. Cook on low for 6-8 hours.

Roast Chicken 5

Prep time: 15 minutes

Cook time: 6-8 hours

Ingredients

1 whole chicken
2 C chicken broth
1 C tomato juice

1 large onion, sliced
1 garlic clove, minced
Salt and pepper to taste

Directions

Combine ingredients together in slow cooker. Cook on low for 6-8 hours.

Roast Chicken 6

Prep time: 15 minutes

Cook time: 6-8 hours

Ingredients

1 whole chicken
2 C chicken broth
½ C orange juice
1 can mandarin oranges

1 large onion, sliced
1 garlic clove, minced
Salt and pepper to taste

Directions

Combine ingredients together in slow cooker. Cook on low for 6-8 hours.

Roast Chicken 7

Prep time: 15 minutes

Cook time: 6-8 hours

Ingredients

1 whole chicken
2 C water
1 tbsp soya sauce

1 large onion, sliced
1 garlic clove, minced
½ tsp ground black pepper

Directions

Combine ingredients together in slow cooker. Cook on low for 6-8 hours.

ROAST CHICKEN 8

Prep time: 15 minutes

Cook time: 6-8 hours

Ingredients
1 whole chicken
3 C chicken broth
1 small onion, sliced

1 garlic clove, minced
1 celery stalk, chopped
Salt and pepper to taste

Directions
Combine ingredients together in slow cooker. Cook on low for 6-8 hours.

ROAST CHICKEN 9

Prep time: 15 minutes

Cook time: 6-8 hours

Ingredients
1 whole chicken
1 C chicken broth
1 C tomato sauce
1 can stewed, diced tomatoes, not drained

1 large onion, sliced
1 garlic clove, minced
Salt and pepper to taste

Directions
Combine ingredients together in slow cooker. Cook on low for 6-8 hours.

ROAST CHICKEN 10

Prep time: 15 minutes

Cook time: 6-8 hours

Ingredients
1 whole chicken
3 C water
2 tbsp chicken bouillon powder
1 large onion, sliced
1 garlic clove, minced

1 tsp paprika
½ tsp thyme
½ tsp poultry seasoning
Salt and pepper to taste

Directions
Combine ingredients together in slow cooker. Cook on low for 6-8 hours.

*I*TALIAN CHICKEN BREAST

Prep time: 10 minutes

Cook time: 4 hours

Ingredients

2 boneless, skinless chicken breasts
2 C spaghetti sauce
½ tsp salt

½ tsp ground black pepper
1 C shredded mozzarella cheese

Directions

Season chicken with salt and pepper. Place 1 C of spaghetti sauce in the slow cooker, followed by the chicken. Pour the rest of the sauce over the chicken. Cook on low for 5 hours, or on high for 3 hours. Before serving, sprinkle with shredded cheese.

*H*ERBED CHICKEN BREAST

Prep time: 10 minutes

Cook time: 4 hours

Ingredients

2 boneless, skinless chicken breasts
3 C chicken broth
½ tsp poultry seasoning
½ tsp salt
½ tsp black pepper

½ tsp rosemary
½ tsp sage
½ tsp garlic powder
1 small onion, sliced

Directions

Combine the broth and seasonings in the slow cooker. Add the chicken and onions, making sure that the broth covers the chicken. Cook on low for 5 hours, or on high for 3 hours.

*S*WEET & SOUR CHICKEN

Prep time: 15 minutes

Cook time: 3 hours

Directions

1 pound boneless, skinless chicken, cut into 1" chunks
1 C ketchup
½ C vinegar
½ C brown sugar, packed
½ C pineapple juice

½ C green pepper, seeded and chopped
½ C chopped green onion
1 tsp salt
½ tsp ground black pepper
½ tsp garlic powder
½ tsp curry powder

Directions

Combine the seasonings, and season chicken chunks with the mixture. Combine ketchup, vinegar, brown sugar, pineapple juice, green pepper, and green onion in the slow cooker, and add the chicken chunks, stirring to make sure all of the chicken is coated in sauce. Cook on low for 3 hours, or on high for 1.5 hours. Serve with rice.

Chicken in Orange Sauce

Prep time: 15 minutes

Cook time: 4-6 hours

Ingredients

3 pounds chicken
1 C water
1 ½ C orange juice
½ C sliced almonds
½ C yellow raisins

2 tbsp margarine
2 tsp salt
½ tsp ground cinnamon
¼ tsp ground ginger
3 tbsp corn starch

Directions

Combine all ingredients except corn starch together in slow cooker. Cook on low for 5-6 hours. Add corn starch to thicken sauce.

Stuffed Chicken Breasts

Prep time: 20 minutes

Cook time: 4-6 hours

Ingredients

4 boneless, skinless chicken breasts (halves)
½ C chicken broth + 2 tbsp
½ C Italian bread crumbs
½ C canned mushrooms, drained

¼ C finely diced onions
1 tbsp corn starch
½ tsp garlic powder
Salt and pepper to taste

Directions

Rinse and dry chicken, and pound flat by placing in a plastic bag and pounding from the center outwards. The chicken should be about 1/8" thick. In a bowl, combine crumbs, salt, mushrooms, onions, and 2 tbsp broth. Place ¼ of this mixture on each chicken breast, wrap, and hold together with toothpicks. Place meat into the slow cooker, and add the remaining broth. Cook at low heat for 4-6 hours. Remove chicken, and strain the sauce. Put the sauce in a sauce pan on the stovetop. Mix corn starch with a bit of water to dissolve, and add to the sauce. Stir constantly until thickened, about 2 minutes.

Chicken and Rice

Prep time: 15 minutes

Cook time: 4-6 hours

Ingredients

2 ½ pounds boneless, skinless chicken breast, cut into 6-8 pieces
3 C chicken broth
1 C uncooked rice
½ C frozen vegetables
½ C dry white wine

1 onion, diced
2 minced garlic cloves
1 red pepper, cut into strips
1 tomato, peeled and chopped
Salt and pepper to taste

Directions

Combine ingredients together in slow cooker. Cook on low for 4-6 hours.

CHICKEN CURRY

Prep time: 10 minutes

Cook time: 4-6 hours

Ingredients

1 pound boneless, skinless chicken breasts, cut into small chunks
1 C 5-minute rice
1 ¼ C water
4 onions, sliced
2 tbsp chopped parsley

1 tbsp soy sauce
1 tsp chili powder
1 tsp curry powder
4 cloves garlic, minced
½ tsp turmeric
½ tsp ground ginger

Directions

Cook rice and set aside. Combine ingredients together in slow cooker. Cook on low for 4-6 hours. Serve with the rice.

LEMON CHICKEN

Prep time: 10 minutes + 12 hours

Cook time: 4-6 hours

Ingredients

4 pounds boneless, skinless chicken breast, cut into chunks
½ C chicken stock

¼ C lemon juice
Salt and pepper to taste

Directions

Mix lemon juice, oil, and ¼ C oil in a bowl. Place chicken in a freezer bag, add the oil mixture, and marinade overnight. Dry the chicken, and save the marinade. Season the chicken with salt and pepper. Combine ingredients together in slow cooker. Cook on low for 4-6 hours.

CHICKEN CACCIATORE (BONELESS)

Prep time: 15 minutes

Cook time: 4-6 hours

Ingredients

2 pounds boneless, skinless chicken breast, cut into chunks
1 C white wine
¼ C chicken stock
1 minced onion

3 tsp garlic powder
1 5-ounce can tomato paste
½ tsp oregano
½ tsp Italian seasoning

Directions

Combine ingredients together in slow cooker. Cook on low for 4-6 hours.

CHICKEN CACCIATORE (BONE-IN)

Prep time: 20 minutes

Cook time: 4-6 hours

Ingredients

4 pounds skinless chicken breasts
2/3 C white wine
1/3 C flour
1 chopped onion
1 large can diced tomatoes

1 small can tomato paste
1 tsp oregano
1 tsp Italian seasoning
2 garlic cloves, minced
Salt and pepper to taste

Directions

Rinse chicken, pat it dry, and shake in flour to coat, and brown on the stovetop. Combine ingredients together in slow cooker. Cook on low for 4-6 hours.

CHICKEN IN DUCK SAUCE

Prep time: 10 minutes

Cook time: 4-6 hours

Ingredients

4 pounds boneless, skinless chicken breast, cut into cubes
½ C duck sauce
¼ C white wine

¼ C chicken stock
¼ tsp marjoram
½ tsp paprika
Salt and pepper to taste

Directions

Combine ingredients together in slow cooker. Cook on low for 4-6 hours.

HERBED CHICKEN

Prep time: 15 minutes

Cook time: 4-6 hours

Ingredients

2 ½ pounds boneless, skinless chicken, cut into chunks
1 ¼ C chicken broth
3 sliced tomatoes

1 tsp dried rosemary
1 tsp dried sage
Cooked rice
Salt and pepper to taste

Directions

Combine ingredients together in slow cooker. Cook on low for 4-6 hours.

Coq Au Vin

Prep time: 15 minutes

Cook time: 4-6 hours

Ingredients

4 pounds boneless, skinless chicken breast, cut into cubes
¼ pound fresh, sliced mushrooms
1 C cooking sherry
2 tbsp extra virgin olive oil
3 slices bacon, minced
1 chopped onion

1 tbsp flour
2 tbsp minced parsley
½ tsp thyme
1 carrot, diced
1 bay leaf
Salt and pepper to taste
More flour for dusting

Directions

Dust chicken cubes with flour and brown. Combine ingredients together in slow cooker. Cook on low for 4-6 hours.

Chicken and Broccoli

Prep time: 15 minutes

Cook time: 4-6 hours

Ingredients

2 boneless, skinless chicken breasts
2 C chicken stock
1 C shredded cheddar cheese
3 C cream cheese, cubed
3 C broccoli
½ C onion, chopped

1 tbsp butter
2 tbsp corn starch
3 tbsp water
½ tsp red pepper flakes
1 tbsp dried parsley
Salt and pepper to taste

Directions

Combine ingredients except broccoli and cheeses, together in slow cooker. Cook on low for 4-6 hours. Remove chicken and cut into chunks. Dissolve corn starch in water, and add to cooker. Simmer until thick, stirring constantly. Add cream cheese, cheddar cheese, and broccoli, and stir until all of the cheese has completely melted. Add chicken and broccoli, and cook simmer for 5 minutes.

Salsa Lime Chicken

Prep time: 10 minutes

Cook time: 4-6 hours

Ingredients

2 frozen, boneless, skinless chicken breasts
½ C salsa
½ C tomato sauce

Juice from 1 lime
1 C mozzarella, grated
Salt and pepper to taste

Directions

Combine ingredients except cheese together in slow cooker. Cook on low for 4-6 hours. Top with cheese before serving.

Teriyaki Chicken Wings

Prep time: 10 minutes + 12 hours

Cook time: 3-4 hours

Ingredients

2 pounds chicken wings
1 C teriyaki sauce
1 tbsp lemon juice

5 tbsp extra virgin olive oil
2 tbsp sugar
Toasted sesame seeds

Directions

Place chicken, 3 tbsp olive oil, teriyaki sauce, lemon juice, and sugar in a freezer bag, and refrigerate overnight. Combine ingredients except sesame seeds together in slow cooker. Cook on low for 3-4 hours. Garnish with sesame seeds.

Honey Garlic Chicken

Prep time: 15 minutes

Cook time: 4-6 hours

Ingredients

3 pounds boneless, skinless chicken breast, cubed
1 C ketchup
1 C soy sauce
1 C raw honey

2 tbsp corn starch
2 tbsp water
3 cloves garlic, minced
2 tbsp extra virgin olive oil

Directions

Combine ingredients together in slow cooker. Cook on low for 4-6 hours.

Chicken and Mushrooms

Prep time: 15 minutes

Cook time: 4-6 hours

Ingredients

4 boneless, skinless chicken breast halves
2 C fresh mushrooms, thinly sliced
2 C chicken stock
¼ C evaporated milk
½ C parmesan cheese, finely grated
6 cloves garlic, minced
2 tbsp white vinegar

1 tbsp tomato paste
2 tbsp corn starch
2 tbsp water
1 onion, minced
Salt and pepper to taste
Cooked rice

Directions

Combine all ingredients, except milk, parmesan cheese, and corn starch, together in slow cooker. Cook on low for 4-6 hours. Add milk to sauce in cooker, and stir in parmesan cheese. Dissolve corn starch in water, and add to sauce mixture. Whisk until mixture is smooth. Cook over medium-low heat, stirring constantly until sauce reaches desired consistency (about 5 minutes).

Thai Chicken Thighs

Prep time: 15 minutes

Cook time: 4-6 hours

Ingredients

2 pounds boneless, skinless chicken thighs
½ C chicken stock
¼ C peanut butter
¼ C soy sauce
¼ C unsalted peanuts, chopped

2 tbsp lime juice
1 tbsp cilantro
1 tbsp corn starch
1 tbsp water
½ tsp red pepper flakes

Directions

Combine all ingredients except corn starch and water together in slow cooker. Cook on low for 4-6 hours. Dissolve corn starch in water, and add to sauce. Set cooker to simmer and bring mixture to a boil. Stir constantly until sauce thickens. Add chicken and stir. Garnish chicken with chopped peanuts.

Chicken Taco Filling

Prep time: 10 minutes

Cook time: 4-6 hours

Ingredients

4 frozen, boneless, skinless chicken breasts
1 can diced tomatoes with green chilies
1 tbsp + 1 tsp chili powder

1 tsp salt
½ tsp black pepper
1 onion, diced

Directions

Combine ingredients together in slow cooker. Cook on low for 4-6 hours.

Braised Quail

Prep time: 20 minutes

Cook time: 6-8 hours

Ingredients

2 quails, cleaned and emptied
½ c sparkling white wine
3.5 ounces pancetta

2 C carrots cut into matchsticks
1 bay leaf
Salt and pepper to taste

Directions

Combine ingredients together in slow cooker. Cook on low for 6-8 hours.

APRICOT CHICKEN

Prep time: 10 minutes

Cook time: 4-6 hours

Ingredients

2 pounds chicken pieces
¼ C chicken stock
¼ C white wine
¼ C apricot jam

2 tbsp white vinegar
2 tbsp raw honey
1 tsp paprika
Salt and pepper to taste

Directions

Combine ingredients together in slow cooker. Cook on low for 4-6 hours.

PAPRIKA CHICKEN

Prep time: 10 minutes

Cook time: 4-6 hours

Ingredients

4 chicken breast halves, with skin and bones
1 C sour cream
2 tbsp flour
1 tbsp tomato paste

1 tbsp paprika
1 onion, diced
1 garlic clove, minced
Salt and pepper to taste

Directions

Combine ingredients together in slow cooker. Cook on low for 4-6 hours.

PUMPKIN CHICKEN

Prep time: 15 minutes

Cook time: 4-6 hours

Ingredients

1 ½ pound boneless, skinless chicken breast, cubed
2 pounds pumpkin, peeled and diced
2 chicken bouillon cubes
1 C tomato sauce

1 C cottage cheese
1 diced onion
2 garlic cloves, minced
Salt and pepper to taste

Directions

Combine all ingredients except cottage cheese together in slow cooker. Cook on low for 4-6 hours. Add the cottage cheese and stir to mix.

CHINESE DUCK

Prep time: 15 minutes

Cook time: 6-8 hours

Ingredients
1 2-pound whole duck
1 small bottle of beer
3 garlic cloves, crushed
1 piece fresh ginger, chopped
2 tbsp chili bean paste
1 tsp chili flakes

1 tsp soy sauce
1 tsp chili powder
1 cinnamon stick
1 tsp black peppercorns
1 carrot, chopped
5 tbsp vegetable oil, divided

Directions
Cut the duck in half, chop to the bone, and skin in 2" sections. Blanch in boiling water for 1 minute and set aside. Blanch carrots in boiling water for 5 minutes, drain, and set aside. Combine ingredients together in slow cooker. Cook on low for 6-8 hours.

FENUGREEK CHICKEN

Prep time: 15 minutes

Cook time: 4-6 hours

Ingredients
1 whole chicken, cut into pieces and skinned
½ C fresh spinach, diced
½ C fresh fenugreek leaves, diced
1 tbsp dried fenugreek leaves
1 C water
¼ C vegetable oil
1 cinnamon stick

5 whole cloves
1 onion, thinly sliced
1 tbsp ginger-garlic paste
4 green chilies, halved
1 tsp chili powder
¼ tsp ground turmeric
Salt and pepper to taste

Directions
Combine ingredients together in slow cooker. Cook on low for 4-6 hours.

TARO BRAISED CHICKEN

Prep time: 10 minutes

Cook time: 4-6 hours

Ingredients
1 whole chicken, rinsed and cut into chunks
½ tbsp soy sauce
1 tsp chili flakes
1 piece fresh ginger, sliced

1 tsp rice wine
1 small taro, peeled, rinsed, and chopped
Pinch salt

Directions
Combine ingredients together in slow cooker. Cook on low for 4-6 hours.

SEASONED CHICKEN

Prep time: 15 minutes   Cook time: 4-6 hours

Ingredients
1 whole chicken   ¼ tsp curry powder
1 ½ C chicken broth   Salt and pepper to taste
½ tsp poultry seasoning

Directions
Combine ingredients together in slow cooker. Cook on low for 4-6 hours.

ITALIAN CHICKEN

Prep time: 15 minutes   Cook time: 4-6 hours

Ingredients
4 boneless, skinless chicken breasts, cubed   1 small onion, diced
1 15-ounce can tomato sauce   2 cloves garlic, crushed
1 C water   ½ tsp black pepper
1 C mozzarella cheese, grated   ½ tsp salt

Directions
Combine ingredients together in slow cooker. Cook on low for 4-6 hours.

DRY GARLIC CHICKEN

Prep time: 15 minutes   Cook time: 4-6 hours

Ingredients
4 boneless, skinless chicken breasts, cubed   1 tbsp extra virgin olive oil
2 C dry garlic sauce   ½ tsp black pepper
1 C water   ½ tsp salt
2 cloves garlic, crushed

Directions
Combine ingredients together in slow cooker. Cook on low for 4-6 hours.

SWEET & SOUR CHICKEN

Prep time: 15 minutes   Cook time: 4-6 hours

Ingredients
4 boneless, skinless chicken breasts, cubed   1 small onion, diced
2 C sweet & sour sauce   ½ tsp black pepper
1 C water   ½ tsp salt

Directions
Combine ingredients together in slow cooker. Cook on low for 4-6 hours.

HONEY CHICKEN

Prep time: 15 minutes   Cook time: 4-6 hours

Ingredients
4 boneless, skinless chicken breasts, cubed
2 C raw honey
1 C water

2 cloves garlic, crushed
½ tsp black pepper
½ tsp salt

Directions
Combine ingredients together in slow cooker. Cook on low for 4-6 hours.

CHICKEN STIR-FRY 1

Prep time: 15 minutes   Cook time: 4 hours

Ingredients
1 pound boneless chicken breast, cut into strips and browned
3 tbsp soya sauce
1 tbsp white sugar
1 tsp ground ginger
2 tsp garlic powder

1 C sliced carrot
1 C chopped broccoli
1 C snow peas
1 C sprouts
1 C shredded red cabbage

Directions
Combine first 6 ingredients in slow cooker. Cook on low for 4 hours. Add remaining vegetables and heat through.

CHICKEN STIR-FRY 2

Prep time: 15 minutes   Cook time: 4 hours

Ingredients
1 pound boneless chicken breast, cut into strips and browned
2 C stir-fry sauce
1 C sliced carrot

1 C chopped broccoli
1 C snow peas
1 C sprouts
1 C shredded red cabbage

Directions
Combine first 3 ingredients in slow cooker. Cook on low for 4 hours. Add remaining vegetables and heat through.

CHICKEN STIR-FRY 3

Prep time: 15 minutes   Cook time: 4 hours

Ingredients
1 pound boneless chicken breast, cut into strips and browned
3 tbsp soya sauce

1 tbsp brown sugar
2 tsp garlic powder
1 C sliced carrot

1 C chopped cauliflower
1 C chopped broccoli
1 C snow peas

1 C sprouts
1 C shredded red cabbage

Directions
Combine first 5 ingredients in slow cooker. Cook on low for 4 hours. Add remaining vegetables and heat through.

CHICKEN STIR-FRY 4

Prep time: 15 minutes

Cook time: 4 hours

Ingredients
1 pound boneless chicken breast, cut into strips and browned
2 C dry garlic sauce
1 C sliced carrot

1 C chopped broccoli
1 C snow peas
1 C sprouts
1 C shredded red cabbage

Directions
Combine first 6 ingredients in slow cooker. Cook on low for 4 hours. Add remaining vegetables and heat through.

CHICKEN STIR-FRY 5

Prep time: 15 minutes

Cook time: 4 hours

Ingredients
1 pound boneless chicken breast, cut into strips and browned
2 C sweet & sour sauce
2 tsp garlic powder
1 C sliced carrot

1 C chopped broccoli
1 C snow peas
1 C sprouts
1 C shredded red cabbage

Directions
Combine first 3 ingredients in slow cooker. Cook on low for 4 hours. Add remaining vegetables and heat through.

CHICKEN STIR-FRY 6

Prep time: 15 minutes

Cook time: 4 hours

Ingredients
1 pound boneless chicken breast, cut into strips and browned
1 C chicken broth
1 C sliced carrot

1 C chopped broccoli
1 C snow peas
1 C sprouts
1 C shredded red cabbage

Directions
Combine first 3 ingredients in slow cooker. Cook on low for 4 hours. Add remaining vegetables and heat through.

CHICKEN STIR-FRY 7

Prep time: 15 minutes   Cook time: 4 hours

Ingredients

1 pound boneless chicken breast, cut into strips and browned
3 tbsp soya sauce
2 tbsp teriyaki sauce
1 tbsp Worcestershire sauce
1 tbsp white sugar

2 tsp garlic powder
1 C sliced carrot
1 C chopped broccoli
1 C snow peas
1 C sprouts
1 C shredded red cabbage

Directions

Combine first 7 ingredients in slow cooker. Cook on low for 4 hours. Add remaining vegetables and heat through.

CHICKEN STIR-FRY 8

Prep time: 15 minutes   Cook time: 4 hours

Ingredients

1 pound boneless chicken breast, cut into strips and browned
1 C chicken gravy
1 C sliced carrot

1 C chopped broccoli
1 C snow peas
1 C sprouts
1 C shredded red cabbage

Directions

Combine first 3 ingredients in slow cooker. Cook on low for 4 hours. Add remaining vegetables and heat through.

CHICKEN STIR-FRY 9

Prep time: 15 minutes   Cook time: 4 hours

Ingredients

1 pound boneless chicken breast, cut into strips and browned
3 tbsp soya sauce
1 C water
2 tsp garlic powder
1 large onion, sliced

1 C sliced carrot
1 C chopped broccoli
1 C snow peas
1 C sprouts
1 C shredded red cabbage

Directions

Combine first 6 ingredients in slow cooker. Cook on low for 4 hours. Add remaining vegetables and heat through.

CHICKEN STIR-FRY 10

Prep time: 15 minutes

Cook time: 4 hours

Ingredients

1 pound steak, cut into strips and browned
2 C General Tau sauce
1 C sliced carrot
1 C chopped broccoli

1 C snow peas
1 C sprouts
1 C shredded red cabbage

Directions

Combine first 6 ingredients in slow cooker. Cook on low for 4 hours. Add remaining vegetables and heat through.

CHICKEN AND NOODLES

Prep time: 15 minutes

Cook time: 4-6 hours

Ingredients

4 boneless, skinless chicken breasts, cubed
2 C dry garlic sauce
2 packages broken Ramen noodles without soup seasoning
1 C water

2 cloves garlic, crushed
1 tbsp extra virgin olive oil
½ tsp black pepper
½ tsp salt

Directions

Combine ingredients except ramen noodles together in slow cooker. Cook on low for 4-6 hours. Stir in noodles and let sit until they are cooked (about 15 minutes).

BARBECUED CHICKEN

Prep time: 15 minutes

Cook time: 4-6 hours

Ingredients

4 boneless, skinless chicken breasts, cubed
2 C barbecue sauce
1 C water
1 small onion, sliced

2 cloves garlic, crushed
½ tsp black pepper
½ tsp salt

Directions

Combine ingredients together in slow cooker. Cook on low for 4-6 hours.

Cheesy Chicken

Prep time: 15 minutes

Cook time: 4-6 hours

Ingredients

4 boneless, skinless chicken breasts, cubed
2 cans cheddar cheese soup
1 C water

2 cloves garlic, crushed
½ tsp black pepper
½ tsp salt

Directions

Combine ingredients together in slow cooker. Cook on low for 4-6 hours.

Spicy Chicken

Prep time: 15 minutes

Cook time: 4-6 hours

Ingredients

4 boneless, skinless chicken breasts, cubed
3 C water
2 tbsp chicken bouillon powder
1 clove garlic, crushed
1 tsp chili powder

1 tbsp red pepper flakes
1 tbsp hot sauce
½ tsp black pepper
½ tsp salt

Directions

Combine ingredients together in slow cooker. Cook on low for 4-6 hours.

Turkey with Gravy

Prep time: 15 minutes

Cook time: 2-3 hours

Ingredients

1 C cooked turkey, cubed
2 C turkey gravy
1 C chicken stock
1 small onion, diced

2 cloves garlic, crushed
1 tbsp extra virgin olive oil
½ tsp black pepper
½ tsp salt

Directions

Combine ingredients together in slow cooker. Cook on low for 2-3 hours.

Turkey Marinara

Prep time: 15 minutes

Cook time: 4-6 hours

Ingredients

1 C cooked turkey, cubed
2 C tomato sauce
1 C chicken stock
1 small onion, diced

2 cloves garlic, crushed
½ tsp black pepper
½ tsp salt
1 C finely grated parmesan cheese

Directions

Combine ingredients together in slow cooker. Cook on low for 4-6 hours.

Turkey with Veggies

Prep time: 15 minutes

Cook time: 4-6 hours

Ingredients

1 C cooked turkey, cubed
3 C chicken stock
1 C frozen mixed vegetables
1 small onion, diced

2 cloves garlic, crushed
½ tsp black pepper
½ tsp salt

Directions

Combine ingredients together in slow cooker. Cook on low for 4-6 hours.

Turkey with Rice

Prep time: 15 minutes

Cook time: 4-6 hours

Ingredients

1 C cooked turkey, cubed
3 C chicken stock
1 C Minute Rice, cooked
½ C sweet & sour sauce

1 small onion, diced
2 cloves garlic, crushed
½ tsp black pepper
½ tsp salt

Directions

Combine ingredients except rice together in slow cooker. Cook on low for 4-6 hours. Serve with cooked rice.

Turkey Stuffed Pasta Shells

Prep time: 15 minutes

Cook time: 3-4

Ingredients

1 pound ground turkey, browned
1 package jumbo pasta shells
3 C spaghetti sauce, separated
1 small onion, finely minced

1 garlic clove, minced
1 tsp ground black pepper
1 tsp salt
2 C shredded mozzarella cheese

Directions

Cook noodles on the stove top and set aside to cool. Mix 1 C sauce with turkey, cheese, salt, and pepper. Stuff meat mixture into cooked pasta shells. Place ½ C sauce on the bottom of the slow cooker, and place stuffed shells on top. Pour remaining sauce on top of shells. Cook on low for 3-4 hours. Stir in cheese, and cook over medium heat until cheese melts.

Turkey Rotini

Prep time: 10 minutes

Cook time: 3-4 hours

Ingredients

1 C cooked turkey, cubed
3 C chicken stock
1 package rotini noodles, cooked
1 small onion, diced
2 cloves garlic, crushed

1 tbsp hot sauce
1 tbsp hot pepper flakes
1 tsp paprika
½ tsp black pepper
½ tsp salt

Directions

Combine ingredients together in slow cooker. Cook on low for 3-4 hours.

Smoked Turkey

Prep time: 15 minutes

Cook time: 3-4 hours

Ingredients

1 C cooked turkey, cubed
3 C chicken stock
3 tbsp liquid smoke
1 small onion, diced

2 cloves garlic, crushed
½ tsp black pepper
½ tsp salt

Directions

Combine ingredients together in slow cooker. Cook on low for 3-4 hours.

ROAST TURKEY BREAST 1

Prep time: 15 minutes

Cook time: 4-6 hours

Ingredients
2 pound turkey breast
2 C chicken broth
½ C orange juice
1 large onion, sliced

1 garlic clove, minced
½ tsp poultry seasoning
Salt and pepper to taste

Directions
Combine ingredients together in slow cooker. Cook on low for 4-6 hours.

ROAST TURKEY BREAST 2

Prep time: 15 minutes

Cook time: 4-6 hours

Ingredients
2 pounds turkey breast
2 C chicken broth
½ C pineapple juice
1 can crushed pineapple
1 large onion, sliced

1 garlic clove, minced
½ tsp poultry seasoning
¼ tsp curry powder
Salt and pepper to taste

Directions
Combine ingredients together in slow cooker. Cook on low for 4-6 hours.

ROAST TURKEY BREAST 3

Prep time: 15 minutes

Cook time: 4-6 hours

Ingredients
2 pounds turkey breast
2 C chicken broth
1 C water
1 large onion, diced
1 garlic clove, minced

½ tsp poultry seasoning
½ tsp thyme
½ tsp sage
½ tsp curry powder
1 tbsp soya sauce

Directions
Combine ingredients together in slow cooker. Cook on low for 4-6 hours.

ROAST TURKEY BREAST 4

Prep time: 15 minutes

Cook time: 4-6 hours

Ingredients
2 pounds turkey breast
1 C chicken broth
½ C orange juice
1 can cream of chicken soup

1 large onion, sliced
1 garlic clove, minced
1 tbsp soya sauce
1 tsp ground black pepper

Directions
Combine ingredients together in slow cooker. Cook on low for 4-6 hours.

ROAST TURKEY BREAST 5

Prep time: 15 minutes

Cook time: 4-6 hours

Ingredients
2 pounds turkey breast
2 C chicken broth
1 C heavy cream

1 large onion, sliced
½ tsp poultry seasoning
Salt and pepper to taste

Directions
Combine ingredients together in slow cooker. Cook on low for 4-6 hours.

ROAST TURKEY BREAST 6

Prep time: 15 minutes

Cook time: 4-6 hours

Ingredients
2 pounds turkey breast
2 C chicken broth
1 C orange juice
1 can mandarin oranges

1 large onion, sliced
½ tsp poultry seasoning
Salt and pepper to taste

Directions
Combine ingredients together in slow cooker. Cook on low for 4-6 hours.

ROAST TURKEY BREAST 7

Prep time: 15 minutes

Cook time: 4-6 hours

Ingredients

2 pounds turkey breast
2 C chicken broth
1 can cream of chicken soup
1 large onion, sliced

½ tsp poultry seasoning
½ tsp thyme
½ tsp rosemary
Salt and pepper to taste

Directions

Combine ingredients together in slow cooker. Cook on low for 4-6 hours.

ROAST TURKEY BREAST 8

Prep time: 15 minutes

Cook time: 4-6 hours

Ingredients

2 pounds turkey breast
2 C chicken broth
1 large can stewed, diced tomatoes, not drained

1 large onion, sliced
½ tsp poultry seasoning
Salt and pepper to taste

Directions

Combine ingredients together in slow cooker. Cook on low for 4-6 hours.

ROAST TURKEY BREAST 9

Prep time: 15 minutes

Cook time: 4-6 hours

Ingredients

2 pounds turkey breast
2 C water
2 tbsp chicken bouillon powder
1 small onion, sliced

½ tsp poultry seasoning
½ tsp thyme
Salt and pepper to taste

Directions

Combine ingredients together in slow cooker. Cook on low for 4-6 hours.

ROAST TURKEY BREAST 10

Prep time: 15 minutes

Cook time: 4-6 hours

Ingredients

2 pounds turkey breast
2 C chicken broth
1 C cream of celery soup
1 celery stalk, diced

1 large onion, sliced
½ tsp poultry seasoning
½ tsp rosemary
Salt and pepper to taste

Directions

Combine ingredients together in slow cooker. Cook on low for 4-6 hours.

TURKEY LEGS 1

Prep time: 10 minutes

Cook time: 4-6 hours

Ingredients

2 turkey legs
1 C chicken broth
1 C water

1 tsp salt
½ tsp black pepper
½ tsp poultry seasoning

Directions

Combine ingredients together in slow cooker. Cook on low for 4-6 hours.

TURKEY LEGS 2

Prep time: 10 minutes

Cook time: 4-6 hours

Ingredients

2 turkey legs
1 C chicken broth
1 can cream of chicken soup

1 tsp salt
½ tsp black pepper
½ tsp poultry seasoning

Directions

Combine ingredients together in slow cooker. Cook on low for 4-6 hours.

TURKEY LEGS 3

Prep time: 10 minutes

Cook time: 4-6 hours

Ingredients

2 turkey legs
2 C chicken broth
½ C orange juice
1 tsp salt

½ tsp black pepper
½ tsp poultry seasoning
½ tsp curry powder

Directions

Combine ingredients together in slow cooker. Cook on low for 4-6 hours.

TURKEY LEGS 4

Prep time: 10 minutes

Cook time: 4-6 hours

Ingredients

2 turkey legs
1 C chicken broth
1 C tomato juice
1 tbsp hot sauce

1 tsp salt
½ tsp black pepper
½ tsp poultry seasoning

Directions

Combine ingredients together in slow cooker. Cook on low for 4-6 hours.

TURKEY LEGS 5

Prep time: 10 minutes

Cook time: 4-6 hours

Ingredients

2 turkey legs
1 C chicken broth
1 C milk
1 can cream of chicken soup

1 tbsp soya sauce
½ tsp black pepper
½ tsp poultry seasoning

Directions

Combine ingredients together in slow cooker. Cook on low for 4-6 hours.

Turkey Legs 6

Prep time: 10 minutes

Cook time: 4-6 hours

Ingredients

2 turkey legs
1 C chicken broth
1 C water

½ C pure maple syrup
1 tsp salt
½ tsp black pepper

Directions

Combine ingredients together in slow cooker. Cook on low for 4-6 hours.

Turkey Legs 7

Prep time: 10 minutes

Cook time: 4-6 hours

Ingredients

2 turkey legs
1 C chicken broth
1 C tomato sauce
1 tbsp sugar
½ tsp ground cloves

½ tsp paprika
1 tsp salt
½ tsp black pepper
½ tsp poultry seasoning

Directions

Combine ingredients together in slow cooker. Cook on low for 4-6 hours.

Turkey Legs 8

Prep time: 10 minutes

Cook time: 4-6 hours

Ingredients

2 turkey legs
2 C chicken broth
1 tsp salt
½ tsp black pepper
½ tsp poultry seasoning

½ tsp curry powder
½ tsp thyme
½ tsp rosemary
½ tsp sage

Directions

Combine ingredients together in slow cooker. Cook on low for 4-6 hours.

*T*URKEY LEGS 9

Prep time: 10 minutes

Cook time: 4-6 hours

Ingredients

2 turkey legs
1 C vegetable broth
1 C water
1 tbsp chicken bouillon powder

1 tsp salt
½ tsp black pepper
½ tsp poultry seasoning

Directions

Combine ingredients together in slow cooker. Cook on low for 4-6 hours.

*T*URKEY LEGS 10

Prep time: 10 minutes

Cook time: 4-6 hours

Ingredients

2 turkey legs
1 C tomato juice
1 C water
¼ C soya sauce

½ tsp black pepper
½ tsp poultry seasoning
½ tsp thyme

Directions

Combine ingredients together in slow cooker. Cook on low for 4-6 hours.

*M*ANDARIN CHICKEN

Prep time: 15 minutes

Cook time: 4-6 hours

Ingredients

1 pound boneless, skinless chicken breast
2 C chicken broth
1 can mandarin oranges, drained
1 C Chinese noodles
4 tbsp corn starch
1 tbsp soy sauce

1 tbsp Balsamic vinegar
1 onion, sliced
1 can mandarin oranges, drained
2 tbsp raw honey
¼ C water
Pepper to taste

Directions

Combine ingredients together in slow cooker. Cook on low for 4-6 hours.

GINGER CHICKEN

Prep time: 10 minutes   Cook time: 4-6 hours

Ingredients

3 pounds boneless, skinless chicken breast, cut
into chunks and browned
¼ C cooking sherry
¼ C soy sauce

¼ C water
1 tbsp raw honey
1 large piece of ginger, grated
Salt and pepper to taste

Directions

Combine ingredients together in slow cooker. Cook on low for 4-6 hours.

SPICY CHICKEN

Prep time: 10 minutes   Cook time: 4-6 hours

Ingredients

1 pound boneless, skinless chicken breast, cut
into chunks
1 C chick broth
1 box angel hair pasta
4 minced garlic cloves
1 hot pepper, chopped

1 ½ C chopped scallions
2 tbsp peanut butter
4 tbsp corn starch
1 tbsp soy sauce
1 tbsp minced ginger
1 tsp crushed pepper flakes

Directions

Combine ingredients together in slow cooker. Cook on low for 4-6 hours.

SPANISH-STYLE CHICKEN FAJITAS

Prep time: 15 minutes   Cook time: 4-6 hours

Ingredients

1 pound boneless, skinless chicken breast, cut
into chunks and browned
½ C raisins
1 15-ounce can diced tomatoes
2 onions, chopped
6 garlic cloves, minced
½ C raisins

2 sweet red peppers, 1 finely chopped and the
other cut in strips
1 chili pepper, finely chopped
1 cinnamon stick
½ tsp red pepper flakes
1 tbsp extra virgin olive oil
Corn tortillas, warmed

Directions

Combine ingredients together in slow cooker. Cook on low for 4-6 hours.

ORIENTAL CORNISH HEN

Prep time: 10 minutes   Cook time: 4-6 hours

Ingredients
1 Cornish hens   ¼ C minced scallions
1 bag frozen snow peas, thawed
    ½ C chicken stock

½ C minced onion   1 tbsp cooking sherry
2 tbsp raw honey   2 cloves garlic, minced
4 tbsp soy sauce   1 ½ tsp fresh ginger, grated
1 ½ tbsp yellow mustard

Directions
Combine ingredients together in slow cooker. Cook on low for 4-6 hours.

CORNISH HENS IN WHITE WINE

Prep time: 10 minutes   Cook time: 6-8 hours

Ingredients
2 Cornish hens   ¼ tsp basil
½ C chicken stock   ¼ tsp thyme
½ C dry white wine   ½ tsp garlic powder
1 tbsp flour   Salt and pepper to taste

Directions
Combine ingredients together in slow cooker. Cook on low for 4-6 hours.

HONEY SESAME CHICKEN

Prep time: 15 minutes   Cook time: 4 hours

Ingredients
2 boneless, skinless chicken breasts, cut into   1 clove garlic, minced
small chunks and browned   3 tbsp water
¼ C soy sauce   2 tbsp corn starch
1/8 C ketchup   1 green onion, chopped
¼ C diced onion   Toasted sesame seeds
½ C raw honey   Salt and pepper to taste

Directions
Combine ingredients together in slow cooker. Cook on low for 4-6 hours.

Braised Chicken Breasts

Prep time: 10 minutes   Cook time: 4-6 hours

Ingredients
4 skinless chicken breasts, bone-in
1/3 C white wine vinegar
1 can chicken broth
1/3 C salted capers, soaked

1 tbsp corn starch
1 tbsp water
1 onion, minced
Salt and pepper to taste

Directions
Combine ingredients except corn starch and water together in slow cooker. Cook on low for 4-6 hours. Dissolve corn starch in water, and add to cooker. Cook for about 2 minutes until sauce has thickened.

Chicken Marsala

Prep time: 10 minutes   Cook time: 4-6 hours

Ingredients
3 pounds boneless, skinless chicken
4 slices bacon, diced and cooked
½ C sweet Marsala wine
1 C chicken broth
1 can sliced mushrooms, drained

3 tbsp butter, divided
2 tbsp corn starch
2 tbsp water
Salt and pepper to taste

Directions
Sprinkle salt and pepper on the chicken, and place in a pan with the bacon grease to brown. Remove chicken and set aside. Add Marsala to the fat in the cooker, allowing it to evaporate to eliminate a lot of the liquid. Combine all ingredients in slow cooker except corn starch and water. Cook on low for 4-6 hours. Dissolve corn starch in water, and to the sauce pan, and bring to a boil, stirring the whole time (about 2 minutes). Add the rest of the butter, and the mushrooms from the cooker. Serve chicken with sauce.

Chicken Marinara

Prep time: 15 minutes   Cook time: 4-6 hours

Ingredients
4 boneless, skinless chicken breasts
1 can crushed tomato puree
1 C water
1 C mozzarella cheese, grated
2 cloves garlic, crushed

1 tsp dried basil
1 tsp onion powder
½ tsp black pepper
½ tsp salt
½ tsp red pepper flakes

Directions
Combine ingredients except cheese together in slow cooker. Cook on low for 4-6 hours. Place chicken in a casserole dish. Turn cooker to simmer, and cook sauce until it is as thick as you like. Pour sauce on chicken, sprinkle with cheese, and bake in an oven that has been pre-heated to broil. Cook for about 2-3 minutes, or until cheese starts to brown.

LOOSE CHICKEN 1

Prep time: 10 minutes   Cook time: 3-4 hour

Ingredients

1 pound ground chicken, browned   Salt and pepper to taste
1 C chicken gravy

Directions

Combine ingredients in slow cooker. Cook on low for 3-4 hours.

LOOSE CHICKEN 2

Prep time: 10 minutes   Cook time: 3-4 hour

Ingredients

1 pound ground chicken, browned   1 tbsp hot sauce
1 C chicken broth

Directions

Combine ingredients in slow cooker. Cook on low for 3-4 hours.

LOOSE CHICKEN 3

Prep time: 10 minutes   Cook time: 3-4 hour

Ingredients

1 pound ground chicken, browned   1 small onion, diced
1 C chicken gravy   1 garlic clove, minced

Directions

Combine ingredients in slow cooker. Cook on low for 3-4 hours.

LOOSE CHICKEN 4

Prep time: 10 minutes   Cook time: 3-4 hour

Ingredients

1 pound ground chicken, browned   Salt and pepper to taste
1 C sweet & sour sauce

Directions

Combine ingredients in slow cooker. Cook on low for 3-4 hours.

Loose Chicken 5

Prep time: 10 minutes

Cook time: 3-4 hour

Ingredients

1 pound ground chicken, browned
1 C dry garlic sauce

Salt and pepper to taste

Directions

Combine ingredients in slow cooker. Cook on low for 3-4 hours.

Loose Chicken 6

Prep time: 10 minutes

Cook time: 3-4 hour

Ingredients

1 pound ground chicken, browned
1 C spaghetti sauce
1 tsp garlic powder

1 tsp onion powder
Salt and pepper to taste

Directions

Combine ingredients in slow cooker. Cook on low for 3-4 hours.

Loose Chicken 7

Prep time: 10 minutes

Cook time: 3-4 hour

Ingredients

1 pound ground chicken, browned
1 C chicken broth
1 small onion, minced

2 garlic cloves, minced
Salt and pepper to taste

Directions

Combine ingredients in slow cooker. Cook on low for 3-4 hours.

Loose Chicken 8

Prep time: 10 minutes

Cook time: 3-4 hour

Ingredients

1 pound ground chicken, browned
1 tbsp soya sauce
1 tbsp Worcestershire sauce

1 C water
½ C tomato sauce

Directions

Combine ingredients in slow cooker. Cook on low for 3-4 hours.

LOOSE CHICKEN 9

Prep time: 10 minutes   Cook time: 3-4 hour

Ingredients

1 pound ground chicken, browned   1 large onion, minced
1 large can stewed diced tomatoes, not drained Salt and pepper to taste

Directions

Combine ingredients in slow cooker. Cook on low for 3-4 hours.

LOOSE CHICKEN 10

Prep time: 10 minutes   Cook time: 3-4 hour

Ingredients

1 pound ground chicken, browned   1 can sliced mushrooms, not drained
1 can cream of mushroom soup   Salt and pepper to taste

Directions

Combine ingredients in slow cooker. Cook on low for 3-4 hours.

Seafood

Salmon Steaks

Prep time: 10 minutes

Cook time: 3 hours

Ingredients
2 2-pound salmon steaks
½ C dry white wine
½ C water

1 lemon, sliced
1 onion, sliced into rings
Salt and pepper to taste

Directions
Combine all ingredients together in slow cooker. Cook on low for 3 hours.

Trout Fillets

Prep time: 10 minutes

Cook time: 3 hours

Ingredients
3-4 pounds trout fillets
1 C water
1 tsp salt

¼ C lemon juice
Salt and pepper to taste

Directions
Combine all ingredients together in slow cooker. Cook on low for 3 hours.

Tuna Casserole

Prep time: 10 minutes

Cook time: 3-4 hours

Ingredients
2 cans tuna packed in water, drained
2 C uncooked pasta
1 can cream of chicken soup

1 can cream of celery soup
1 C water
Salt and pepper to taste

Directions
Combine all ingredients together in slow cooker. Cook on low for 3 hours.

Boiled Haddock

Prep time: 5 minutes

Cook time: 3 hours

Ingredients
2 pounds haddock
3 C water

1 tsp salt

Directions
Combine all ingredients together in slow cooker. Cook on low for 3 hours.

BOILED POLLOCK

Prep time: 5 minutes   Cook time: 3 hours

Ingredients
2 pounds pollock   1 tsp salt
3 C water

Directions
Combine all ingredients together in slow cooker. Cook on low for 3 hours.

STEAMED MUSSELS

Prep time: 10 minutes   Cook time: 2-3 hours

Ingredients
1 pound mussels in shells   3 tbsp butter
3 C water   1 tsp salt

Directions
Combine all ingredients together in slow cooker. Cook on low for 3-4 hours or until shells open on their own.

STEAMED CLAMS

Prep time: 10 minutes   Cook time: 2-3 hours

Ingredients
1 pound clams in shells   3 tbsp butter
3 C water   1 tsp salt

Directions
Combine all ingredients together in slow cooker. Cook on low for 2-3 hours or until shells open on their own.

LEMON BUTTER TROUT

Prep time: 10 minutes   Cook time: 3 hours

Ingredients
1 pound trout, cleaned and skinned   1 C fish stock
½ C butter

Directions
Combine all ingredients together in slow cooker. Cook on low for 3 hours.

Lobster Tail

Prep time: 10 minutes

Cook time: 5 minutes

Ingredients
4 lobster tails
1 C water
½ C white wine

½ tsp salt
¼ C melted butter

Directions
Combine all ingredients together in slow cooker. Cook on low for 3-4 hours.

King Crab

Prep time: 5 minutes

Cook time: 3-4 hours

Ingredients
4 pounds king crab legs
1 C water
Lemon wedges

½ C melted butter
½ tsp salt

Directions
Break crab legs in half and place in slow cooker with water and salt. Cook on low for 3-4 hours. Serve with melted butter and lemon wedges.

Fish Chowder 1

Prep time: 10 minutes

Cook time: 3-4 hours

Ingredients
1 pound fresh or frozen haddock or Pollock
1 can clams, not drained
Juice from 2 cans of tuna
3 potatoes, cubed
1 C frozen corn
3 C water
1 C milk

1 can 2% evaporated milk
1 onion, thinly sliced
1 tsp garlic powder
1 tsp paprika
1 tbsp flour
1 tbsp butter
Salt and pepper to taste

Directions
Combine all ingredients together in slow cooker. Cook on low for 3-4 hours.

FISH CHOWDER 2

Prep time: 10 minutes

Cook time: 3-4 hours

Ingredients

1 can lobster
1 C fresh shrimp
4 potatoes, diced
3 C water
1 C milk
1 can 2% evaporated milk

1 onion, diced
1 tsp garlic powder
1 tbsp flour
1 tbsp butter
Salt and pepper to taste

Directions

Combine all ingredients together in slow cooker. Cook on low for 3-4 hours.

FISH CHOWDER 3

Prep time: 15 minutes

Cook time: 3-4 hours

Ingredients

1 C scallops
1 C whole clams
1 C whole shrimp, shells removed
1 C whole mussels
1 C chopped salmon
2 C water

1 C chicken stock
½ C white wine
3 garlic cloves, minced
¾ C frozen corn
1 can tomato paste
Salt and pepper to taste

Directions

Combine all ingredients together in slow cooker. Cook on low for 3-4 hours.

FISH CHOWDER 4

Prep time: 10 minutes

Cook time: 3-4 hours

Ingredients

1 can tuna
1 can chopped clams
1 can salmon
1 shrimp
½ pound chopped haddock
1 C scallops
2 C water

1 C milk
1 can 2% evaporated milk
1 small onion, diced
1 tbsp flour
1 tbsp butter
Salt and pepper to taste

Directions

Combine all ingredients together in slow cooker. Cook on low for 3-4 hours.

FISH CHOWDER 5

Prep time: 10 minutes

Cook time: 3-4 hours

Ingredients

1 C chopped haddock
1 C chopped salmon
1 C chopped Pollock
1 C whole clams
1 C water
1 C chicken stock
1 C cream
1 can 2% evaporated milk

1 onion, thinly sliced
2 garlic cloves, minced
1 tbsp lemon juice
½ tsp paprika
1 tbsp flour
1 tbsp butter
Salt and pepper to taste

Directions

Combine all ingredients together in slow cooker. Cook on low for 3-4 hours.

FISH CHOWDER 6

Prep time: 10 minutes

Cook time: 3-4 hours

Ingredients

1 C chopped lobster
1 C baby scallops
1 C baby clams
1 C deboned baby shrimp
1 C vegetable stock
2 C water

1 C milk
1 tbsp flour
1 tbsp butter
1 C mixed frozen vegetables
Salt and pepper to taste

Directions

Combine all ingredients together in slow cooker. Cook on low for 3-4 hours.

FISH CHOWDER 7

Prep time: 10 minutes

Cook time: 3-4 hours

Ingredients

1 pound cod fillets, chopped
½ pound smoked cod, skinned and deboned, chopped
1 C milk
1 C heavy cream

1 small onion, diced
1 tbsp flour
1 tbsp butter
2-3 large potatoes
Salt and pepper to taste

Directions

Combine all ingredients together in slow cooker. Cook on low for 3-4 hours.

FISH CHOWDER 8

Prep time: 10 minutes

Cook time: 3-4 hours

Ingredients

1 pound red snapper fillets, chopped
1 can stewed tomatoes
4 C clam juice
3 tbsp tomato paste
2 tbsp Worcestershire sauce
3 celery stalks, chopped
3 carrots, chopped

1 green pepper, chopped
4 garlic cloves, minced
3 small potatoes, peeled and cubed
1 jalapeno pepper, seeded and minced
2 tbsp extra virgin olive oil
1 bay leaf
Salt and pepper to taste

Directions

Combine all ingredients together in slow cooker. Cook on low for 3-4 hours.

FISH CHOWDER 9

Prep time: 10 minutes

Cook time: 3-4 hours

Ingredients

1 can whole clams
1 C haddock, chopped
1 C baby shrimp
1 C baby scallops
1 C water
1 C vegetable broth

1 C Clamato juice
1 C frozen corn
1 tbsp flour
1 tbsp butter
Salt and pepper to taste

Directions

Combine all ingredients together in slow cooker. Cook on low for 3-4 hours.

FISH CHOWDER 10

Prep time: 10 minutes

Cook time: 3-4 hours

Ingredients

1 C whole clams
1 C deboned shrimp
1 C scallops
1 C trout, chopped
1 C imitation crab meat
2 C water
1 C chicken stock
1 C tomato juice

1 small onion, diced
2 garlic cloves, minced
1 C frozen corn
1 C finely chopped carrots
1 tbsp soya sauce
1 tbsp flour
1 tbsp butter
Salt and pepper to taste

Directions

Combine all ingredients together in slow cooker. Cook on low for 3-4 hours.

FISH CHOWDER 11

Prep time: 10 minutes

Cook time: 3-4 hours

Ingredients

1 C fresh lobster
1 C fresh or frozen haddock
1 C scallops
2 C clam slices
2 C water
1 C heavy cream

1 can 2% evaporated milk
3 potatoes, chopped
1 tbsp flour
1 tbsp butter
Salt and pepper to taste

Directions

Combine all ingredients together in slow cooker. Cook on low for 3-4 hours.

FISH CHOWDER 12

Prep time: 10 minutes

Cook time: 3-4 hours

Ingredients

1 pound shark meat, chopped
1 C haddock, chopped
3 potatoes, chopped
1 onion, chopped
2 garlic cloves, minced
3 C water

1 C heavy cream
1 tsp paprika
1 tbsp flour
1 tbsp butter
Salt and pepper to taste

Directions

Combine all ingredients together in slow cooker. Cook on low for 3-4 hours.

FISH CHOWDER 13

Prep time: 10 minutes

Cook time: 3-4 hours

Ingredients

1 pound smoked salmon, chopped
10 slices bacon, finely chopped
3 carrots, chopped
3 green onions, chopped
5 C fish stock
2 C milk

2 tbsp lemon juice
10 small red potatoes, chopped
3 tbsp flour
3 tbsp butter
Salt and pepper to taste

Directions

Combine all ingredients together in slow cooker. Cook on low for 3-4 hours.

FISH CHOWDER 14

Prep time: 10 minutes

Cook time: 3-4 hours

Ingredients

2 pounds mix of halibut, flounder, pike, and rainbow trout, chopped
1 16-ounce can stewed tomatoes
1 C clam juice
½ C heavy cream
1 small onion, chopped
½ C chopped carrots

½ C chopped celery
½ C dry white wine
2 tbsp flour
2 tbsp butter
1 tbsp fresh parsley
½ tsp dried rosemary

Directions

Combine all ingredients together in slow cooker. Cook on low for 3-4 hours.

FISH CHOWDER 15

Prep time: 10 minutes

Cook time: 3-4 hours

Ingredients

1 C trout, chopped
1 C salmon, chopped
1 C perch, chopped
1 C clam juice
1 C fish stock
1 C milk

2 potatoes, sliced
2 tbsp flour
2 tbsp butter
2 tbsp lemon juice
Salt and pepper to taste

Directions

Combine all ingredients together in slow cooker. Cook on low for 3-4 hours.

FISH CHOWDER 16

Prep time: 10 minutes

Cook time: 3-4 hours

Ingredients

1 16-ounce can diced tomatoes
½ pound frozen cod fillets, thawed and chopped
2 celery stalks, chopped

1 small onion, diced
1 tbsp soya sauce
½ tsp black pepper

Directions

Combine all ingredients together in slow cooker. Cook on low for 3-4 hours.

FISH CHOWDER 17

Prep time: 10 minutes

Cook time: 3-4 hours

Ingredients

3 pounds chopped catfish fillets
2 C water
2 16-ounce cans stewed tomatoes
1 C frozen corn
1 can beer
2 tbsp extra virgin olive oil
1 onion, diced

2 carrots, diced
2 garlic cloves, minced
1 tsp oregano
1 tsp sea salt
2 tbsp parsley
½ tsp black pepper

Directions

Combine all ingredients together in slow cooker. Cook on low for 3-4 hours.

FISH CHOWDER 18

Prep time: 10 minutes

Cook time: 3-4 hours

Ingredients

1 pound cod fillets, chopped
2 C whole milk
½ C water
1 C frozen corn
3 potatoes, chopped
2 C chicken broth

6 slices bacon, diced
1 onion, diced
2 garlic cloves, minced
2 tbsp butter
Salt and pepper to taste

Directions

Combine all ingredients together in slow cooker. Cook on low for 3-4 hours.

FISH CHOWDER 19

Prep time: 10 minutes

Cook time: 3-4 hours

Ingredients

2 pounds catfish fillets, chopped
2 C shredded cheddar cheese
3 C milk, divided
2 tbsp flour
2 tbsp butter
1 C water

2 C chicken broth
½ C chopped celery
1 C sliced carrots
2 potatoes, chopped
Salt and pepper to taste

Directions

Combine all ingredients together in slow cooker. Cook on low for 3-4 hours.

FISH CHOWDER 20

Prep time: 10 minutes   Cook time: 3-4 hours

Ingredients

1 pound cod fillets, chopped   1 C evaporated milk
1 C whole milk   2 small potatoes, cubed
1 ½ C water, divided   Salt and pepper to taste

Directions

Combine all ingredients together in slow cooker. Cook on low for 3-4 hours.

Soups and Stews

BEEF BROTH

Prep time: 10 minutes   Cook time: 4 hours

Ingredients
1 pound beef bones   1 tbsp sea salt
1 large onion, peeled and cut in half   1 tsp whole black peppercorns
4 large carrots, cut into 4" pieces   2 bay leaves
4 celery stalks, cut into 4" pieces   6 quarts water
4 cloves garlic, halved

Directions
Bake bones in the oven at 425 degrees for 15 minutes. Combine all ingredients together in slow cooker. Cook on low for 4 hours.

CHICKEN BROTH

Prep time: 15 minutes   Cook time: 4 hours

Ingredients
3 pounds chicken wings   1 C chopped onion
1 C chopped carrots   1 tbsp sea salt
1 C chopped celery   ½ tsp whole black peppercorns

Directions
Combine all ingredients together in slow cooker. Cook on low for 4 hours.

VEGETABLE BROTH

Prep time: 15 minutes   Cook time: 4 hours

Ingredients
4 ½ C water   3 celery stalks, cut in half
2 medium carrots, peeled and chopped   10 peppercorns
1 large onion, peeled and cut in half   1 bay leaf

Directions
Combine all ingredients together in slow cooker. Cook on low for 4 hours.

FISH STOCK

Prep time: 15 minutes

Cook time: 4 hours

Ingredients

2 pounds seafood meat, bones, etc.
6 C water
1 onion, sliced
1 stalk celery, chopped
1 carrot, chopped

1 bay leaf
1 tsp thyme
5 peppercorns
½ tsp salt

Directions

Combine all ingredients together in slow cooker. Cook on low for 4 hours.

SPLIT PEA SOUP

Prep time: 15 minutes

Cook time: 4-6 hours

Ingredients

8 C water
1 pound dried split peas
1 ham hock
1 diced onion

2 celery stalks, diced
½ tsp garlic powder
Salt and pepper to taste

Directions

Combine all ingredients together in slow cooker. Cook on low for 4-6 hours.

CREAM OF CARROT SOUP

Prep time: 20 minutes

Cook time: 4-6 hours

Ingredients

10 C vegetable stock
6 C baby carrots
4 C heavy whipping cream
1 large potato, peeled and diced
2 ½ C diced onions

6 chopped green onions
¼ C butter
8 cloves garlic
Salt and pepper to taste

Directions

Combine all ingredients together in slow cooker. Cook on low for 4 hours.

CREAMY TOMATO SOUP

Prep time: 10 minutes

Cook time: 4-6 hours

Ingredients
4 C canned pureed tomatoes
1 C chicken broth
1 ½ C milk

½ C heavy whipping cream
½ tsp baking soda
Salt and pepper to taste

Directions
Combine all ingredients together in slow cooker. Cook on low for 4 hours. Blend with a hand blender until creamy.

KOSHER CHICKEN SOUP

Prep time: 30 minutes

Cook time: 4 hours

Ingredients
1 small chicken, cut up
3 quarts water
2 small onions, diced
2 celery stalks, diced

3 carrots, diced
1 bay leaf
1 bunch fresh dill

Directions
Combine all ingredients together in slow cooker. Cook on low for 4 hours.

LENTIL SOUP

Prep time: 20 minutes

Cook time: 4-6 hours

Ingredients
2 C red lentils
1 chopped onion
4 tbsp extra virgin olive oil
1 1-ounce package dry onion soup mix

Juice from 1 lemon
1 tsp ground cumin
Salt and pepper to taste

Directions
Combine all ingredients together in slow cooker. Cook on low for 4-6 hours.

VEGETABLE SOUP

Prep time: 20 minutes

Cook time: 4 hours

Ingredients

2 C stewed tomatoes
1 C fresh green beans, chopped
1 C diced carrots
½ C diced onions
½ C tomato puree (or tomato paste)
3 beef bouillon cubes
1 celery stalk, chopped

1 clove garlic, chopped
¼ gallon water
1 tbsp barley
1 tbsp Worcestershire sauce
1 tbsp floour
Salt and pepper to taste

Directions

Combine all ingredients together in slow cooker. Cook on low for 4 hours.

CHICKEN SOUP WITH WILD RICE

Prep time: 15 minutes

Cook time: 4-6 hours

Ingredients

2 14-ounce cans chicken broth
2 boneless, skinless chicken breasts, uncooked, diced
1 C chopped onion
1 C diced carrots
1 C diced celery
1 6-ounce package long grain and wild rice

2 C whole milk
2 tbsp water
2 tbsp corn starch
2 tbsp butter
1 tsp salt
½ tsp pepper
1 tbsp parsley flakes

Directions

Combine all ingredients together in slow cooker. Cook on low for 4-6 hours.

TURKEY NOODLE SOUP

Prep time: 20 minutes

Cook time: 4 hours

Ingredients

2 C diced raw turkey
6 C turkey stock
2 C cooked egg noodles
4 carrots, peeled and sliced

1 large onion, diced
1 celery stalk, diced
1 tbsp butter
Salt and pepper to taste

Directions

Combine all ingredients together in slow cooker. Cook on low for 4 hours.

CHICKEN NOODLE SOUP 1

Prep time: 20 minutes

Cook time: 4 hours

Ingredients

2 C cooked egg noodles
6 C chicken stock
2 C diced, raw chicken
1 tbsp butter

4 carrots, peeled and sliced
1 large onion, diced
1 celery stalk, diced
Salt and pepper to taste

Directions

Combine all ingredients together in slow cooker. Cook on low for 4 hours.

CHICKEN NOODLE SOUP 2

Prep time: 20 minutes

Cook time: 4 hours

Ingredients

2 C cooked egg noodles
6 C chicken stock
2 C diced, raw chicken
1 tbsp butter

1 C mixed frozen veggies
1 celery stalk, diced
Salt and pepper to taste

Directions

Combine all ingredients together in slow cooker. Cook on low for 4 hours.

CHICKEN NOODLE SOUP 3

Prep time: 20 minutes

Cook time: 4 hours

Ingredients

2 C cooked egg noodles
6 C chicken stock
2 C diced, raw chicken
1 tbsp butter
2 carrots, peeled and sliced

1 large potato, diced
½ C diced turnip
1 large onion, diced
1 celery stalk, diced
Salt and pepper to taste

Directions

Combine all ingredients together in slow cooker. Cook on low for 4 hours.

CHICKEN NOODLE SOUP 4

Prep time: 20 minutes

Cook time: 4 hours

Ingredients

2 C cooked egg noodles
3 C chicken stock
3 C tomato juice
½ C hot sauce
2 C diced, raw chicken

1 tbsp butter
4 carrots, peeled and sliced
1 large onion, diced
1 celery stalk, diced
Salt and pepper to taste

Directions

Combine all ingredients together in slow cooker. Cook on low for 4 hours.

CHICKEN NOODLE SOUP 5

Prep time: 20 minutes

Cook time: 4 hours

Ingredients

2 C cooked egg noodles
6 C chicken stock
2 C diced, raw chicken
1 small onion, sliced

1 tbsp butter
1 tsp celery salt
½ tsp ground black pepper

Directions

Combine all ingredients together in slow cooker. Cook on low for 4 hours.

CHICKEN NOODLE SOUP 6

Prep time: 20 minutes

Cook time: 4 hours

Ingredients

2 C cooked egg noodles
5 C chicken stock
1 can cream of chicken soup
2 C diced, cooked chicken
2 carrots, peeled and sliced

1 tbsp butter
1 large onion, diced
1 celery stalk, chopped
Salt and pepper to taste

Directions

Combine all ingredients together in slow cooker. Cook on low for 4 hours.

Chicken Noodle Soup 7

Prep time: 20 minutes

Cook time: 4 hours

Ingredients
6 C chicken stock
2 C diced, cooked chicken
½ C Minute Rice
1 tbsp butter

4 carrots, peeled and sliced
1 large onion, diced
1 celery stalk, diced
Salt and pepper to taste

Directions
Combine all ingredients together in slow cooker. Cook on low for 4 hours.

Chicken Noodle Soup 8

Prep time: 20 minutes

Cook time: 4 hours

Ingredients
2 C cooked egg noodles
3 C chicken stock
3 C tomato juice
1 C tomato sauce
2 C diced, cooked chicken

1 tsp celery salt
1 tsp garlic powder
1 tsp onion powder
½ tsp ground black pepper

Directions
Combine all ingredients together in slow cooker. Cook on low for 4 hours.

Chicken Noodle Soup 9

Prep time: 20 minutes

Cook time: 4 hours

Ingredients
2 C cooked egg noodles
6 C chicken stock
2 C diced, cooked chicken
1 can stewed diced tomatoes, drained

1 tsp celery salt
1 tsp garlic powder
1 tsp onion powder
½ tsp ground black pepper

Directions
Combine all ingredients together in slow cooker. Cook on low for 4 hours.

CHICKEN NOODLE SOUP 10

Prep time: 20 minutes

Cook time: 4 hours

Ingredients

2 C cooked egg noodles
6 C chicken stock
2 C diced, cooked chicken
1 C frozen peas
1 C frozen corn

1 small onion, diced
1 garlic clove, minced
1 tsp celery salt
½ tsp ground black pepper

Directions

Combine all ingredients together in slow cooker. Cook on low for 4 hours.

SPICY CHICKEN SOUP

Prep time: 20 minutes

Cook time: 4 hours

Ingredients

4 boneless, skinless chicken breasts, diced
2 14-ounce cans diced tomatoes
2 14-ounce cans chicken broth
2 16-ounce cans black beans, drained
1 15-ounce bag frozen corn
1 16-ounce jar chunky salsa
2 tbsp extra virgin olive oil
1 large onion, diced

3 cloves garlic, minced
1 tsp ground black pepper
1 tsp garlic powder
1 tbsp flaked parsley
1 tbsp onion powder
½ tsp sea salt
1 tbsp chili powder

Directions

Combine all ingredients together in slow cooker. Cook on low for 4 hours.

POTATO SOUP

Prep time: 10 minutes

Cook time: 4 hours

Ingredients

12 ounces evaporated skim milk
3 C chicken broth
4 C peeled, diced potatoes
½ C finely diced celery

1 C finely chopped onion
2 tbsp vegetable oil
Salt and pepper to taste

Directions

Combine all ingredients together in slow cooker. Cook on low for 4 hours.

POTATO AND CHEESE SOUP

Prep time: 20 minutes   Cook time: 4 hours

Ingredients

6 C potatoes, peeled and cubed
2 14-ounce cans chicken broth
2 C half and half
1 C shredded cheddar cheese
1 C frozen corn
2 tbsp butter

2 tbsp corn starch
2 tbsp water
3 ounces cream cheese, cubed
6 slices cooked bacon, crumbled
½ C chopped onion
Salt and pepper to taste

Directions

Combine all ingredients except cheeses together in slow cooker. Cook on low for 4 hours. Stir in cheeses and heat through.

CREAMY CHICKEN AND WILD RICE SOUP

Prep time: 20 minutes   Cook time: 4-6 hours

Ingredients

2 boneless, skinless chicken breasts, raw and diced
2 14-ounce cans chicken broth
1 6-ounce package long grain and wild rice
1 C chopped onion
1 C diced carrots

1 C diced celery
2 tbsp butter
2 tbsp corn starch
2 tbsp water
1 tsp sea salt
½ tsp pepper

Directions

Combine all ingredients together in slow cooker. Cook on low for 4-6 hours.

WHITE BEAN AND LAMB STEW

Prep time: 15 minutes   Cook time: 4 hours

Ingredients

4 lamb chops, fat trimmed off
1 ½ C dry white beans, washed
2 C canned diced tomatoes
1 C diced onion
1 C diced leek
2 tbsp chopped garlic

2 tsp Worcestershire sauce
1 sprig each thyme and savory
1 tsp herbes de Provence
1 ½ tsp sea salt
1 tsp pepper
3 C water

Directions

Combine all ingredients together in slow cooker. Cook on low for 4 hours.

BUTTERNUT SQUASH BISQUE

Prep time: 15 minutes

Cook time: 4 hours

Ingredients

5 C vegetable stock
3 pounds butternut squash, cut into 1" pieces
3 granny smith apples, cut into 1" pieces
2 C kale
2 onions, chopped
1 pint whole milk

2 tbsp pure maple syrup
2 tsp ground ginger
1 ½ tsp ground cumin
½ tsp nutmeg
1 tbsp extra virgin olive oil

Directions

Combine all ingredients except maple syrup and milk together in slow cooker. Cook on low for 4 hours. Pour ingredients into a blender, add maple syrup and milk, and puree until smooth.

POTATO, LEEK, AND PEA SOUP

Prep time: 10 minutes

Cook time: 4 hours

Ingredients

4 C chicken stock
1 C milk
1 pound potatoes, peeled and cubed
1 C frozen peas, thawed

2 tbsp extra virgin olive oil
1 onion, diced
4 leeks, finely chopped
Salt and pepper to taste

Directions

Combine all ingredients together in slow cooker. Cook on low for 4 hours. Puree mixture in a food processer.

FRENCH ONION SOUP

Prep time: 10 minutes

Cook time: 4 hours

Ingredients

6 C chicken stock
½ C parmesan cheese, finely grated
5 onions, sliced

3 tbsp butter
2 tbsp cooking sherry
6 slices toasted French bread

Directions

Combine all ingredients together in slow cooker. Cook on low for 4 hours. Serve with parmesan cheese and French bread.

TORTILLA SOUP

Prep time: 10 minutes

Cook time: 4 hours

Ingredients

1 pound grated cheddar cheese
1 15-ounce can stewed tomatoes, drained
Chopped cilantro
1/3 C cooking oil

3 quarts chicken broth
4 garlic cloves
2 diced onions

Directions

Combine all ingredients except cheese together in slow cooker. Cook on low for 4 hours. Serve with cheese.

CLAM CHOWDER

Prep time: 15 minutes

Cook time: 4 hours

Ingredients

2 ½ C fish stock
1 C minced clams
¼ C celery, finely diced
¼ C green pepper, finely diced
1 potato, diced
1 14-ounce can tomatoes, chopped

1 tbsp flour
1 onion, chopped
6 slices of bacon, diced
1 clove of garlic, minced
Salt and pepper to taste

Directions

Combine all ingredients together in slow cooker. Cook on low for 4 hours.

BEEF STEW

Prep time: 15 minutes

Cook time: 4-5 hours

Ingredients

1 pound stew beef
2 C frozen peas
½ C tomato sauce
½ C cooking sherry
½ C water
2 tbsp cooking oil
1 onion, minced

2 garlic cloves, minced
5 carrots, diced
1 potato, cubed
2 bay leaves
1 tsp Worcestershire sauce
Salt and pepper to taste

Directions

Combine all ingredients together in slow cooker. Cook on low for 4-5 hours.

MEATBALL STEW

Prep time: 15 minutes

Cook time: 4 hours

Ingredients

1 package frozen meatballs, thawed and
browned
¾ C frozen peas
½ C beef stock
¼ C dry white wine
2 carrots, chopped

2 potatoes, cut in 1" cubes
1 bay leaf
2 cloves of garlic, minced
1 onion, diced
Salt and pepper

Directions

Combine all ingredients together in slow cooker. Cook on low for 4 hours.

LAMB STEW

Prep time: 10 minutes

Cook time: 4-6 hours

Ingredients

3 pounds lamb stew meat, cut into 2" slices
and browned
2 tbsp extra virgin olive oil
6 tbsp lemon juice

8 tbsp chicken stock
3 cloves garlic, peeled and crushed
Salt and pepper to taste

Directions

Combine all ingredients together in slow cooker. Cook on low for 4-6 hours.

YOGURT AND BARLEY SOUP

Prep time: 10 minutes

Cook time: 4 hours

Ingredients

6 C chicken stock
3 C plain yogurt
½ C finely diced onion

4 tbsp pearl barley, rinsed
2 tbsp butter
Salt and pepper to taste

Directions

Combine all ingredients except yogurt, salt, and pepper, together in slow cooker. Cook on low for 4 hours. Cool mixture, and refrigerate until chilled. Add yogurt, salt, and pepper. Serve cold.

VEGETABLE STEW

Prep time: 15 minutes   Cook time: 4 hours

Ingredients
½ C vegetable stock   2 garlic cloves, minced
4 tbsp extra virgin olive oil, divided   2 tomatoes, chopped
2 green peppers, cut into strips   1 eggplant, cut into 1" cubes
1 potato, diced   2 zucchini, cut into ½" slices
1 onion, chopped

Directions
Combine all ingredients together in slow cooker. Cook on low for 4 hours.

BEEF AND BARLEY STEW

Prep time: 15 minutes   Cook time: 4 hours

Ingredients
1 28-ounce can crushed tomatoes   2 celery stalks, chopped
2 ½ C water   1 onion, chopped
½ C barley   1 garlic clove, minced
1 ½ pound lean ground beef   ½ tsp basil
2 tbsp extra virgin olive oil   ½ tsp thyme
3 carrots, chopped   Salt and pepper to taste

Directions
Combine all ingredients together in slow cooker. Cook on low for 4 hours.

CHICKEN BOUILLABAISSE

Prep time: 10 minutes   Cook time: 4 hours

Ingredients
10 ounces kielbasa sausage, cut into 1" chunks   ½ C chopped carrot
4 skinless chicken thighs   ¼ C chopped celery
1 C diced tomatoes   1 tbsp extra virgin olive oil
¾ C water   1 tbsp chopped garlic
½ C dry white wine   1 tsp lemon zest
6 potatoes, peeled and quartered   Salt and pepper to taste
½ C chopped onion

Directions
Combine all ingredients together in slow cooker. Cook on low for 4 hours.

CHICKEN STEW 1

Prep time: 10 minutes

Cook time: 3-4 hours

Ingredients

2 C leftover chicken, cubed
1 small onion, sliced
2 medium potatoes, cubed

4 C chicken broth
1 tsp salt
½ tsp ground black pepper

Directions

Combine all ingredients in slow cooker. Cook on low for 3-4 hours.

CHICKEN STEW 2

Prep time: 10 minutes

Cook time: 3-4 hours

Ingredients

2 C leftover chicken, cubed
1 small onion, sliced
2 medium potatoes, cubed
1 C frozen corn kernels
1 C sliced carrot

4 C chicken broth
1 tsp salt
½ tsp ground black pepper
½ tsp poultry seasoning
½ tsp curry powder

Directions

Combine all ingredients in slow cooker. Cook on low for 3-4 hours.

CHICKEN STEW 3

Prep time: 10 minutes

Cook time: 3-4 hours

Ingredients

2 C leftover chicken, cubed
1 small onion, sliced
2 medium potatoes, cubed
4 C chicken broth

1 can cream of chicken soup
1 tsp salt
½ tsp ground black pepper
½ tsp poultry seasoning

Directions

Combine all ingredients in slow cooker. Cook on low for 3-4 hours.

CHICKEN STEW 4

Prep time: 10 minutes

Cook time: 3-4 hours

Ingredients

2 C leftover chicken, cubed
1 small onion, sliced
2 medium potatoes, cubed
1 C sliced carrots
1 C mixed frozen vegetables

4 C chicken broth
1 tsp salt
½ tsp ground black pepper
2 tbsp hot sauce

Directions

Combine all ingredients in slow cooker. Cook on low for 3-4 hours.

CHICKEN STEW 5

Prep time: 10 minutes

Cook time: 3-4 hours

Ingredients

2 C leftover chicken, cubed
1 small onion, sliced
2 medium potatoes, cubed
4 C chicken broth
1 small can stewed diced tomatoes, drained

1 tsp salt
½ tsp ground black pepper
½ tsp poultry seasoning
½ tsp sage

Directions

Combine all ingredients in slow cooker. Cook on low for 3-4 hours.

CHICKEN STEW 6

Prep time: 10 minutes

Cook time: 3-4 hours

Ingredients

2 C leftover chicken, cubed
1 small onion, sliced
1 garlic clove, minced
2 medium potatoes, cubed
4 C chicken broth

1 C tomato juice
1 tsp salt
½ tsp ground black pepper
½ tsp poultry seasoning

Directions

Combine all ingredients in slow cooker. Cook on low for 3-4 hours.

CHICKEN STEW 7

Prep time: 10 minutes

Cook time: 3-4 hours

Ingredients

2 C leftover chicken, cubed
1 small onion, sliced
2 medium red potatoes, cubed
2 C chicken broth
2 C vegetable broth

1 tsp salt
½ tsp ground black pepper
½ tsp poultry seasoning
½ tsp sage
½ tsp thyme

Directions

Combine all ingredients in slow cooker. Cook on low for 3-4 hours.

CHICKEN STEW 8

Prep time: 10 minutes

Cook time: 3-4 hours

Ingredients

2 C leftover chicken, cubed
1 small onion, sliced
2 medium potatoes, cubed
2 garlic cloves, minced
2 C cherry tomatoes
3 C chicken broth

1 C milk
1 tsp salt
½ tsp ground black pepper
½ tsp poultry seasoning
½ tsp sage
½ tsp thyme

Directions

Combine all ingredients in slow cooker. Cook on low for 3-4 hours.

CHICKEN STEW 9

Prep time: 10 minutes

Cook time: 3-4 hours

Ingredients

2 C leftover chicken, cubed
1 small onion, sliced
3 medium potatoes, cubed
4 C chicken broth
1 tbsp soya sauce

1 tbsp chicken bouillon powder
½ tsp ground black pepper
½ tsp poultry seasoning
½ tsp sage
½ tsp thyme

Directions

Combine all ingredients in slow cooker. Cook on low for 3-4 hours.

CHICKEN STEW 10

Prep time: 10 minutes

Cook time: 3-4 hours

Ingredients

2 C leftover chicken, cubed
1 small onion, sliced
2 large potatoes, cubed
2 garlic cloves, minced
4 C chicken broth
1 can cream of celery soup
1 celery stalk, chopped

1 bay leaf
1 tsp salt
½ tsp ground black pepper
½ tsp poultry seasoning
½ tsp sage
½ tsp thyme

Directions

Combine all ingredients in slow cooker. Cook on low for 3-4 hours.

BEEF STEW 1

Prep time: 10 minutes

Cook time: 3-4 hours

Ingredients

2 cubed stewing beef, browned
1 large onion, chopped
2 large potatoes, cubed
4 C beef broth

1 can cream of celery soup
1 celery stalk, chopped
1 tbsp soya sauce
½ tsp ground black pepper

Directions

Combine all ingredients in slow cooker. Cook on low for 3-4 hours.

BEEF STEW 2

Prep time: 10 minutes

Cook time: 3-4 hours

Ingredients

2 cubed stewing beef, browned
1 large onion, chopped
2 large potatoes, cubed
3 C beef broth

1 can cream of beef soup
1 tbsp soya sauce
½ tsp ground black pepper
½ tsp chili powder

Directions

Combine all ingredients in slow cooker. Cook on low for 3-4 hours.

BEEF STEW 3

Prep time: 10 minutes

Cook time: 3-4 hours

Ingredients

2 cubed stewing beef, browned
1 large onion, chopped
2 large potatoes, cubed

4 C beef broth
1 tbsp soya sayce
½ tsp ground black pepper

Directions

Combine all ingredients in slow cooker. Cook on low for 3-4 hours.

BEEF STEW 4

Prep time: 10 minutes

Cook time: 3-4 hours

Ingredients

2 cubed stewing beef, browned
1 large onion, chopped
2 large potatoes, cubed
1 large can stewed diced tomatoes, drained

4 C beef broth
1 tbsp soya sauce
½ tsp ground black pepper

Directions

Combine all ingredients in slow cooker. Cook on low for 3-4 hours.

BEEF STEW 5

Prep time: 10 minutes

Cook time: 3-4 hours

Ingredients

2 cubed stewing beef, browned
1 large onion, chopped
2 large potatoes, cubed
4 C beef broth

1 can cream of mushroom soup
1 can sliced mushrooms, not drained
1 tbsp soya sauce
½ tsp ground black pepper

Directions

Combine all ingredients in slow cooker. Cook on low for 3-4 hours.

*B*EEF STEW 6

Prep time: 10 minutes   Cook time: 3-4 hours

Ingredients

2 cubed stewing beef, browned   1 C vegetable broth
1 large onion, chopped   1 tsp salt
2 large potatoes, cubed   ½ tsp ground black pepper
3 C beef broth

Directions

Combine all ingredients in slow cooker. Cook on low for 3-4 hours.

*B*EEF STEW 7

Prep time: 10 minutes   Cook time: 3-4 hours

Ingredients

2 cubed stewing beef, browned   3 C beef broth
1 large onion, chopped   1 tbsp Worcestershire sauce
2 large potatoes, cubed   ½ tsp ground black pepper
1 large can stewed diced tomatoes, not drained

Directions

Combine all ingredients in slow cooker. Cook on low for 3-4 hours.

*B*EEF STEW 8

Prep time: 10 minutes   Cook time: 3-4 hours

Ingredients

2 cubed stewing beef, browned   1 tsp paprika
1 large onion, chopped   1 tsp cayenne pepper
2 large potatoes, cubed   ½ tsp chili powder
4 C beef broth   1 tbsp hot sauce
1 tsp salt   ½ tsp ground black pepper

Directions

Combine all ingredients in slow cooker. Cook on low for 3-4 hours.

BEEF STEW 9

Prep time: 10 minutes

Cook time: 3-4 hours

Ingredients

2 cubed stewing beef, browned
1 large onion, chopped
2 large potatoes, cubed
4 C beef broth

1 tbsp teriyaki sauce
1 tbsp soya sauce
½ tsp ground black pepper
1 C uncooked pasta

Directions

Combine all ingredients in slow cooker. Cook on low for 3-4 hours.

BEEF STEW 10

Prep time: 10 minutes

Cook time: 3-4 hours

Ingredients

2 cubed stewing beef, browned
1 large onion, chopped
2 large potatoes, cubed
2 garlic cloves, minced
1 celery stalk, chopped

2 C sliced carrots
4 C beef broth
1 tsp salt
½ tsp ground black pepper

Directions

Combine all ingredients in slow cooker. Cook on low for 3-4 hours.

TURKEY STEW 1

Prep time: 10 minutes

Cook time: 3-4 hours

Ingredients

2 C leftover turkey, cubed
2 large potatoes, cubed
2 garlic cloves, minced
1 C sliced carrot
4 C chicken broth
1 can cream of celery soup
1 celery stalk, chopped

1 bay leaf
1 tsp salt
½ tsp ground black pepper
½ tsp poultry seasoning
½ tsp sage
½ tsp thyme

Directions

Combine all ingredients in slow cooker. Cook on low for 3-4 hours.

TURKEY STEW 2

Prep time: 10 minutes

Cook time: 3-4 hours

Ingredients

2 C leftover turkey, cubed
1 large onion, chopped
2 large potatoes, cubed
4 C chicken broth
1 can cream of celery soup
1 celery stalk, chopped

1 tbsp soya sayce
½ tsp ground black pepper
½ tsp poultry seasoning
½ tsp sage
½ tsp thyme

Directions

Combine all ingredients in slow cooker. Cook on low for 3-4 hours.

TURKEY STEW 3

Prep time: 10 minutes

Cook time: 3-4 hours

Ingredients

2 C leftover turkey, cubed
1 large onion, chopped
2 large potatoes, cubed
4 C chicken broth
1 can cream of chicken
½ tsp ground black pepper
½ tsp poultry seasoning

½ tsp sage
½ tsp thyme
1 tsp paprika
½ tsp chili powder
½ tsp cayenne pepper
1 tsp curry powder

Directions

Combine all ingredients in slow cooker. Cook on low for 3-4 hours.

TURKEY STEW 4

Prep time: 10 minutes

Cook time: 3-4 hours

Ingredients

2 C leftover turkey, cubed
1 large onion, chopped
2 large potatoes, cubed
2 C chicken broth
1 can cream of celery soup
1 C cream

1 tsp salt
2 tbsp hot sauce
½ tsp ground black pepper
½ tsp poultry seasoning
½ tsp sage
½ tsp thyme

Directions

Combine all ingredients in slow cooker. Cook on low for 3-4 hours.

TURKEY STEW 5

Prep time: 10 minutes

Cook time: 3-4 hours

Ingredients

2 C leftover turkey, cubed
1 large onion, chopped
2 large potatoes, cubed
4 C chicken broth

2 cans cream of chicken soup
1 celery stalk, chopped
1 tbsp soya sayce
½ tsp ground black pepper

Directions

Combine all ingredients in slow cooker. Cook on low for 3-4 hours.

TURKEY STEW 6

Prep time: 10 minutes

Cook time: 3-4 hours

Ingredients

2 C leftover turkey, cubed
1 large onion, chopped
2 large potatoes, cubed
4 C chicken broth
1 large can stewed, diced tomatoes, not drained

1 celery stalk, chopped
1 tbsp soya sayce
½ tsp ground black pepper
½ tsp poultry seasoning
½ tsp sage
½ tsp thyme

Directions

Combine all ingredients in slow cooker. Cook on low for 3-4 hours.

TURKEY STEW 7

Prep time: 10 minutes

Cook time: 3-4 hours

Ingredients

2 C leftover turkey, cubed
1 large onion, chopped
2 large potatoes, cubed
4 C chicken broth
1 can cream of celery soup
½ C tomato juice

1 celery stalk, chopped
½ tsp poultry seasoning
½ tsp sage
½ tsp thyme
Salt and pepper to taste

Directions

Combine all ingredients in slow cooker. Cook on low for 3-4 hours.

TURKEY STEW 8

Prep time: 10 minutes

Cook time: 3-4 hours

Ingredients

2 C leftover turkey, cubed
1 large onion, chopped
2 large potatoes, cubed
2 C chicken broth
½ C orange juice
1 C water

2 tbsp chicken bouillon powder
½ tsp ground black pepper
½ tsp poultry seasoning
½ tsp sage
½ tsp thyme

Directions

Combine all ingredients in slow cooker. Cook on low for 3-4 hours.

TURKEY STEW 9

Prep time: 10 minutes

Cook time: 3-4 hours

Ingredients

2 C leftover turkey, cubed
1 large onion, chopped
2 large potatoes, cubed
4 C chicken broth
1 can cream of mushroom soup

1 C sliced mushrooms
1 tbsp soya sauce
½ tsp poultry seasoning
½ tsp sage
½ tsp thyme

Directions

Combine all ingredients in slow cooker. Cook on low for 3-4 hours.

TURKEY STEW 10

Prep time: 10 minutes

Cook time: 3-4 hours

Ingredients

2 C leftover turkey, cubed
1 large onion, chopped
2 large potatoes, cubed
4 C chicken broth

½ tsp poultry seasoning
½ tsp sage
½ tsp thyme

Directions

Combine all ingredients in slow cooker. Cook on low for 3-4 hours.

Casseroles and Pasta Dishes

Mock Lasagna

Prep time: 15 minutes

Cook time: 5-6 hours

Ingredients

1 pound lean ground beef
1 package lasagna noodles, broken and
uncooked
1 jar spaghetti sauce
1 tbsp soya sauce
1 onion, thinly sliced

2 garlic cloves, minced
1 celery stalk, chopped
1 tsp paprika
½ tsp chili powder
½ tsp cayenne pepper
½ tsp black pepper

Directions

Combine all ingredients together in slow cooker. Cook on low for 5-6 hours.

Lasagna

Prep time: 15 minutes

Cook time: 5-6 hours

Ingredients

1 pound lean ground beef, cooked on stove top
1 package no-boil lasagna noodles, uncooked
2 C shredded mozzarella cheese

½ C finely grated parmesan cheese
2-3 C spaghetti sauce

Directions

Layer ingredients in slow cooker as you would a traditional lasagna. Cook on low for 5-6 hours.

Spaghetti Casserole

Prep time: 15 minutes

Cook time: 3-4 hours

Ingredients

1 pound lean ground beef, cooked
1 box spaghetti, uncooked and broken into bite
sized pieces
2 C spaghetti sauce
1 small onion, minced
1 garlic clove, minced
1 tbsp soya sauce

2 tbsp extra virgin olive oil
1 tsp paprika
1 tsp cayenne pepper
½ tsp black pepper
½ tsp ground cloves
1 tbsp white sugar

Directions

Combine all ingredients together in slow cooker. Cook on low for 3-4 hours.

BEEF CASSEROLE 1

Prep time: 15 minutes

Cook time: 5-6 hours

Ingredients

1 pound lean ground beef, cooked
1 small onion, minced
1 garlic clove, minced
3 C beef broth
1 ½ C uncooked egg noodles

1 C frozen vegetables
1 tbsp soya sauce
1 tsp paprika
½ tsp chili powder
½ tsp black pepper

Directions

Combine all ingredients together in slow cooker. Cook on low for 5-6 hours.

BEEF CASSEROLE 2

Prep time: 15 minutes

Cook time: 5-6 hours

Ingredients

1 pound stew beef, cut into small cubes and browned on the stovetop
2 ½ C beef broth
½ C vegetable juice
2 C elbow macaroni, uncooked

1 tbsp soya sauce
1 onion, diced
1 garlic clove, minced
½ tsp black pepper

Directions

Combine all ingredients together in slow cooker. Cook on low for 5-6 hours.

BEEF CASSEROLE 3

Prep time: 15 minutes

Cook time: 5-6 hours

Ingredients

1 pound lean ground beef, cooked
2 tbsp extra virgin olive oil
1 onion, thinly sliced
2 garlic cloves, minced
2 celery stalks, chopped
1 package cream cheese, softened and cubed

2 C beef broth
1 C frozen vegetables
3 potatoes, peeled and cubed
1 tbsp soya sauce
½ tsp black pepper

Directions

Combine all ingredients except cream cheese together in slow cooker. Cook on low for 5-6 hours. Stir in cream cheese, and cook for 30 minutes.

BEEF CASSEROLE 4

Prep time: 15 minutes

Cook time: 5-6 hours

Ingredients
1 pound lean ground beef, cooked
3 C leftover mashed potatoes
2 C frozen vegetables

2 onions, thinly sliced
2 C shredded cheese (any kind)

Directions
Layer ingredients in dish as follows: beef, onions, vegetables, potatoes, cheese. Cook on low for 5-6 hours.

BEEF CASSEROLE 5

Prep time: 15 minutes

Cook time: 5-6 hours

Ingredients
1 pound lean ground beef, cooked
1 can tomato soup
1 C water
½ C milk or cream
1 C pasta, uncooked

1 onion, minced
1 garlic clove, minced
Salt and pepper to taste
1 C shredded cheddar cheese

Directions
Combine all ingredients except cheese together in slow cooker. Cook on low for 5-6 hours. Stir in cheese and serve.

CHICKEN CASSEROLE 1

Prep time: 10 minutes

Cook time: 5-6 hours

Ingredients
1 pound boneless, skinless chicken breast, cooked and shredded
1 tsp salt
½ tsp black pepper
1 small onion, diced

1 garlic clove, minced
3 C chicken broth
1 can cream of chicken soup
3 C cooked egg noodles

Directions
Combine all ingredients together in slow cooker. Cook on low for 5-6 hours.

CHICKEN CASSEROLE 2

Prep time: 10 minutes   Cook time: 5-6 hours

Ingredients

1 pound boneless, skinless chicken breast, cut into 1" chunks and browned
2 tbsp extra virgin olive oil
1 package cream cheese, cubed
1 small onion, diced

½ tsp salt
½ tsp black pepper
1 can cream of chicken soup
3 C chicken broth
2 C uncooked elbow macaroni

Directions

Combine all ingredients except cream cheese together in slow cooker. Cook on low for 5-6 hours. Stir in cream cheese.

CHICKEN CASSEROLE 3

Prep time: 10 minutes   Cook time: 5-6 hours

Ingredients

1 pound boneless, skinless chicken breast, cut into 1" chunks and browned
1 small onion, diced
½ tsp salt
½ tsp black pepper

1 can cream of celery soup
1 can cream of chicken soup
2 C chicken broth
2 C uncooked elbow macaroni

Directions

Combine all ingredients together in slow cooker. Cook on low for 5-6 hours.

CHICKEN CASSEROLE 4

Prep time: 10 minutes   Cook time: 5-6 hours

Ingredients

1 pound boneless, skinless chicken breast, cut into 1" chunks and browned
1 small onion, diced
1 clove garlic, minced
½ tsp salt

½ tsp black pepper
3 C chicken broth
1 C heavy cream
2 C uncooked pasta

Directions

Combine all ingredients together in slow cooker. Cook on low for 5-6 hours.

CHICKEN CASSEROLE 5

Prep time: 10 minutes   Cook time: 5-6 hours

Ingredients
1 pound boneless, skinless chicken breast, cut into 1" chunks and browned
2 tbsp extra virgin olive oil
1 small onion, diced
1 clove garlic, minced

½ tsp salt
½ tsp black pepper
3 C chicken broth
1 C tomato juice
2 C uncooked egg noodles

Directions
Combine all ingredients together in slow cooker. Cook on low for 5-6 hours.

TURKEY CASSEROLE 1

Prep time: 10 minutes   Cook time: 5-6 hours

Ingredients
2 C cooked turkey, cubed
1 small onion, diced
1 clove garlic, minced
½ tsp salt

½ tsp black pepper
3 C chicken broth
1 small can tomato paste
2 C uncooked pasta

Directions
Combine all ingredients together in slow cooker. Cook on low for 5-6 hours.

TURKEY CASSEROLE 2

Prep time: 10 minutes   Cook time: 5-6 hours

Ingredients
2 C cooked turkey, cubed
1 small onion, diced
1 clove garlic, minced
½ tsp salt
½ tsp black pepper

3 C chicken broth
½ C orange juice
1 can mandarin oranges
2 C uncooked egg noodles

Directions
Combine all ingredients together in slow cooker. Cook on low for 5-6 hours.

TURKEY CASSEROLE 3

Prep time: 10 minutes

Cook time: 5-6 hours

Ingredients

1 pound cooked turkey breast, cubed
1 small onion, diced
1 clove garlic, minced
½ tsp salt

½ tsp black pepper
3 C spaghetti sauce
1 small can tomato paste
2 C uncooked rotini pasta

Directions

Combine all ingredients together in slow cooker. Cook on low for 5-6 hours.

TURKEY CASSEROLE 4

Prep time: 10 minutes

Cook time: 5-6 hours

Ingredients

1 pound cooked turkey breast, cubed
1 small onion, diced
1 clove garlic, minced
½ tsp salt
½ tsp black pepper
½ tsp curry powder

½ tsp cayenne pepper
1 tsp paprika
2 C chicken broth
1 C tomato sauce
1 C shredded mozzarella cheese
2 C uncooked pasta

Directions

Combine all ingredients together in slow cooker. Cook on low for 5-6 hours.

TURKEY CASSEROLE 5

Prep time: 10 minutes

Cook time: 5-6 hours

Ingredients

1 pound cooked turkey breast, cubed
1 small onion, diced
1 clove garlic, minced
½ tsp salt
½ tsp black pepper

2 C chicken broth
1 C milk
¼ C hot sauce
2 C uncooked egg noodles

Directions

Combine all ingredients together in slow cooker. Cook on low for 5-6 hours.

HAMBURGER CASSEROLE

Prep time: 15 minutes

Cook time: 5-6 hours

Ingredients

1 pound lean ground beef, browned
1 onion, thinly sliced
2 C spaghetti sauce
1 C ketchup

1 C elbow macaroni
1 tsp salt
½ tsp black pepper

Directions

Combine all ingredients together in slow cooker. Cook on low for 5-6 hours.

CHEESEBURGER CASSEROLE

Prep time: 15 minutes

Cook time: 5-6 hours

Ingredients

1 pound lean ground beef, browned
1 onion, thinly sliced
2 C spaghetti sauce
1 C ketchup

1 C shredded sharp cheddar cheese
1 C elbow macaroni
1 tsp salt
½ tsp black pepper

Directions

Combine all ingredients together in slow cooker. Cook on low for 5-6 hours.

TACO CASSEROLE

Prep time: 10 minutes

Cook time: 5-6 hours

Ingredients

1 pound lean ground beef, browned
1 C elbow macaroni, uncooked
1 C broken taco shells
1 small onion, finely diced
1 garlic clove, minced
½ C diced green pepper

½ C diced red pepper
1 package taco seasoning
2 C water
1 C tomato sauce
1 C shredded sharp cheddar cheese
1 C taco sauce

Directions

Combine all ingredients together in slow cooker. Cook on low for 5-6 hours.

Sweet & Sour Beef Casserole

Prep time: 10 minutes

Cook time: 5-6 hours

Ingredients

1 pound stew beef, cubed and browned
2 tbsp extra virgin olive oil
1 can pineapple chunks, not drained
1 C ketchup
½ C vinegar

½ C packed brown sugar
2 green onions, diced
1 tsp fresh grated ginger
1 C egg noodles, uncooked

Directions

Combine all ingredients together in slow cooker. Cook on low for 5-6 hours.

Sweet & Sour Chicken Casserole

Prep time: 10 minutes

Cook time: 5-6 hours

Ingredients

1 pound boneless, skinless chicken breast, cubed and browed
1 small onion, thinly sliced
1 green onion, chopped

3 C sweet & sour sauce
½ C water
2 C Chinese noodles
1 C frozen vegetables

Directions

Combine all ingredients together in slow cooker. Cook on low for 5-6 hours.

Sweet & Sour Pork Casserole

Prep time: 10 minutes

Cook time: 5-6 hours

Ingredients

1 pound boneless pork tenderloin, cubed and browned
1 small onion, thinly sliced
1 garlic clove, minced
1 tsp fresh grated ginger
1 C white vinegar

1 C packed brown sugar
½ C pineapple juice
½ C raw honey
1 green onion, chopped
1 ½ C elbow macaroni, uncooked

Directions

Combine all ingredients together in slow cooker. Cook on low for 5-6 hours.

BEEF CANNELLONI

Prep time: 20 minutes

Cook time: 5-6 hours

Ingredients
1 pound lean ground beef, browned
1 package cannelloni noodles, uncooked
1 small onion, minced
2 garlic cloves, minced
3 C spaghetti sauce
3 C grated mozzarella cheese

1 tsp cayenne pepper
1 tsp paprika
½ tsp chili pepper
1 tbsp soya sauce
½ tsp black pepper

Directions
Combine beef, onion, garlic, 2 C spaghetti sauce, 2 C mozzarella, and seasonings. Stuff mixture into cannelloni. Place remaining sauce in slow cooker, and add the stuffed shells. Top with more sauce and remaining cheese. Cook on low for 5-6 hours.

STUFFED PASTA SHELLS

Prep time: 20 minutes

Cook time: 5-6 hours

Ingredients
1 pound lean ground beef, browned
1 package large shell noodles, cooked
1 small onion, minced
2 garlic cloves, minced
3 C spaghetti sauce
2 C grated mozzarella cheese

1 tsp cayenne pepper
1 tsp paprika
½ tsp chili pepper
1 tbsp soya sauce
½ tsp black pepper

Directions
Combine beef, onion, garlic, 2 C spaghetti sauce, 2 C mozzarella, and seasonings. Stuff mixture into shells. Place remaining sauce in slow cooker, and add the stuffed shells. Top with more sauce and remaining cheese. Cook on low for 5-6 hours.

BEEF AND POTATO CASSEROLE

Prep time: 15 minutes

Cook time: 3-4 hours

Ingredients
1 pound lean ground beef, browned
1 medium size onion, chopped
4-5 medium size potatoes, peeled and thinly sliced
1 C frozen corn
1 C frozen peas

1 C frozen carrots
3 C shredded cheese (your choice)
2 C beef broth
1 tsp garlic powder
1 tsp chili powder
Salt and pepper to taste

Directions
Spread a layer of potatoes on the bottom of the slow cooker, followed by a layer of cheese, a layer of corn, a layer of potatoes, a layer of meat, a layer of cheese, a layer of peas, a layer of potatoes, a layer of meat, a layer of cheese, and a layer of carrots. Top with remaining cheese. Cook on low for 3-4 hours.

MAC & CHEESE 1

Prep time: 15 minutes

Cook time: 4-5 hours

Ingredients

2 tbsp extra virgin olive oil
1 small onion, diced
1 garlic clove, minced
2 C shredded cheddar cheese

2 C uncooked macaroni
1 C water
3 C milk

Directions

Combine all ingredients together in slow cooker. Cook on low for 4-5 hours.

MAC & CHEESE 2

Prep time: 15 minutes

Cook time: 4-5 hours

Ingredients

½ pound ground beef, browned
1 small onion, diced
1 garlic clove, minced
2 C shredded cheddar cheese

2 C uncooked macaroni
1 C water
3 C milk

Directions

Combine all ingredients together in slow cooker. Cook on low for 4-5 hours.

MAC & CHEESE 3

Prep time: 15 minutes

Cook time: 4-5 hours

Ingredients

½ pound bacon, chopped and cooked
1 small onion, diced
1 garlic clove, minced
2 C shredded cheddar cheese

2 C uncooked macaroni
1 C water
3 C milk

Directions

Combine all ingredients except cheese together in slow cooker. Cook on low for 4-5 hours. Stir in cheese before serving.

Macaroni and Cheese 4

Prep time: 5 minutes

Cook time: 4-5 hours

Ingredients

3 C chicken broth
1 pound pasta
2 C water
1 C heavy whipping cream

3 C sharp shredded cheddar cheese
4 ounces cream cheese
Salt and pepper to taste

Directions

Combine all ingredients together in slow cooker. Cook on low for 4-5 hours.

Macaroni and Cheese 5

Prep time: 5 minutes

Cook time: 4-5 hours

Ingredients

3 C chicken broth
1 pound pasta
2 C water
1 C heavy whipping cream
3 C sharp shredded cheddar cheese

4 ounces cream cheese
Salt and pepper to taste
2 tsp paprika
1 tsp garlic powder

Directions

Combine all ingredients together in slow cooker. Cook on low for 4-5 hours.

Macaroni and Cheese 6

Prep time: 5 minutes

Cook time: 4-5 hours

Ingredients

3 C chicken broth
1 pound pasta
2 C water
1 C heavy whipping cream
3 C sharp shredded cheddar cheese

1 tsp chili powder
1 tsp paprika
½ tsp cayenne pepper
Salt and pepper to taste

Directions

Combine all ingredients together in slow cooker. Cook on low for 4-5 hours.

Macaroni and Cheese 7

Prep time: 5 minutes

Cook time: 4-5 hours

Ingredients

3 C chicken broth
1 pound pasta
2 C water
1 C milk

3 C sharp shredded cheddar cheese
½ C sour cream
1 clove garlic, minced
Salt and pepper to taste

Directions

Combine all ingredients together in slow cooker. Cook on low for 4-5 hours.

Macaroni and Cheese 8

Prep time: 5 minutes

Cook time: 4-5 hours

Ingredients

3 C chicken broth
1 pound pasta
2 C water
1 C heavy whipping cream

3 C sharp shredded cheddar cheese
3 tbsp taco seasoning
Salt and pepper to taste

Directions

Combine all ingredients together in slow cooker. Cook on low for 4-5 hours.

Macaroni and Cheese 8

Prep time: 5 minutes

Cook time: 4-5 hours

Ingredients

3 C chicken broth
1 pound pasta
2 C water
1 can evaporated milk

3 C sharp shredded cheddar cheese
2 ounces cream cheese
½ C cottage cheese
Salt and pepper to taste

Directions

Combine all ingredients together in slow cooker. Cook on low for 4-5 hours.

Macaroni and Cheese 9

Prep time: 5 minutes

Cook time: 4-5 hours

Ingredients
3 C vegetable broth
1 pound pasta
2 C water
1 C heavy whipping cream

3 C sharp shredded cheddar cheese
1 C mixed frozen vegetables
Salt and pepper to taste

Directions
Combine all ingredients together in slow cooker. Cook on low for 4-5 hours.

Macaroni and Cheese 10

Prep time: 5 minutes

Cook time: 4-5 hours

Ingredients
3 C beef broth
1 pound pasta
2 C water
1 C heavy whipping cream

3 C sharp shredded cheddar cheese
4 ounces cream cheese
2 C cooked ground beef
Salt and pepper to taste

Directions
Combine all ingredients together in slow cooker. Cook on low for 4-5 hours.

Spaghetti 1

Prep time: 15 minutes

Cook time: 3-4 hours

Ingredients
1 pound lean ground beef, browned
1 C onion, chopped
2 8-ounce cans tomato sauce
2 C cooking sherry
1 clove garlic, crushed
1 C water
1 pound uncooked spaghetti

2 tsp chili powder
1 tsp salt
1 tbsp sugar
1 tsp ground cloves
½ tsp ground black pepper
¼ C parmesan cheese, finely grated

Directions
Combine all ingredients together in slow cooker. Cook on low for 3-4 hours.

SPAGHETTI 2

Prep time: 15 minutes   Cook time: 3-4 hours

Ingredients

1 pound lean ground beef, browned   1 clove garlic, crushed
1 C onion, chopped   1 C water
2 8-ounce cans prepared spaghetti sauce   1 pound uncooked spaghetti

Directions

Combine all ingredients together in slow cooker. Cook on low for 3-4 hours.

SPAGHETTI 3

Prep time: 15 minutes   Cook time: 3-4 hours

Ingredients

1 pound frozen meatballs, thawed and browned 1 small onion, chopped
1 C onion, chopped   1 C water
2 8-ounce cans prepared spaghetti sauce   1 pound uncooked spaghetti
2 cloves garlic, crushed

Directions

Combine all ingredients together in slow cooker. Cook on low for 3-4 hours.

SPAGHETTI 4

Prep time: 15 minutes   Cook time: 3-4 hours

Ingredients

1 pound ground sausage, browned   1 C water
1 C onion, chopped   1 pound uncooked angel hair spaghetti
2 C prepared spaghetti sauce   1 C shredded mozzarella cheese
1 clove garlic, crushed   ½ C grated parmesan cheese

Directions

Combine all ingredients together in slow cooker. Cook on low for 3-4 hours.

SPAGHETTI 5

Prep time: 15 minutes

Cook time: 3-4 hours

Ingredients

2 C cooked, chopped chicken, browned
1 C onion, chopped
2 8-ounce cans prepared Alfredo sauce
1 clove garlic, crushed

1 C water
1 pound uncooked spaghetti
1 C grated parmesan cheese

Directions

Combine all ingredients together in slow cooker. Cook on low for 3-4 hours.

SPAGHETTI 6

Prep time: 15 minutes

Cook time: 3-4 hours

Ingredients

1 pound lean ground beef, browned
1 C onion, chopped
2 C beef broth

1 clove garlic, crushed
1 C water
1 pound uncooked spaghetti

Directions

Combine all ingredients together in slow cooker. Cook on low for 3-4 hours.

SPAGHETTI 7

Prep time: 15 minutes

Cook time: 3-4 hours

Ingredients

2 C chopped cooked chicken, browned
1 C onion, chopped
2 C chicken broth

1 clove garlic, crushed
1 C water
1 pound uncooked spaghetti

Directions

Combine all ingredients together in slow cooker. Cook on low for 3-4 hours.

SPAGHETTI 8

Prep time: 15 minutes

Cook time: 3-4 hours

Ingredients

1 pound lean ground beef, browned
1 C onion, chopped
2 8-ounce cans prepared spaghetti sauce
1 clove garlic, crushed
2 tbsp hot sauce

1 tbsp taco seasoning
1 tsp chili powder
1 C water
1 pound uncooked spaghetti

Directions

Combine all ingredients together in slow cooker. Cook on low for 3-4 hours.

SPAGHETTI 9

Prep time: 15 minutes

Cook time: 3-4 hours

Ingredients

1 C onion, chopped
2 C prepared spaghetti sauce
2 tbsp extra virgin olive oil
1 C chopped pepperoni
1 clove garlic, crushed

1 tsp black pepper
1 tbsp soya sauce
1 C water
1 pound uncooked spaghetti

Directions

Combine all ingredients together in slow cooker. Cook on low for 3-4 hours.

SPAGHETTI 10

Prep time: 15 minutes

Cook time: 3-4 hours

Ingredients

2 C chopped cooked ham
1 C onion, chopped
2 C cream of chicken soup

1 clove garlic, crushed
1 C water
1 pound uncooked spaghetti

Directions

Combine all ingredients together in slow cooker. Cook on low for 3-4 hours.

LINGUINE WITH CLAMS

Prep time: 15 minutes

Cook time: 4-5 hours

Ingredients

2 cans clams, not drained
3 C fish broth
1 tsp garlic powder

1 tsp onion powder
1 package uncooked linguini

Directions

Combine all ingredients together in slow cooker. Cook on low for 4-5 hours.

FETTUCINE WITH TUNA

Prep time: 15 minutes

Cook time: 4-5 hours

Ingredients

2 cans solid white tuna, not drained
3 C fish broth
1 tsp garlic powder

1 tsp onion powder
1 package uncooked fettucine

Directions

Combine all ingredients together in slow cooker. Cook on low for 4-5 hours.

BOWTIE PASTA

Prep time: 5 minutes

Cook time: 3-4 hours

Ingredients

1 16-ounce package bowtie pasta
1 14-ounce can tomato puree
2 garlic cloves, crushed

1 tsp hot pepper flakes
1 tsp salt
Extra virgin olive oil

Directions

Combine all ingredients together in slow cooker. Cook on low for 3-4 hours.

PASTA WITH TUNA

Prep time: 10 minutes

Cook time: 4-5 hours

Ingredients

2 C tomato puree
1 tbsp extra virgin olive oil
3 anchovies, browned with 1 clove minced garlic
1 tsp salt

2 5.5-ounce cans tuna, packed in oil
2 C fusilli pasta
2 tbsp capers
Water

Directions

Combine all ingredients except 1 can of tuna and capers together in slow cooker. Cook on low for 4-5 hours. Stir in tuna and capers before serving.

ITALIAN MACARONI AND CHEESE

Prep time: 10 minutes

Cook time: 4-5 hours

Ingredients
2 C uncooked elbow macaroni
1 C ricotta cheese
1 tbsp extra virgin olive oil

½ Romano cheese, finely grated
Salt and pepper to taste

Directions
Combine all ingredients together in slow cooker. Cook on low for 4-5 hours.

SWEET & SOUR PASTA

Prep time: 5 minutes

Cook time: 4-5 hours

Ingredients
3 C chicken broth
1 pound pasta
1 C water
½ C ketchup

¼ C white vinegar
½ C raw honey
¼ C chopped green onion
Salt and pepper to taste

Directions
Combine all ingredients together in slow cooker. Cook on low for 4-5 hours.

CASHEW PASTA

Prep time: 5 minutes

Cook time: 4-5 hours

Ingredients
3 C chicken broth
1 pound pasta
1 C water
2 tbsp soya sauce

1 tbsp teriyaki sauce
½ C unsalted cashews
Salt and pepper to taste

Directions
Combine all ingredients together in slow cooker. Cook on low for 4-5 hours.

PESTO PASTA

Prep time: 5 minutes

Cook time: 4-5 hours

Ingredients
3 C chicken broth
1 pound pasta
1 C water

Salt and pepper to taste
1 C pesto

Directions
Combine all ingredients together in slow cooker. Cook on low for 4-5 hours.

GARLIC PASTA

Prep time: 5 minutes   Cook time: 4-5 hours

Ingredients
3 C chicken broth   3 cloves garlic, minced
1 pound pasta   ½ C cream cheese
1 C water   Salt and pepper to taste

Directions
Combine all ingredients together in slow cooker. Cook on low for 4-5 hours.

PASTA AND TOMATOES

Prep time: 5 minutes   Cook time: 4-5 hours

Ingredients
3 C chicken broth   1 can stewed diced tomatoes
1 pound pasta   Salt and pepper to taste
1 C water

Directions
Combine all ingredients together in slow cooker. Cook on low for 4-5 hours.

PASTA AND VEGGIES

Prep time: 5 minutes   Cook time: 4-5 hours

Ingredients
3 C chicken broth   1 C mixed frozen veggies
1 pound pasta   2 C sharp shredded cheddar cheese
1 C water   Salt and pepper to taste

Directions
Combine all ingredients together in slow cooker. Cook on low for 4-5 hours.

PIZZA PASTA

Prep time: 10 minutes   Cook time: 2 hours

Ingredients
2 C cooked pasta   1 C sliced pepperoni
1 egg   1 C shredded mozzarella cheese
1 C pizza sauce

Directions
Mix pasta and egg, and spread in bottom of slow cooker. Spread sauce on top of pasta, followed by pepperoni and cheese (you can add other pizza toppings if you like). Close and lock lid, bring to high pressure, reduce heat, and cook on low for 2 hours.

BUTTER PASTA

Prep time: 5 minutes   Cook time: 4-5 hours

Ingredients
3 C chicken broth   ½ C parsley (fresh or dried)
1 pound pasta   Salt and pepper to taste
4 tbsp butter

Directions
Combine all ingredients together in slow cooker. Cook on low for 4-5 hours.

PASTA SALAD

Prep time: 5 minutes   Cook time: 4-5 hours

Ingredients
3 C chicken broth   1 C Miracle Whip
1 pound pasta   1/3 C white sugar
2 C water   3 squirts soya sauce
Salt and pepper to taste   3 squirts teriyaki sauce
1 C mixed frozen veggies   2 tsp paprika
1 C sharp cheddar cheese, cubed   2 cans tuna, drained
4-5 hard boiled eggs   ½ C cottage cheese

Directions
Place first 5 ingredients inside the slow cooker. Cook on low for 4-5 hours Drain and rinse in cold water. In a separate bowl, combine remaining ingredients. Mix with pasta, and refrigerate until ready to serve.

PASTA WITH MEATBALLS

Prep time: 5 minutes   Cook time: 4-5 hours

Ingredients
3 C chicken broth   2 C water
1 pound pasta   2 C spaghetti sauce
1 package frozen meatballs, thawed and 1 C shredded mozzarella cheese
browned   Salt and pepper to taste

Directions
Combine all ingredients together in slow cooker. Cook on low for 4-5 hours.

BACON PASTA

Prep time: 5 minutes

Cook time: 4-5 hours

Ingredients
3 C chicken broth
1 pound pasta
1 C water

1 C cream cheese, cubed
2 C bacon, chopped and cooked
Salt and pepper to taste

Directions
Combine all ingredients together in slow cooker. Cook on low for 4-5 hours.

BOWTIES AND TOMATOES

Prep time: 5 minutes

Cook time: 4-5 hours

Ingredients
2 C chicken broth
1 pound bowtie pasta
2 cans stewed diced tomatoes
1 C grape tomatoes

1 C heavy whipping cream
2 cloves garlic, minced
1 small onion, diced
Salt and pepper to taste

Directions
Combine all ingredients together in slow cooker. Cook on low for 4-5 hours.

BROKEN LASAGNA

Prep time: 5 minutes

Cook time: 4-5 hours

Ingredients
3 C water
1 pound broken lasagna noodles
1 C spaghetti sauce
2 C shredded mozzarella cheese
1 pound lean ground beef, browned

1 garlic clove, minced
1 small onion, diced
½ C cottage cheese
Salt and pepper to taste

Directions
Layer ingredients like a traditional lasagna in slow cooker. Cook on low for 4-5 hours.

Nacho Cheese Pasta

Prep time: 5 minutes

Cook time: 4-5 hours

Ingredients

3 C beef broth
1 pound pasta
1 pound lean ground beef, browned
2 C water
1 C nacho cheese sauce
3 C sharp shredded cheddar cheese

2 cloves garlic, minced
1 tsp chili powder
1 tsp paprika
1 tsp cayenne pepper
Salt and pepper to taste

Directions

Combine all ingredients together in slow cooker. Cook on low for 4-5 hours.

Fettucine with Sausage Meatballs

Prep time: 5 minutes

Cook time: 4-5 hours

Ingredients

3 C beef broth
1 pound fettucine noodles
1 pound ground sausage
1 C Italian bread crumbs

2 tbsp extra virgin olive oil
2 C water
1 bottle prepares spaghetti sauce
Salt and pepper to taste

Directions

Mix sausage and bread crumbs, form into 2" meatballs, and brown on the stovetop. Combine all ingredients together in slow cooker. Cook on low for 4-5 hours.

Fettucine with Meat Sauce

Prep time: 5 minutes

Cook time: 4-5 hours

Ingredients

3 C beef broth
1 pound fettucine noodles
1 pound lean ground beef, browned
2 tbsp extra virgin olive oil

2 C water
1 jar prepared spaghetti sauce
Salt and pepper to taste

Directions

Combine all ingredients together in slow cooker. Cook on low for 4-5 hours.

*F*ETTUCINE WITH CHEESE SAUCE

Prep time: 5 minutes

Cook time: 10 minutes

Ingredients
3 C beef broth
1 pound fettucine noodles
1 pound lean ground beef, browned

2 C water
1 jar prepared cheese sauce
Salt and pepper to taste

Directions
Combine all ingredients together in slow cooker. Cook on low for 4-5 hours.

*C*HEESY ROTINI

Prep time: 5 minutes

Cook time: 4-5 hours

Ingredients
3 C chicken broth
1 pound rotini pasta
2 C water

1 C finely grated parmesan cheese
1 C shredded mozzarella cheese
Salt and pepper to taste

Directions
Combine all ingredients together in slow cooker. Cook on low for 4-5 hours.

*H*AM AND CHEESE ROTINI

Prep time: 5 minutes

Cook time: 4-5 hours

Ingredients
3 C chicken broth
1 pound rotini pasta
1 pound cooked ham, cubed

2 C water
1 C shredded cheddar cheese
Salt and pepper to taste

Directions
Combine all ingredients except cheese together in slow cooker. Cook on low for 4-5 hours. Stir in cheese and heat until cheese is melted.

*S*PAGHETTI WITH CHICKEN

Prep time: 10 minutes

Cook time: 3-4 hours

Ingredients
1 pound spaghetti
2 C cooked chicken, cubed
4 C water
3 tbsp chicken bouillon powder

1 large onion, diced
1 garlic clove, minced
1 C finely grated parmesan cheese

Directions
Combine all ingredients together in slow cooker. Cook on low for 3-4 hours.

CREAM OF CHICKEN PASTA

Prep time: 10 minutes   Cook time: 4-5 hours

Ingredients

1 pound pasta   1 small onion, diced
1 C cooked chicken, diced   1 garlic clove, minced
2 C water   1 tsp paprika
2 cans cream of chicken soup   Salt and pepper to taste

Directions

Combine all ingredients together in slow cooker. Cook on low for 4-5 hours.

BEEFY PASTA

Prep time: 10 minutes   Cook time: 4-5 hours

Ingredients

1 pound macaroni   1 small onion, diced
1 pound lean stewing beef, cut into 1" cubes   1 garlic clove, minced
and browned   1 tbsp soya sauce
4 C water   ½ tsp ground black pepper
3 tbsp beef bouillon powder

Directions

Combine all ingredients together in slow cooker. Cook on low for 4-5 hours.

PASTA WITH CLAMS

Prep time: 10 minutes   Cook time: 4-5 hours

Ingredients

1 pound pasta   1 C clam juice
3 C water   Salt and pepper to taste
2 cans clams with juice   1 C finely grated parmesan cheese

Directions

Combine all ingredients together in slow cooker. Cook on low for 4-5 hours.

Vegetables

Mashed Potatoes 1

Prep time: 10 minutes

Cook time: 3 hours, 15 minutes

Ingredients
3 C water
½ C whole milk
3 ½ pounds potatoes, peeled and sliced

¼ C butter
2 tsp sea salt
½ tsp white pepper

Directions
Boil potatoes with salt for 15 minutes. Transfer to slow cooker and add remaining ingredients. Cook on low for 3 hours.

Mashed Potatoes 2

Prep time: 10 minutes

Cook time: 3 hours, 15 minutes

Ingredients
3 C water
3 ½ pounds potatoes, peeled and sliced
¼ C butter
2 tsp sea salt

½ tsp white pepper
1 C shredded white cheddar cheese (sharp)
1 C cubed cream cheese

Directions
Boil potatoes with salt for 15 minutes. Transfer to slow cooker and add remaining ingredients. Cook on low for 3 hours.

Mashed Potatoes 3

Prep time: 10 minutes

Cook time: 3 hours, 15 minutes

Ingredients
5 large potatoes, peeled and quartered
1 can evaporated milk
3 tbsp butter
1 tsp extra virgin olive oil

1 clove garlic, minced
½ C chopped green onion
Salt to taste

Directions
Boil potatoes with salt for 15 minutes. Transfer to slow cooker and add remaining ingredients. Cook on low for 3 hours.

Mashed Potatoes 4

Prep time: 10 minutes

Cook time: 3 hours, 15 minutes

Ingredients

5 large potatoes, peeled and quartered
1 can evaporated milk
3 tbsp butter
1 tsp extra virgin olive oil

½ C corn niblets, drained
½ C frozen peas, thawed
Salt to taste

Directions

Boil potatoes with salt for 15 minutes. Transfer to slow cooker and add remaining ingredients. Cook on low for 3 hours.

Mashed Potatoes 5

Prep time: 10 minutes

Cook time: 3 hours, 15 minutes

Ingredients

5 large potatoes, peeled and quartered
5 cloves garlic, whole
1 can evaporated milk
3 tbsp butter

1 C chopped chicken or turkey
½ C mixed frozen vegetables, thawed
1 tsp extra virgin olive oil
Salt to taste

Directions

Boil potatoes with salt for 15 minutes. Transfer to slow cooker and add remaining ingredients. Cook on low for 3 hours.

Mashed Potatoes 6

Prep time: 10 minutes

Cook time: 3 hours, 15 minutes

Ingredients

5 large potatoes, peeled and quartered
5 cloves garlic, whole
½ can evaporated milk
½ C cream cheese

4 tbsp fresh or dried parsley
3 tbsp butter
1 tsp extra virgin olive oil
Salt to taste

Directions

Boil potatoes with salt for 15 minutes. Transfer to slow cooker and add remaining ingredients. Cook on low for 3 hours.

Mashed Potatoes 7

Prep time: 10 minutes

Cook time: 3 hours, 15 minutes

Ingredients

5 large potatoes, peeled and quartered
5 cloves garlic, whole
1 can evaporated milk
1 C shredded cheddar cheese
3 cloves garlic, minced

3 tbsp butter
1 tsp extra virgin olive oil
Salt to taste
1 C chicken gravy

Directions

Boil potatoes with salt for 15 minutes. Transfer to slow cooker and add remaining ingredients. Cook on low for 3 hours.

Mashed Potatoes 8

Prep time: 10 minutes

Cook time: 3 hours, 35 minutes

Ingredients

5 large potatoes, peeled and quartered
5 cloves garlic, whole
1 C evaporated milk
1 C cream cheese
3 cloves garlic, minced

1 small onion, minced
3 tbsp butter
1 tsp extra virgin olive oil
Salt to taste
½ C Tex Mex blend shredded cheese

Directions

Preheat oven to 400 degrees. Boil potatoes with salt for 15 minutes. Transfer to slow cooker and add remaining ingredients except cheese. Cook on low for 3 hours. Place potatoes in a greased casserole dish, and sprinkle with cheese. Bake for 20 minutes, or until cheese is golden and bubbly.

Mashed Potatoes 9

Prep time: 10 minutes

Cook time: 3 hours, 15 minutes

Ingredients

5 large potatoes, peeled and quartered
5 cloves garlic, whole
1 C evaporated milk
1 C chopped onion

½ C chopped green pepper
½ C chopped red pepper
Salt to taste

Directions

Boil potatoes with salt for 15 minutes. Transfer to slow cooker and add remaining ingredients. Cook on low for 3 hours.

Mashed Potatoes 10

Prep time: 10 minutes

Cook time: 3 hours, 15 minutes

Ingredients

5 large potatoes, peeled and quartered
5 cloves garlic, whole
1 C evaporated milk
3 cloves garlic, minced
1 C green onion, finely chopped

1 C corn niblets, drained
3 tbsp butter
1 tsp extra virgin olive oil
Salt to taste

Directions

Boil potatoes with salt for 15 minutes. Transfer to slow cooker and add remaining ingredients. Cook on low for 3 hours.

Potato Salad

Prep time: 15 minutes

Cook time: 6 hours

Ingredients

2 lb. potatoes, peeled and sliced
1 C celery, sliced
1 C onion, chopped
½ C green bell pepper, seeded and chopped
½ C balsamic vinegar

½ C extra-virgin olive oil
¼ tsp. red pepper flakes, crushed
Salt and freshly ground black pepper, to taste
6 cooked bacon slices. Crumbled
2 tbsp. fresh parsley, chopped

Directions

In a slow cooker, add potatoes, celery, onion, bell pepper, vinegar, oil, red pepper flakes, salt and black pepper and mix well. Cook on low for 5-6 hours.
Top with bacon and parsley and serve.

Red Cabbage Salad

Prep time: 10 minutes

Cook time: 2 hours

Ingredients

2 C red cabbage, shredded
¼ C chopped onion
1 tbsp oil

2 tsp red wine vinegar
½ tsp brown sugar
Salt and pepper to taste

Directions

Combine all ingredients together in slow cooker. Cook on low for 2 hours.

FRESH VEGGIE MIX

Prep time: 20 minutes

Cook time: 2 hours

Ingredients
1 C chicken stock
¾ C red split lentils
½ C canola oil
¼ C fresh dill, finely chopped
1 tsp fresh basil, chopped
1 onion, chopped
1 clove garlic, chopped

3 tomatoes, cut into chunks, seeded
2 zucchini, cut into chunks
4 potatoes, peeled, and cut into ½" slices
2 carrots, sliced
3 celery stalks, chopped
2 C frozen peas, thawed
Salt and pepper to taste

Directions
Combine all ingredients together in slow cooker. Cook on low for 2 hours.

SAVORY POTATOES

Prep time: 10 minutes

Cook time: 3 hours

Ingredients
4 C thinly sliced potatoes
½ C finely chopped onion
½ C chicken stock
1 tbsp extra virgin olive oil

¼ pound fresh mushrooms, trimmed, stemmed, and sliced
2 tbsp minced parsley
Salt and pepper to taste

Directions
Combine all ingredients together in slow cooker. Cook on low for 3 hours.

STIR-FRIED BROCCOLI

Prep time: 10 minutes

Cook time: 3 hours

Ingredients
6 tbsp chicken stock
2 tbsp extra virgin olive oil
1 large garlic clove, peeled and crushed

1 slice fresh ginger, peeled
1 bunch of broccoli stems, cut into florettes
2 tbsp soy sauce

Directions
Combine all ingredients except broccoli together in slow cooker. Cook on low for 3 hours. Stir in broccoli and heat through.

CANDIED YAMS

Prep time: 5 minutes

Cook time: 3 hours

Ingredients

1 C orange juice
2 large sweet potatoes, peeled and halved lengthwise
½ C brown sugar

2 tbsp butter
1 tsp grated orange zest
Salt to taste

Directions

Combine all ingredients together in slow cooker. Cook on low for 3 hours.

ROASTED GARLIC

Prep time: 5 minutes

Cook time: 3 hours

Ingredients

4 large garlic bulbs
1 C water

Extra virgin olive oil

Directions

Combine all ingredients together in slow cooker. Cook on low for 3 hours.

ZUCCHINI SPAGHETTI SAUCE

Prep time: 10 minutes

Cook time: 4 hours

Ingredients

1 ½ pounds chopped zucchini
¾ C water
1 tbsp extra virgin olive oil
1 chopped onion

1 bunch of basil leaves
2 garlic cloves, minced
1 tsp salt

Directions

Combine all ingredients together in slow cooker. Cook on low for 4 hours.

BAKED POTATOES

Prep time: 5 minutes   Cook time: 5-6 hours

Ingredients
2 pounds baking potatoes

Directions
Wash potatoes, place in slow cooker, and pierce the tops with a fork. Cook on low for 5-6 hours.

GLAZED CARROTS

Prep time: 5 minutes   Cook time: 4-5 hours

Ingredients
2 pounds carrots   ½ C brown sugar
1 C water   ½ C honey
1 tbsp butter   ¼ tsp salt

Directions
Wash and peel carrots, and slice them on a diagonal. Combine all ingredients together in slow cooker. Cook on low for 4-5 hours.

HONEY GLAZED CARROTS

Prep time: 5 minutes   Cook time: 4-5 hours

Ingredients
2 pounds carrots   1 C raw honey
1 C water   ¼ tsp salt
1 tbsp butter

Directions
Wash and peel carrots, and slice them on a diagonal. Combine all ingredients together in slow cooker. Cook on low for 4-5 hours.

Maple Glazed Carrots

Prep time: 5 minutes

Cook time: 4-5 hours

Ingredients

2 pounds carrots
1 C water
1 tbsp butter

1 C maple syrup
¼ tsp salt

Directions

Wash and peel carrots, and slice them on a diagonal. Combine all ingredients together in slow cooker. Cook on low for 4-5 hours.

Brown Sugar Glazed Carrots

Prep time: 5 minutes

Cook time: 4-5 hours

Ingredients

2 pounds carrots
1 C water
1 tbsp butter

1 C brown sugar
¼ tsp salt

Directions

Wash and peel carrots, and slice them on a diagonal. Combine all ingredients together in slow cooker. Cook on low for 4-5 hours.

Sweet & Sour Carrots

Prep time: 5 minutes

Cook time: 4-5 hours

Ingredients

2 pounds carrots
1 C water
1 tbsp butter

½ C sweet and sour sauce
¼ tsp salt

Directions

Wash and peel carrots, and slice them on a diagonal. Place carrots, water, butter, salt, and sweet and sour sauce in pressure cooker. Close and lock lid, bring to low pressure, reduce heat, and cook for 4 minutes. Use a quick pressure release.

CINNAMON AND BROWN SUGAR GLAZED CARROTS

Prep time: 5 minutes

Cook time: 4-5 hours

Ingredients
2 pounds carrots
1 C water
1 tbsp butter
1 C brown sugar

1 tsp ground cinnamon
½ tsp ground cloves
¼ tsp salt

Directions
Wash and peel carrots, and slice them on a diagonal. Combine all ingredients together in slow cooker. Cook on low for 4-5 hours.

ORANGE GLAZED CARROTS

Prep time: 5 minutes

Cook time: 4-5 hours

Ingredients
2 pounds carrots
1 C water
1 tbsp butter
½ C raw honey

½ C frozen orange juice concentrate (thawed, not mixed with water)
¼ tsp salt

Directions
Wash and peel carrots, and slice them on a diagonal. Combine all ingredients together in slow cooker. Cook on low for 4-5 hours.

CARROTS IN GRAVY

Prep time: 5 minutes

Cook time: 4-5 hours

Ingredients
2 pounds carrots
1 C water
1 tbsp butter

¼ tsp salt
1 C chicken or beef gravy

Directions
Wash and peel carrots, and slice them on a diagonal. Combine all ingredients together in slow cooker. Cook on low for 4-5 hours.

BUTTERED CARROTS

Prep time: 5 minutes

Cook time: 4-5 hours

Ingredients

2 pounds carrots
1 C water
½ C butter

1 tbsp brown sugar
¼ tsp salt
¼ tsp ground black pepper

Directions

Wash and peel carrots, and slice them on a diagonal. Combine all ingredients together in slow cooker. Cook on low for 4-5 hours.

CARROTS IN BARBECUE SAUCE

Prep time: 5 minutes

Cook time: 4-5 hours

Ingredients

2 pounds carrots
1 C water
1 tbsp butter

½ C barbecue sauce
¼ tsp salt

Directions

Wash and peel carrots, and slice them on a diagonal. Combine all ingredients together in slow cooker. Cook on low for 4-5 hours.

Rice, Beans, and Grains

MUSHROOM RISOTTO

Prep time: 15 minutes

Cook time: 4 hours

Ingredients

¼ C butter, divided
1 onion, diced
2 garlic cloves, minced
1 C portabella mushrooms, sliced

1 ½ C Arborio rice
3 C chicken broth
1 C dry white wine
½ C parmesan cheese, grated

Directions

Combine all ingredients together in slow cooker. Cook on low for 4 hours.

RICE PILAF 1

Prep time: 10 minutes

Cook time: 4 hours

Ingredients

3 C chicken stock
2 C long grain white rice
3 tbsp frozen peas

1 onion, diced
1 tbsp extra virgin olive oil
1 tbsp butter

Directions

Combine all ingredients together in slow cooker. Cook on low for 4 hours.

RICE PILAF 2

Prep time: 10 minutes

Cook time: 4 hours

Ingredients

3 C beef stock
2 C long grain white rice
1 C mixed frozen vegetables

1 onion, diced
1 tbsp butter

Directions

Combine all ingredients together in slow cooker. Cook on low for 4 hours.

RICE PILAF 3

Prep time: 10 minutes

Cook time: 4 hours

Ingredients

3 C chicken stock
2 C long grain white rice
1 can sliced mushrooms, drained

1 garlic clove, minced
1 onion, diced
1 tbsp butter

Directions

Combine all ingredients together in slow cooker. Cook on low for 4 hours.

Rice Pilaf 4

Prep time: 10 minutes

Cook time: 4 hours

Ingredients

2 C chicken stock
1 large can stewed, diced tomatoes, not drained
2 C long grain white rice

3 tbsp frozen peas
1 onion, diced
1 tbsp butter

Directions

Combine all ingredients together in slow cooker. Cook on low for 4 hours.

Rice Pilaf 5

Prep time: 10 minutes

Cook time: 4 hours

Ingredients

2 C chicken stock
1 C tomato juice
1 tbsp soya sauce

2 C long grain white rice
1 tbsp butter

Directions

Combine all ingredients together in slow cooker. Cook on low for 4 hours.

Rice Pilaf 6

Prep time: 10 minutes

Cook time: 4 hours

Ingredients

3 C vegetable stock
2 C long grain white rice
3 tbsp frozen carrots

1 onion, diced
1 garlic clove, minced
1 tbsp butter

Directions

Combine all ingredients together in slow cooker. Cook on low for 4 hours.

RICE PILAF 7

Prep time: 10 minutes

Cook time: 4 hours

Ingredients

3 C chicken stock
2 C long grain white rice
1 C sliced mushrooms
1 celery stalk, chopped

1 tsp salt
½ tsp ground black pepper
3 tbsp frozen peas
1 tbsp butter

Directions

Combine all ingredients together in slow cooker. Cook on low for 4 hours.

RICE PILAF 8

Prep time: 10 minutes

Cook time: 4 hours

Ingredients

1 C water
2 large cans stewed, diced tomatoes, not drained
2 C long grain white rice

1 C mixed frozen vegetables
1 onion, diced
1 tbsp soya sauce
1 tsp ground black pepper

Directions

Combine all ingredients together in slow cooker. Cook on low for 4 hours.

RICE PILAF 9

Prep time: 10 minutes

Cook time: 4 hours

Ingredients

3 C fish stock
2 C long grain white rice
1 C frozen corn niblets

Salt and pepper to taste
1 tbsp butter

Directions

Combine all ingredients together in slow cooker. Cook on low for 4 hours.

Rice Pilaf 10

Prep time: 10 minutes

Cook time: 4 hours

Ingredients

2 C chicken stock
1 can cream of chicken soup
2 C long grain white rice
3 tbsp frozen peas
1 onion, diced

1 tbsp butter
1 tsp salt
½ tsp ground black pepper
½ tsp paprika

Directions

Combine all ingredients together in slow cooker. Cook on low for 4 hours.

Dirty Rice

Prep time: 10 minutes

Cook time: 4 hours

Ingredients

1 ¼ C chopped chicken livers
½ C chopped bacon
1 ¼ C long grain rice
2 ½ C vegetable stock
1 onion, chopped
2 stalks of celery, chopped
2 cloves of garlic, minced

1 sprig chopped parsley
1 tbsp extra virgin olive oil
1 tsp paprika
½ tsp oregano
½ tsp thyme
½ tsp cayenne pepper
Salt and pepper to taste

Directions

Combine all ingredients together in slow cooker. Cook on low for 4 hours.

Jambalaya

Prep time: 20 minutes

Cook time: 4 hours

Ingredients

½ pound boneless, skinless chicken breast, cubed (1" chunks)
½ pound Italian sausage, cooked and sliced
½ pound raw shrimp, peeled and deveined
1 C long grain rice
2 C canned diced tomatoes in juice
1 C chicken stock
1 tbsp vegetable oil

1 green bell pepper, chopped
3 cloves garlic, minced
3 celery stalks, chopped
1 onion, chopped
2 tsp Creole seasoning
½ tsp cayenne pepper
1 tsp paprika

Directions

Combine all ingredients together in slow cooker. Cook on low for 4 hours.

RICE WITH VEGETABLES

Prep time: 10 minutes

Cook time: 4 hours

Ingredients
2 C chicken stock
1 C rice
1 2-ounce package sliced, blanched almonds
½ C diced carrots
½ C diced celery

½ C diced green pepper
½ C green onion, sliced
1 tomato, peeled, seeded, and diced
1 ½ C water
¼ C fresh chopped parsley

Directions
Combine all ingredients together in slow cooker. Cook on low for 4 hours.

BARLEY CASSEROLE

Prep time: 20 minutes

Cook time: 5 hours

Ingredients
1 C uncooked pearl barley
1 ½ C vegetable juice
1 C chopped mushrooms
1 ½ C chicken stock
¼ C chopped walnuts
2 celery stalks, chopped

1 carrot, chopped
1 onion, chopped
1 green pepper, chopped
2 cloves garlic, minced
Salt and pepper to taste

Directions
Combine all ingredients except nuts together in slow cooker. Cook on low for 5 hours. Add nuts just prior to serving.

BAKED BEANS

Prep time: 10 minutes + 8-10 hours

Cook time: 5-6 hours

Ingredients
2 C dried white beans
1 onion, diced
1 garlic clove, minced
1 ¾ C water
2 ounces tomato paste (1/2 small can)
3 tbsp canola oil

3 tbsp brown sugar
2 tbsp molasses
½ tsp yellow mustard
¼ tsp cumin
¼ tsp chili powder

Directions
Rinse the beans and soak them in water for 8-12 hours to soften, then drain. Combine all ingredients together in slow cooker. Cook on low for 5-6 hours.

PAELLA

Prep time: 20 minutes

Cook time: 4 hours

Ingredients

2 C rice
4 C fish stock or chicken broth
½ pound firm white fish (halibut is a good option), cut into 1" chunks
½ pound shrimp, shelled and peeled
8 mussels or clams
2 tbsp extra virgin olive oil

1 onion, chopped
3 cloves garlic, minced
1 tomato, skinned, seeded, and chopped
½ C frozen peas, thawed
½ tsp paprika
Salt and pepper to taste

Directions

Combine all ingredients together in slow cooker. Cook on low for 4 hours.

HUMMUS

Prep time: 10 minutes + 4 hours

Cook time: 4-5

Ingredients

¾ C dried chickpeas
1/3 C canola oil
1/3 C extra virgin olive oil
1/3 C tahini
1/3 C water

4 tbsp lemon juice
2 cloves garlic, minced
½ tsp cumin
Salt and pepper to taste

Directions

Soak chickpeas in water for 4 hours or longer, drain, and rinse. Place chickpeas and 3 ½ C water in the pressure cooker. Cook on low for 4-5 hours. Transfer cooked chickpeas to a blender and mix with the other ingredients until creamy.

INDIAN CURRY

Prep time: 10 minutes

Cook time: 4 hours

Ingredients

2 C warm water
1 C quinoa
1 C canned chickpeas, drained
½ C raisins
½ C green beans
½ C diced onios
½ hot pepper, sliced
1 pinch saffron threads
1 tsp coconut extract
1 small eggplant, cubed
1 small acorn squash, cubed

1 small sweet potato, cubed
1 5-ounce can evaporated milk
1 tsp cumin seeds
1 tbsp butter
2/3 tsp hot curry powder
½ tsp curry powder

Directions

Soak saffron threads in 2 C water. Place chickpeas, quinoa, raisins, coconut water, vegetables, and saffron water (from soaking the threads) into the slow cooker. Cook on low for 4 hours. While this is cooking, saute cumin seeds and onions in a sauce pan until the onions are soft. Add evaporated milk and remaining spices, and simmer for 10 minutes. Toss everything together and serve.

POLENTA

Prep time: 5 minutes   Cook time: 4 hours

Ingredients
2 C coarse polenta corn flour   2 tsp salt
8 C water

Directions
Combine all ingredients together in slow cooker. Cook on low for 4 hours.

SOLID POLENTA

Prep time: 5 minutes   Cook time: 4 hours

Ingredients
Basic polenta

Directions
Make the basic polenta recipe. Press polenta mixture into a casserole dish, flattening quickly. Allow mixture to cool for an hour. Cut and serve.

OVEN-BAKED POLENTA

Prep time: 5 minutes   Cook time: 4 hours + 10 minutes

Ingredients
Basic polenta

Directions
Make the basic polenta recipe. Place into individual heat-proof dishes, and bake in an oven pre-heated to 350 degrees F until crispy but not brown (about 10 minutes).

GRILLED POLENTA

Prep time: 5 minutes   Cook time: 4 hours + 10 minutes

Ingredients
Basic polenta

Directions
Make the basic polenta recipe. Press into a casserole dish, and cut into shapes. Brush with olive oil, and place on the barbecue grill until lightly browned on both sides (about 5-10 minutes).

*F*RIED POLENTA

Prep time: 5 minutes

Cook time: 4 hours + 10 minutes

Ingredients
Basic Polenta

Directions
Make the basic polenta recipe, then the solid recipe. Cut solid polenta into ½" thick sticks, and pan fry in extra virgin olive oil until lightly browned and crispy (about 5-10 minutes).

*Q*UINOA WITH OATS & APRICOTS

Prep time: 10 minutes

Cook time: 2 hours 8 minutes

Ingredients
¾ C red quinoa, rinsed
¾ C steel cut oats
1 C dried apricots, chopped
6 C water

2 tbsp. honey
1 tsp. vanilla extract
Salt, to taste

Directions
Combine all ingredients in slow cooker. Cook on low for 8-10 hours.

*S*TEAMED RICE

Prep time: 5 minutes

Cook time: 4 hours

Ingredients
1 C long grain white rice
1 ½ C water

1 tbsp extra virgin olive oil

Directions
Combine all ingredients together in slow cooker. Cook on low for 4 hours.

*R*ISOTTO

Prep time: 10 minutes

Cook time: 4 hours

Ingredients
2 C short grain white pearl rice
1 chopped onion
1 tbsp white wine

1 tbsp parmesan cheese, finely grated
Salt and pepper to taste

Directions
Combine all ingredients together in slow cooker. Cook on low for 4 hours.

SPANISH RICE

Prep time: 10 minutes

Cook time: 4 hours

Ingredients
2 C long grain white rice
1 C chopped canned tomatoes in juice
2 ½ C water

1 tsp salt
1 chopped onion
½ tsp oregano

Directions
Combine all ingredients together in slow cooker. Cook on low for 4 hours.

LEEK RISOTTO

Prep time: 10 minutes

Cook time: 2 hours 8 minutes

Ingredients
¼ C butter, divided
3 leeks, sliced thinly (white part only)
2 garlic cloves, minced
2 C Arborio rice
1 C white wine
1 tsp. fresh thyme, minced

Salt and freshly ground black pepper, to taste
5½ Chot chicken broth
1 C Parmesan cheese, grated
1 tbsp. fresh lemon juice
2 tsp. fresh lemon peel, grated finely

Directions:
In a large nonstick skillet, melt 2 tbsp. of butter on medium heat. Add leeks and garlic and sauté for about 2-3 minutes.
Add rice and sauté for about 1-2 minutes.
Stir in wine and cook, stirring continuously for about 3 minutes or till all the liquid is absorbed.
Transfer the rice mixture into a greased slow cooker.
Add thyme, salt, black pepper and hot broth and mix well. Cook on high for 2 hours.
Uncover and immediately, stir in remaining butter, cheese and lemon juice.
Serve with the topping of lemon peel.

BASIC BROWN RICE

Prep time: 5 minutes

Cook time: 5 hours

Ingredients
1 C brown rice
1 ¾ C boiling water

1 tbsp extra virgin olive oil
Salt and pepper to taste

Directions
Combine all ingredients together in slow cooker. Cook on low for 5 hours.

Couscous 1

Prep time: 5 minutes

Cook time: 2-3 hours

Ingredients

2 ½ C chicken stock
1 16-ounce package couscous

2 tbsp butter
Salt and pepper to taste

Directions

Combine all ingredients together in slow cooker. Cook on low for 2-3 hours.

Couscous 2

Prep time: 5 minutes

Cook time: 2-3 hours

Ingredients

2 ½ C beef stock
1 16-ounce package couscous

2 tbsp butter
Salt and pepper to taste

Directions

Combine all ingredients together in slow cooker. Cook on low for 2-3 hours.

Couscous 3

Prep time: 5 minutes

Cook time: 2-3 hours

Ingredients

2 ½ C vegetable stock
1 16-ounce package couscous

2 tbsp butter
Salt and pepper to taste

Directions

Combine all ingredients together in slow cooker. Cook on low for 2-3 hours.

Couscous 4

Prep time: 5 minutes

Cook time: 2-3 hours

Ingredients

2 ½ C fish stock
1 16-ounce package couscous

2 tbsp butter
Salt and pepper to taste

Directions

Combine all ingredients together in slow cooker. Cook on low for 2-3 hours.

COUSCOUS 5

Prep time: 5 minutes

Cook time: 2-3 hours

Ingredients

2 ½ C chicken stock
1 16-ounce package couscous
1 garlic clove, minced

1 small onion, minced
2 tbsp butter
Salt and pepper to taste

Directions

Combine all ingredients together in slow cooker. Cook on low for 2-3 hours.

COUSCOUS 6

Prep time: 5 minutes

Cook time: 2-3 hours

Ingredients

2 ½ C tomato juice
1 16-ounce package couscous

2 tbsp butter
Salt and pepper to taste

Directions

Combine all ingredients together in slow cooker. Cook on low for 2-3 hours.

COUSCOUS 7

Prep time: 5 minutes

Cook time: 2-3 hours

Ingredients

2 ½ C stewed diced tomatoes, not drained
1 16-ounce package couscous

2 tbsp butter
Salt and pepper to taste

Directions

Combine all ingredients together in slow cooker. Cook on low for 2-3 hours.

COUSCOUS 8

Prep time: 5 minutes

Cook time: 2-3 hours

Ingredients

2 ½ C water
1 tsp garlic powder
1 tsp onion powder
1 tbsp soya sauce

1 16-ounce package couscous
2 tbsp butter
Salt and pepper to taste

Directions

Combine all ingredients together in slow cooker. Cook on low for 2-3 hours.

Couscous 9

Prep time: 5 minutes

Cook time: 2-3 hours

Ingredients

2 ½ C chicken stock
1 16-ounce package couscous
2 C mixed frozen vegetables
1 small onion, minced

1 tbsp hot sauce
2 tbsp butter
Salt and pepper to taste

Directions

Combine all ingredients together in slow cooker. Cook on low for 2-3 hours.

Couscous 10

Prep time: 5 minutes

Cook time: 2-3 hours

Ingredients

2 ½ C chicken stock
1 16-ounce package couscous
2 tbsp butter
1 tsp garlic powder

1 tsp paprika
1 tsp curry powder
1 tsp onion powder
Salt and pepper to taste

Directions

Combine all ingredients together in slow cooker. Cook on low for 2-3 hours.

Sauces

SPAGHETTI SAUCE 1

Prep time: 15 minutes   Cook time: 2-3 hours

Ingredients
1 large can stewed tomatoes   1 tsp onion powder
1 small can tomato paste   ½ tsp ground cloves
1 tbsp soy sauce   ½ tsp oregano
2 tbsp white sugar   ½ tsp paprika
1 tsp garlic powder   ½ tsp chili powder

Directions
Place tomatoes in a blender and mix until liquefied. Combine all ingredients in slow cooker. Cook on low for 2-3 hours.

SPAGHETTI SAUCE 2

Prep time: 15 minutes   Cook time: 2-3 hours

Ingredients
1 large can stewed tomatoes   ¼ C chopped green pepper
1 small can tomato paste   1 small can diced tomatoes
1 tbsp soya sauce   2 garlic cloves, minced
¼ C minced onion   1 tsp chili powder

Directions
Place tomatoes in a blender and mix until liquefied. Combine all ingredients in slow cooker. Cook on low for 2-3 hours.

SPAGHETTI SAUCE 3

Prep time: 15 minutes   Cook time: 2-3 hours

Ingredients
2 pound lean ground beef   1 C tomato paste
1 tbsp extra virgin olive oil   3 C diced tomatoes
1 onion, finely chopped   ¼ C white sugar
1 green pepper, finely chopped   2 tbsp oregano
3 garlic cloves, minced   Salt and pepper to taste
4 C tomato sauce

Directions
Place tomatoes in a blender and mix until liquefied. Combine all ingredients in slow cooker. Cook on low for 2-3 hours.

SPAGHETTI SAUCE 4

Prep time: 15 minutes

Cook time: 2-3 hours

Ingredients

1 pound ground sausage
1 pound lean ground beef
3 C tomato sauce
2 C tomato paste
1 C water
3 cloves garlic, minced

1 large onion, minced
3 celery stalks, minced
2 tsp oregano
1 tsp chili pepper
1 tsp cayenne pepper
½ tsp paprika

Directions

Place tomatoes in a blender and mix until liquefied. Combine all ingredients in slow cooker. Cook on low for 2-3 hours.

SPAGHETTI SAUCE 5

Prep time: 15 minutes

Cook time: 2-3 hours

Ingredients

2 pounds lean ground beef
2 C tomato sauce
1 C tomato paste
½ C water
1 tbsp white sugar

¼ tsp ground cloves
1 tsp garlic powder
2 tsp onion powder
1 tsp chili powder

Directions

Place tomatoes in a blender and mix until liquefied. Combine all ingredients in slow cooker. Cook on low for 2-3 hours.

SPAGHETTI SAUCE 6

Prep time: 15 minutes

Cook time: 2-3 hours

Ingredients

1 pound fresh plum tomatoes
1 can tomato paste
3 tbsp white sugar
1 tbsp brown sugar
3 garlic cloves, minced
1 small onion, minced

½ C minced green pepper
½ C chopped mushrooms
1 tbsp soya sauce
½ tsp ground cloves
1 tsp oregano

Directions

Chop tomatoes and remove seeds. Puree in a blender until smooth. Combine all ingredients in slow cooker. Cook on low for 2-3 hours.

SPAGHETTI SAUCE 7

Prep time: 15 minutes

Cook time: 2-3 hours

Ingredients
1 pound lean ground beef
1 large onion, chopped
1 green pepper, chopped
2 cloves garlic, minced

5 large cans diced tomatoes
2 tbsp brown sugar
2 C beef broth
2 tbsp extra virgin olive oil

Directions
Place 4 cans of tomatoes in a blender and mix until liquefied. Combine all ingredients in slow cooker. Cook on low for 2-3 hours.

SPAGHETTI SAUCE 8

Prep time: 15 minutes

Cook time: 2-3 hours

Ingredients
1 pound lean ground beef
1 pound ground sausage
5 C tomato sauce
2 C tomato paste
2 medium onions, minced

4 cloves garlic, minced
2 tsp oregano
1 tsp Italian seasoning
2 tsp parsley
Salt and pepper to taste

Directions
Place tomatoes in a blender and mix until liquefied. Combine all ingredients in slow cooker. Cook on low for 2-3 hours.

SPAGHETTI SAUCE 9

Prep time: 15 minutes

Cook time: 2-3 hours

Ingredients
1 large can stewed tomatoes
1 large can diced tomatoes
2 small cans tomato paste
½ C water
2 tbsp white sugar
1 tbsp brown sugar

5 garlic cloves, minced
1 onion, minced
2 celery stalks, minced
2 tsp Italian seasoning
1 tsp oregano
Salt and pepper to taste

Directions
Place tomatoes in a blender and mix until liquefied. Combine all ingredients in slow cooker. Cook on low for 2-3 hours.

SPAGHETTI SAUCE 10

Prep time: 15 minutes

Cook time: 2-3 hours

Ingredients

1 pound ground turkey
2 tbsp extra virgin olive oil
3 C tomato sauce
1 C tomato paste
½ C water
3 tbsp brown sugar

1 tsp ground cloves
1 tbsp soya sauce
1 onion, minced
3 garlic cloves, minced
1 tsp salt
½ tsp ground black pepper

Directions

Place tomatoes in a blender and mix until liquefied. Combine all ingredients in slow cooker. Cook on low for 2-3 hours.

SPAGHETTI SAUCE 11

Prep time: 15 minutes

Cook time: 2-3 hours

Ingredients

1 pound ground beef
½ pound ground sausage
2 tbsp extra virgin olive oil
3 C tomato sauce
1 C tomato paste
½ C water
3 tbsp brown sugar

1 tsp ground cloves
1 tbsp soya sauce
1 tsp onion powder
1 tsp garlic powder
1 tsp salt
½ tsp ground black pepper

Directions

Place tomatoes in a blender and mix until liquefied. Combine all ingredients in slow cooker. Cook on low for 2-3 hours.

SPAGHETTI SAUCE 12

Prep time: 15 minutes

Cook time: 2-3 hours

Ingredients

1 pound ground pork
2 tbsp extra virgin olive oil
3 C tomato sauce
1 C tomato paste
½ C water
3 tbsp white sugar

1 tsp ground cloves
1 tbsp soya sauce
1 large onion, sliced
3 garlic cloves, minced
1 tsp salt
½ tsp ground black pepper

Directions

Place tomatoes in a blender and mix until liquefied. Combine all ingredients in slow cooker. Cook on low for 2-3 hours.

SPAGHETTI SAUCE 13

Prep time: 15 minutes   Cook time: 2-3 hours

Ingredients

1 pound ground beef
2 tbsp extra virgin olive oil
3 C tomato sauce
1 C tomato paste
½ C water

1 tbsp soya sauce
1 onion, minced
2 garlic cloves, minced
1 tsp salt
½ tsp ground black pepper

Directions

Place tomatoes in a blender and mix until liquefied. Combine all ingredients in slow cooker. Cook on low for 2-3 hours.

SPAGHETTI SAUCE 14

Prep time: 15 minutes   Cook time: 2-3 hours

Ingredients

1 pound ground beef
2 tbsp extra virgin olive oil
3 C tomato sauce
1 C tomato paste
½ C water
3 tbsp brown sugar
1 tsp ground cloves

1 tsp onion powder
1 tsp garlic powder
1 tsp Italian seasoning
1 tsp paprika
1 tsp salt
½ tsp ground black pepper

Directions

Place tomatoes in a blender and mix until liquefied. Combine all ingredients in slow cooker. Cook on low for 2-3 hours.

SPAGHETTI SAUCE 15

Prep time: 15 minutes   Cook time: 2-3 hours

Ingredients

1 pound ground beef
2 tbsp extra virgin olive oil
2 C tomato sauce
1 C tomato paste
1 can diced stewed tomatoes

½ C water
3 tbsp white sugar
1 tsp ground cloves
1 onion, minced
3 garlic cloves, minced

Directions

Place tomatoes in a blender and mix until liquefied. Combine all ingredients in slow cooker. Cook on low for 2-3 hours.

$\mathcal{S}$PAGHETTI SAUCE 16

Prep time: 15 minutes

Cook time: 2-3 hours

Ingredients

2 tbsp extra virgin olive oil
3 C tomato sauce
1 C tomato paste
½ C water
3 tbsp brown sugar

1 tsp ground cloves
1 tbsp soya sauce
1 tsp garlic powder
1 tsp onion powder

Directions

Place tomatoes in a blender and mix until liquefied. Combine all ingredients in slow cooker. Cook on low for 2-3 hours.

$\mathcal{S}$PAGHETTI SAUCE 17

Prep time: 15 minutes

Cook time: 2-3 hours

Ingredients

3 C tomato sauce
1 C tomato paste
½ C water
3 tbsp brown sugar

1 tsp ground cloves
1 tbsp soya sauce
1 onion, minced
½ tsp ground black pepper

Directions

Place tomatoes in a blender and mix until liquefied. Combine all ingredients in slow cooker. Cook on low for 2-3 hours.

$\mathcal{S}$PAGHETTI SAUCE 18

Prep time: 15 minutes

Cook time: 2-3 hours

Ingredients

3 C tomato sauce
1 C tomato paste
1 can stewed diced tomatoes
½ C water
3 tbsp white sugar

1 tsp ground cloves
1 tbsp soya sauce
1 onion, minced
3 garlic cloves, minced
½ tsp ground black pepper

Directions

Place tomatoes in a blender and mix until liquefied. Combine all ingredients in slow cooker. Cook on low for 2-3 hours.

SPAGHETTI SAUCE 19

Prep time: 15 minutes

Cook time: 2-3 hours

Ingredients

3 C tomato sauce
1 C tomato paste
1 C chopped plum tomatoes
1 C water
3 tbsp brown sugar
1 tsp ground cloves
1 tbsp soya sauce

1 onion, minced
2 tsp garlic powder
1 tsp paprika
1 tsp chili powder
1 tsp cayenne pepper
1 tsp salt
½ tsp ground black pepper

Directions

Place tomatoes in a blender and mix until liquefied. Combine all ingredients in slow cooker. Cook on low for 2-3 hours.

SPAGHETTI SAUCE 20

Prep time: 15 minutes

Cook time: 2-3 hours

Ingredients

3 C tomato sauce
1 C tomato paste
1 ½ C water
5 tbsp brown sugar
2 tsp ground cloves

1 tbsp soya sauce
1 onion, minced
3 garlic cloves, minced
1 tbsp beef bouillon powder
1 tsp ground black pepper

Directions

Place tomatoes in a blender and mix until liquefied. Combine all ingredients in slow cooker. Cook on low for 2-3 hours.

BARBECUE SAUCE 1

Prep time: 10 minutes

Cook time: 2-3 hours

Ingredients

1 C ketchup
½ C tomato paste
¼ C soy sauce

2 cloves garlic, minced
¼ C liquid smoke
½ C brown sugar

Directions

Combine all ingredients in slow cooker. Cook on low for 2-3 hours.

Barbecue Sauce 2

Prep time: 10 minutes

Cook time: 2-3 hours

Ingredients

1 C ketchup
½ C raw honey
¼ C white vinegar

¼ C liquid smoke
1 small onion, minced
3 garlic cloves, minced

Directions

Combine all ingredients in slow cooker. Cook on low for 2-3 hours.

Barbecue Sauce 3

Prep time: 10 minutes

Cook time: 2-3 hours

Ingredients

1 C ketchup
½ C tomato paste
2 tbsp soya sauce
½ C brown sugar

¼ C liquid smoke
2 tsp onion powder
1 tsp garlic powder

Directions

Combine all ingredients in slow cooker. Cook on low for 2-3 hours.

Barbecue Sauce 4

Prep time: 10 minutes

Cook time: 2-3 hours

Ingredients

1 C ketchup
½ C tomato paste
½ C dark molasses
¼ C corn syrup

1 small onion, finely diced
1 tsp chili powder
¼ C liquid smoke

Directions

Combine all ingredients in slow cooker. Cook on low for 2-3 hours.

BARBECUE SAUCE 5

Prep time: 10 minutes

Cook time: 2-3 hours

Ingredients
1 C ketchup
½ C spaghetti sauce
½ C brown sugar
2 tsp garlic powder

1 tsp chili powder
1 tsp oregano
1 tsp onion powder
1 tbsp soya sauce

Directions
Combine all ingredients in slow cooker. Cook on low for 2-3 hours.

BARBECUE SAUCE 6

Prep time: 10 minutes

Cook time: 2-3 hours

Ingredients
1 C ketchup
½ C brown sugar
1 tbsp soya sauce
¼ C molasses

2 tsp garlic powder
¼ C raw honey
¼ C white vinegar

Directions
Combine all ingredients in slow cooker. Cook on low for 2-3 hours.

BARBECUE SAUCE 7

Prep time: 10 minutes

Cook time: 2-3 hours

Ingredients
1 C ketchup
¼ C water
¼ C white vinegar
¼ C brown sugar

1 tbsp honey mustard
½ tsp onion powder
½ tsp paprika

Directions
Combine all ingredients in slow cooker. Cook on low for 2-3 hours.

Barbecue Sauce 8

Prep time: 10 minutes

Cook time: 2-3 hours

Ingredients

1 C ketchup
½ C apple cider vinegar
½ C water
¼ C onion, finely diced
2 tbsp minced garlic

2 tbsp molasses
2 tbsp brown sugar
1 tsp chili powder
Salt and pepper to taste

Directions

Combine all ingredients in slow cooker. Cook on low for 2-3 hours.

Barbecue Sauce 9

Prep time: 10 minutes

Cook time: 2-3 hours

Ingredients

1 C ketchup
¾ C water
¼ C white vinegar
½ C brown sugar

½ tsp cayenne pepper
½ tsp chili pepper
½ tsp ground black pepper
1 tbsp liquid smoke

Directions

Combine all ingredients in slow cooker. Cook on low for 2-3 hours.

Barbecue Sauce 10

Prep time: 10 minutes

Cook time: 2-3 hours

Ingredients

1 C ketchup
1 C water
½ C white vinegar
¼ C butter
¼ C onion, finely minced
2 tbsp Worcestershire sauce

2 tbsp raw honey
1 beef bouillon cube
2 tsp paprika
2 tsp chili powder
Salt and pepper to taste

Directions

Combine all ingredients in slow cooker. Cook on low for 2-3 hours.

BARBECUE SAUCE 11

Prep time: 10 minutes

Cook time: 2-3 hours

Ingredients
1 C ketchup
4 tbsp cider vinegar
1/3 C water
2 tbsp vegetable oil

1 tbsp butter
¾ tsp paprika
¾ tsp minced garlic
½ tsp tabasco sauce

Directions
Combine all ingredients in slow cooker. Cook on low for 2-3 hours.

BARBECUE SAUCE 12

Prep time: 10 minutes

Cook time: 2-3 hours

Ingredients
2 C cola
2 C ketchup
½ C white vinegar
¼ C molasses

1 onion, chopped
2 tsp black pepper
2 tbsp salt
2 tbsp chili powder

Directions
Combine all ingredients in slow cooker. Cook on low for 2-3 hours.

BARBECUE SAUCE 13

Prep time: 10 minutes

Cook time: 2-3 hours

Ingredients
2/3 C hoisin sauce
2/3 C soy sauce
½ C cooking sherry
½ C white sugar

3 garlic cloves, minced
2 tbsp black bean paste
2 tsp Chinese 5-spice mix
1 tsp salt

Directions
Combine all ingredients in slow cooker. Cook on low for 2-3 hours.

BARBECUE SAUCE 14

Prep time: 10 minutes

Cook time: 2-3 hours

Ingredients

2 C raw honey
1 small can tomato paste
½ C brown sugar
1/3 C jerk seasoning

¼ C rye whiskey
1 tbsp yellow mustard
2 tsp garlic powder
2 tsp cayenne pepper

Directions

Combine all ingredients in slow cooker. Cook on low for 2-3 hours.

BARBECUE SAUCE 15

Prep time: 10 minutes

Cook time: 2-3 hours

Ingredients

1 C ketchup
1 C water
½ C cider vinegar
1 tbsp extra virgin olive oil
1 onion, chopped
3 garlic cloves, minced

¼ C white sugar
1 tbsp freshly grated ginger
1 tsp salt
1 tsp cayenne pepper
Juice from ½ lemon

Directions

Combine all ingredients in slow cooker. Cook on low for 2-3 hours.

BARBECUE SAUCE 16

Prep time: 10 minutes

Cook time: 2-3 hours

Ingredients

1 C ketchup
1 C water
½ C cider vinegar
1 tbsp extra virgin olive oil

1 onion, chopped
¼ C white sugar
1 tsp salt

Directions

Combine all ingredients in slow cooker. Cook on low for 2-3 hours.

BARBECUE SAUCE 17

Prep time: 10 minutes   Cook time: 2-3 hours

Ingredients
1 C ketchup   1 tsp onion powder
1 C water   1 tsp garlic powder
½ C white vinegar   ¼ C white sugar
1 tbsp extra virgin olive oil

Directions
Combine all ingredients in slow cooker. Cook on low for 2-3 hours.

BARBECUE SAUCE 18

Prep time: 10 minutes   Cook time: 2-3 hours

Ingredients
1 C ketchup   1 onion, chopped
1 C water   1 garlic clove, minced
½ C cider vinegar   ¼ C brown sugar
1 tbsp extra virgin olive oil   1 tbsp freshly grated ginger

Directions
Combine all ingredients in slow cooker. Cook on low for 2-3 hours.

BARBECUE SAUCE 19

Prep time: 10 minutes   Cook time: 2-3 hours

Ingredients
1 C ketchup   3 garlic cloves, minced
1 C water   ¼ C brown sugar
½ C white vinegar   1 tsp salt
1 tbsp extra virgin olive oil   ½ tsp ground black pepper
1 onion, chopped   1 tsp Italian seasoning

Directions
Combine all ingredients in slow cooker. Cook on low for 2-3 hours.

Barbecue Sauce 20

Prep time: 10 minutes

Cook time: 2-3 hours

Ingredients
1 C ketchup
1 C water
½ C white vinegar

1 tbsp extra virgin olive oil
1 tsp onion powder
¼ C molasses

Directions
Combine all ingredients in slow cooker. Cook on low for 2-3 hours.

Sweet & Sour Sauce 1

Prep time: 10 minutes

Cook time: 2-3 hours

Ingredients
1 C pineapple juice
1 C water
3 tbsp white vinegar

1 tbsp soy sauce
½ C brown sugar, packed
3 tbsp corn starch

Directions
Combine all ingredients except corn starch in slow cooker. Cook on low for 2-3 hours. Mix corn starch with 3 tbsp water, and add to sauce. Stir until sauce thickens.

Sweet & Sour Sauce 2

Prep time: 10 minutes

Cook time: 2-3 hours

Ingredients
1 C ketchup
½ C white vinegar
1 C brown sugar, packed

2 tbsp corn starch
2 tbsp water

Directions
Combine all ingredients except corn starch in slow cooker. Cook on low for 2-3 hours. Mix corn starch with 3 tbsp water, and add to sauce. Stir until sauce thickens.

SWEET & SOUR SAUCE 3

Prep time: 10 minutes

Cook time: 2-3 hours

Ingredients

1 C ketchup
½ C pineapple juice
½ C crushed pineapple
½ C white vinegar

½ C raw honey
3 tbsp corn starch
3 tbsp water

Directions

Combine all ingredients except corn starch in slow cooker. Cook on low for 2-3 hours. Mix corn starch with 3 tbsp water, and add to sauce. Stir until sauce thickens.

SWEET & SOUR SAUCE 4

Prep time: 10 minutes

Cook time: 2-3 hours

Ingredients

¾ C white sugar
¼ C soy sauce
1/3 C white vinegar

2/3 C water
2 tbsp ketchup
3 tbsp corn starch

Directions

Combine all ingredients except corn starch in slow cooker. Cook on low for 2-3 hours. Mix corn starch with 3 tbsp water, and add to sauce. Stir until sauce thickens.

SWEET & SOUR SAUCE 5

Prep time: 10 minutes

Cook time: 2-3 hours

Ingredients

2 C water
1 ½ C white sugar
½ C white vinegar
1 6-ounce can tomato paste

1 8-ounce can pineapple tidbits
3 tbsp corn starch
3 tbsp water

Directions

Combine all ingredients except corn starch in slow cooker. Cook on low for 2-3 hours. Mix corn starch with 3 tbsp water, and add to sauce. Stir until sauce thickens.

SWEET & SOUR SAUCE 6

Prep time: 10 minutes   Cook time: 2-3 hours

Ingredients

2 C water   1 6-ounce can tomato paste
1 ½ C white sugar   1 C pineapple juice
½ C brown sugar   3 tbsp corn starch
½ C white vinegar   3 tbsp water

Directions

Combine all ingredients except corn starch in slow cooker. Cook on low for 2-3 hours. Mix corn starch with 3 tbsp water, and add to sauce. Stir until sauce thickens.

SWEET & SOUR SAUCE 7

Prep time: 10 minutes   Cook time: 2-3 hours

Ingredients

2 C water   1 C pineapple juice
1 ½ C white sugar   3 tbsp corn starch
1 C white vinegar   3 tbsp water
¾ C ketchup

Directions

Combine all ingredients except corn starch in slow cooker. Cook on low for 2-3 hours. Mix corn starch with 3 tbsp water, and add to sauce. Stir until sauce thickens.

SWEET & SOUR SAUCE 8

Prep time: 10 minutes   Cook time: 2-3 hours

Ingredients

2 C water   1 6-ounce can tomato paste
1 ½ C white sugar   1 C pineapple juice
¼ C Karo syrup   3 tbsp corn starch
½ C white vinegar   3 tbsp water

Directions

Combine all ingredients except corn starch in slow cooker. Cook on low for 2-3 hours. Mix corn starch with 3 tbsp water, and add to sauce. Stir until sauce thickens.

SWEET & SOUR SAUCE 9

Prep time: 10 minutes

Cook time: 2-3 hours

Ingredients

3 C water
2 C white sugar
1 C white vinegar
½ C ketchup

2 tbsp mustard
1 8-ounce can pineapple tidbits
3 tbsp corn starch
3 tbsp water

Directions

Combine all ingredients except corn starch in slow cooker. Cook on low for 2-3 hours. Mix corn starch with 3 tbsp water, and add to sauce. Stir until sauce thickens.

SWEET & SOUR SAUCE 10

Prep time: 10 minutes

Cook time: 2-3 hours

Ingredients

2 C water
1 ½ C white sugar
½ C white vinegar
1 C tomato paste
1 C crushed pineapple

1 tsp onion powder
1 tbsp chicken bouillon powder
3 tbsp corn starch
3 tbsp water

Directions

Combine all ingredients except corn starch in slow cooker. Cook on low for 2-3 hours. Mix corn starch with 3 tbsp water, and add to sauce. Stir until sauce thickens.

DRY GARLIC SAUCE 1

Prep time: 10 minutes

Cook time: 2-3 hours

Ingredients

1 ½ C brown sugar
1 ½ C water
5 cloves garlic, minced

4 tbsp soy sauce
1 tbsp dry mustard

Directions

Combine all ingredients in slow cooker. Cook on low for 2-3 hours.

DRY GARLIC SAUCE 2

Prep time: 10 minutes

Cook time: 2-3 hours

Ingredients

1 C brown sugar
1 C water
¼ C molasses

5 garlic cloves, minced
1 tbsp soy sauce

Directions

Combine all ingredients in slow cooker. Cook on low for 2-3 hours.

DRY GARLIC SAUCE 3

Prep time: 10 minutes

Cook time: 2-3 hours

Ingredients

1 C molasses
½ C water

1 tbsp raw honey
5 garlic cloves, minced

Directions

Combine all ingredients in slow cooker. Cook on low for 2-3 hours.

DRY GARLIC SAUCE 4

Prep time: 10 minutes

Cook time: 2-3 hours

Ingredients

1 C soy sauce
½ C hoisin sauce

5 tsp garlic powder
1 tsp onion powder

Directions

Combine all ingredients in slow cooker. Cook on low for 2-3 hours.

DRY GARLIC SAUCE 5

Prep time: 10 minutes

Cook time: 2-3 hours

Ingredients

1 C molasses
¼ C soy sauce
5 garlic cloves, minced
1 tsp garlic powder

1 tsp onion powder
2 tbsp brown sugar
1 tbsp raw honey

Directions

Combine all ingredients in slow cooker. Cook on low for 2-3 hours.

DRY GARLIC SAUCE 6

Prep time: 10 minutes   Cook time: 2-3 hours

Ingredients
½ C molasses   3 garlic cloves, minced
½ C brown sugar   1 tbsp raw honey
¼ C soy sauce

Directions
Combine all ingredients in slow cooker. Cook on low for 2-3 hours.

DRY GARLIC SAUCE 7

Prep time: 10 minutes   Cook time: 2-3 hours

Ingredients
1 C molasses   ¼ C white sugar
¼ C soy sauce   4 garlic cloves, minced

Directions
Combine all ingredients in slow cooker. Cook on low for 2-3 hours.

DRY GARLIC SAUCE 8

Prep time: 10 minutes   Cook time: 2-3 hours

Ingredients
1 C molasses   1 tbsp raw honey
¼ C soy sauce   2 tbsp brown sugar
3 tsp garlic powder   ½ tsp onion powder

Directions
Combine all ingredients in slow cooker. Cook on low for 2-3 hours.

DRY GARLIC SAUCE 9

Prep time: 10 minutes   Cook time: 2-3 hours

Ingredients
½ C molasses   ¼ C soy sauce
½ C brown sugar   3 garlic cloves, minced
¼ C Karo syrup   1 large onion, sliced

Directions
Combine all ingredients in slow cooker. Cook on low for 2-3 hours.

Dry Garlic Sauce 10

Prep time: 10 minutes   Cook time: 2-3 hours

Ingredients
1 C molasses   1 C water
¼ C soy sauce   6 garlic cloves, minced

Directions
Combine all ingredients in slow cooker. Cook on low for 2-3 hours.

Honey Garlic Sauce 1

Prep time: 10 minutes   Cook time: 2-3 hours

Ingredients
2 C chicken broth   5 garlic cloves, minced
½ C brown sugar   1 tsp powdered ginger
½ C raw honey   2 tbsp corn starch
¼ C soy sauce   2 tbsp water

Directions
Combine all ingredients except corn starch and water in slow cooker. Cook on low for 2-3 hours. Mix corn starch with water, add to sauce, and stir until thickened.

Honey Garlic Sauce 2

Prep time: 10 minutes   Cook time: 2-3 hours

Ingredients
1 C chicken broth   1 tsp crushed red pepper flakes
2/3 C raw honey   2 tbsp white vinegar
2 tbsp soy sauce   2 tbsp brown sugar
2 tbsp extra virgin olive oil   2 tbsp corn starch
5 garlic cloves, minced   2 tbsp water

Directions
Combine all ingredients except corn starch and water in slow cooker. Cook on low for 2-3 hours. Mix corn starch with water, add to sauce, and stir until thickened.

*H*ONEY GARLIC SAUCE 3

Prep time: 10 minutes

Cook time: 2-3 hours

Ingredients
1 C beef broth
2/3 C raw honey
2 tbsp soy sauce
5 garlic cloves, minced

2 tbsp white vinegar
2 tbsp brown sugar
2 tbsp corn starch
2 tbsp water

Directions
Combine all ingredients except corn starch and water in slow cooker. Cook on low for 2-3 hours. Mix corn starch with water, add to sauce, and stir until thickened.

*H*ONEY GARLIC SAUCE 4

Prep time: 10 minutes

Cook time: 2-3 hours

Ingredients
1 C chicken broth
2/3 C raw honey
2 tbsp soy sauce

3 tsp garlic powder
2 tbsp corn starch
2 tbsp water

Directions
Combine all ingredients except corn starch and water in slow cooker. Cook on low for 2-3 hours. Mix corn starch with water, add to sauce, and stir until thickened.

*H*ONEY GARLIC SAUCE 5

Prep time: 10 minutes

Cook time: 2-3 hours

Ingredients
1 C chicken broth
½ C C raw honey
½ C molasses
2 tbsp soy sauce

2 tbsp extra virgin olive oil
3 garlic cloves, minced
2 tbsp corn starch
2 tbsp water

Directions
Combine all ingredients except corn starch and water in slow cooker. Cook on low for 2-3 hours. Mix corn starch with water, add to sauce, and stir until thickened.

Basic White Sauce

Prep time: 5 minutes

Cook time: 2-3 hours

Ingredients
1 C milk
2 tbsp flour

2 tbsp butter
Pinch salt

Directions
Combine all ingredients in slow cooker. Cook on low for 2-3 hours.

Mushroom Sauce

Prep time: 10 minutes

Cook time: 2-3 hours

Ingredients
1 C fresh mushrooms, roughly chopped
1 C heavy cream
2 tsp yellow mustard

2 cloves garlic, minced
Salt and pepper to taste

Directions
Combine all ingredients in slow cooker. Cook on low for 2-3 hours.

Sesame Ginger Sauce

Prep time: 10 minutes

Cook time: 2-3 hours

Ingredients
5 tbsp soy sauce
5 tbsp rice vinegar
5 tbsp peanut oil
5 tbsp water

5 tbsp tahini
5 tsp chopped fresh ginger
2 tsp garlic minced garlic
½ tsp red chili flakes

Directions
Combine all ingredients in slow cooker. Cook on low for 2-3 hours.

Hollandaise Sauce

Prep time: 10 minutes

Cook time: 2-3 hours

Ingredients
½ C butter
3 egg yolks

1 tbsp lemon juice

Directions
Melt butter in microwave. Whisk egg yolks until thick, and add to butter with lemon juice. Combine all ingredients in slow cooker. Cook on low for 2-3 hours.

STIR-FRY SAUCE

Prep time: 10 minutes

Cook time: 2-3 hours

Ingredients
6 tbsp soy sauce
2 tbsp chicken bouillon
1 tbsp garlic powder
1 tbsp ground ginger

Enough water to bring mixture to 2 C
3 tbsp corn starch
3 tbsp cold water

Directions
Combine all ingredients except corn starch and water in slow cooker. Cook on low for 2-3 hours. Mix corn starch and water, and stir into sauce. Heat until thickened.

ALFREDO SAUCE 1

Prep time: 10 minutes

Cook time: 2-3 hours

Ingredients
¾ C milk
¾ C half and half
1 ½ C finely grated parmesan cheese

1 ounce cream cheese
3 cloves garlic, minced
Salt and pepper to taste

Directions
Combine all ingredients in slow cooker. Cook on low for 2-3 hours.

ALFREDO SAUCE 2

Prep time: 10 minutes

Cook time: 2-3 hours

Ingredients
¾ C milk
¾ C heavy cream
2 C finely grated parmesan cheese

4 cloves garlic, minced
Salt and pepper to taste

Directions
Combine all ingredients in slow cooker. Cook on low for 2-3 hours.

WHITE WINE SAUCE

Prep time: 5 minutes

Cook time: 2-3 hours

Ingredients
½ C chicken broth
¼ C dry white wine
2 tbsp white wine vinegar

2 tbsp butter
1/3 C minced onion

Directions
Combine all ingredients in slow cooker. Cook on low for 2-3 hours.

ORANGE SAUCE 1

Prep time: 10 minutes

Cook time: 2-3 hours

Ingredients

1 ½ C chicken broth
6 tbsp orange marmalade
2 tbsp fresh ginger, grated

2 tbsp soy sauce
2 tbsp lemon juice
1 tsp hot chili sauce

Directions

Combine all ingredients in slow cooker. Cook on low for 2-3 hours.

ORANGE SAUCE 2

Prep time: 10 minutes

Cook time: 2-3 hours

Ingredients

2 C orange marmalade
½ C pineapple juice
½ C rice wine vinegar
2 tbsp soy sauce
2 tbsp ketchup

1 tbsp sesame seeds
2 tsp red pepper flakes
1 tbsp corn starch
1 tbsp water

Directions

Combine all ingredients except corn starch and water in slow cooker. Cook on low for 1-2 hours. Dissolve corn starch in water and add to mixture. Stir until thickened.

LEMON BUTTER SAUCE

Prep time: 5 minutes

Cook time: 2-3 hours

Ingredients

20 tbsp melted butter
10 tsp fresh lemon juice

Salt and pepper to taste/2

Directions

Combine all ingredients in slow cooker. Cook on low for 2-3 hours.

CHEDDAR CHEESE SAUCE

Prep time: 10 minutes

Cook time: 2-3 hours

Ingredients

2 C milk
¼ C butter
¼ C flour

1 C shredded sharp cheddar cheese
1 tsp paprika
Salt and pepper to taste

Directions

Combine all ingredients in slow cooker. Cook on low for 2-3 hours.

*F*ISH SAUCE

Prep time: 5 minutes

Cook time: 2-3 hours

Ingredients

2 C water
1 C white sugar
¾ C fish sauce

½ C white vinegar
1 tbsp lemon juice
Salt and pepper to taste

Directions

Combine all ingredients in slow cooker. Cook on low for 2-3 hours.

*P*ARMESAN SAUCE

Prep time: 5 minutes

Cook time: 2-3 hours

Ingredients

1 C chicken stock
1 pint heavy cream
¼ C finely grated parmesan cheese

½ C flour
Salt and pepper to taste

Directions

Combine all ingredients in slow cooker. Cook on low for 2-3 hours.

*C*REAMY BACON SAUCE

Prep time: 15 minutes

Cook time: 2-3 hours

Ingredients

1 C sliced zucchini
1 C sliced leek
1 C button mushrooms, halved
5 slices bacon, chopped and cooked
3 cloves garlic, minced

1 tbsp yellow mustard
1 tsp chicken bouillon powder
1 ¼ C sour cream
¾ C milk
1 tbsp extra virgin olive oil

Directions

Combine all ingredients in slow cooker. Cook on low for 2-3 hours. Puree in a food processor until creamy.

*S*WEET CHILI SAUCE

Prep time: 5 minutes

Cook time: 2-3 hours

Ingredients

5 C apple cider vinegar
4 pounds white sugar
1 ½ C red chili pepper, seeded

5 cloves garlic, minced
2 tsp grated fresh ginger

Directions

Heat 1 C vinegar in slow cooker, and add ginger, garlic, and chilies. Cook for about 1 hour, or until ingredients are soft. Puree ingredients. Add remaining vinegar and sugar, stirring to mix. Cook on low for 1-2 hours.

TERIYAKI SAUCE

Prep time: 5 minutes

Cook time: 2-3 hours

Ingredients

1/3 C soy sauce
¼ C white sugar
2 C beef stock

2 garlic cloves, minced
3 tbsp flour

Directions

Combine all ingredients in slow cooker. Cook on low for 2-3 hours.

PEANUT SAUCE

Prep time: 10 minutes

Cook time: 2-3 hours

Ingredients

¼ C raw honey
¼ C water
½ C dark sesame oil
6 tbsp dark soy sauce
3 tbsp light soy sauce

6 tbsp tahini
7 tbsp peanut butter
1 tbsp rice wine vinegar
2 tsp fresh ginger, minced
½ C hot water

Directions

Combine all ingredients in slow cooker. Cook on low for 2-3 hours.

DUMPLING SAUCE

Prep time: 10 minutes

Cook time: 2-3 hours

Ingredients

¼ C soy sauce
1 tbsp rice wine
1 tbsp rice wine vinegar
3 tbsp sugar

1 tbsp minced scallion
2 tbsp minced garlic
3 tbsp sesame oil
1 tbsp chili paste

Directions

Combine all ingredients in slow cooker. Cook on low for 2-3 hours.

DARK HOISIN SAUCE

Prep time: 5 minutes

Cook time: 2-3 hours

Ingredients

1 C hoisin sauce
1 C ketchup
4 tbsp rice vinegar

5 tbsp raw honey
1 tbsp dark soy sauce

Directions

Combine all ingredients in slow cooker. Cook on low for 2-3 hours.

Manchurian Sauce

Prep time: 10 minutes

Cook time: 2-3 hours

Ingredients
1 C soy sauce
1 C vegetable stock
1 C chopped green onion

1 tbsp minced ginger root
2 tsp minced garlic
1 tsp wasabi

Directions
Combine all ingredients in slow cooker. Cook on low for 2-3 hours.

Soy Dipping Sauce

Prep time: 10 minutes

Cook time: 1-2 hours

Ingredients
1 C light soy sauce
½ C vegetable stock
2 tbsp rice wine
4 tbsp rice vinegar

4 tbsp sesame oil
2 tbsp raw honey
2 tbsp oil

Directions
Combine all ingredients in slow cooker. Cook on low for 1-2 hours.

Spicy Stir-Fry Sauce

Prep time: 5 minutes

Cook time: 2-3 hours

Ingredients
½ C chicken stock
½ C cooking sherry
½ C soy sauce
2 tbsp vegetable oil

2 tsp minced garlic
2 tsp minced ginger
2 tbsp sliced green onion
1 tbsp hot pepper sauce

Directions
Combine all ingredients except corn starch and water in slow cooker. Cook on low for 2-3 hours. Dissolve corn starch in water, and add to sauce. Stir until thickened.

LOBSTER SAUCE

Prep time: 10 minutes

Cook time: 2-3 hours

Ingredients

½ C fermented black beans
¼ C vegetable oil
1 tbsp minced garlic
1/3 C cooking sherry
¼ C chicken broth

¼ C dark soy sauce
2 tbsp brown sugar, packed
1 tbsp sesame oil
3 tbsp corn starch
3 tbsp water

Directions

Rinse and drain black beans, and then mash. Combine all ingredients except corn starch and water in slow cooker. Cook on low for 2-3 hours. Dissolve corn starch in water, and add to sauce. Stir until thickened.

DUCK SAUCE

Prep time: 10 minutes

Cook time: 2-3 hours

Ingredients

1 13-ounce can peaches, drained
1 14-ounce can plums, drained
1 C red bell peppers, diced

1 C dried apricots, chopped
2/3 C white vinegar
2 tsp candied ginger

Directions

Chop canned fruits. You should have about 5 C of fruit. Combine all ingredients in the slow cooker. Cook on low for 2-3 hours.

HOISIN SAUCE

Prep time: 10 minutes

Cook time: 2-3 hours

Ingredients

½ C red bean paste
½ C white sugar
3 tbsp white vinegar
3 tbsp water

2 tbsp soy sauce
2 tbsp corn oil
3 garlic cloves, minced
5 dried chili peppers

Directions

Combine all ingredients in slow cooker. Cook on low for 2-3 hours. Puree sauce in a food processor.

Hot Mustard Sauce

Prep time: 5 minutes

Cook time: 2-3 hours

Ingredients
½ C hot mustard powder
½ C water

2 tsp white vinegar
2 tsp sesame oil

Directions
Mix mustard powder and water until smooth. Add all ingredients into slow. Cook on low for 2-3 hours.

Hot Chili Sauce

Prep time: 10 minutes

Cook time: 2-3 hours

Ingredients
1 C warm water
60 dried hot chili peppers
2/3 C corn oil
6 garlic cloves, minced

1 pound red bell peppers, seeded and coarsely chopped
2/3 C soy sauce

Directions
Soak peppers in warm water until they are soft, and then drain and chop. Combine all ingredients in slow cooker. Cook on low for 2-3 hours.

Soy Sauce Dip

Prep time: 10 minutes

Cook time: 1-2 hours

Ingredients
2/3 C soy sauce
4 tbsp white vinegar
4 tbsp white sugar

4 tbsp fresh ginger, minced
2 tbsp minced garlic
2 tbsp crushed hot chili flakes

Directions
Combine all ingredients in slow cooker. Cook on low for 1-2 hours.

Garlic Sauce 1

Prep time: 10 minutes

Cook time: 2-3 hours

Ingredients
1 C chicken broth
4 tbsp minced garlic

1 tsp minced ginger
6 tbsp oyster sauce

Directions
Combine all ingredients in slow cooker. Cook on low for 2-3 hours.

Garlic Sauce 2

Prep time: 10 minutes

Cook time: 2-3 hours

Ingredients

1 C beef broth
4 tbsp minced garlic
1 tsp minced ginger

6 tbsp fish sauce
½ tsp onion powder

Directions

Combine all ingredients in slow cooker. Cook on low for 2-3 hours.

Honey Sauce 1

Prep time: 10 minutes

Cook time: 2-3 hours

Ingredients

1 C soy sauce
1 ½ C ketchup
½ C raw honey

1 tbsp yellow mustard
1 large onion, finely chopped

Directions

Combine all ingredients in slow cooker. Cook on low for 2-3 hours.

Honey Sauce 2

Prep time: 10 minutes

Cook time: 2-3 hours

Ingredients

1 C soy sauce
1 ½ C ketchup

1 C raw honey
1 garlic clove, minced

Directions

Combine all ingredients in slow cooker. Cook on low for 2-3 hours.

Lemon Sauce 1

Prep time: 5 minutes

Cook time: 1-2 hours

Ingredients

2 C chicken broth
½ C lemon juice
¾ C white sugar

Zest of 1 lemon
3 tbsp corn starch
3 tbsp water

Directions

Combine all ingredients except corn starch and water in slow cooker. Cook on low for 1-2 hours. Dissolve corn starch in water and add to mixture. Stir until thickened.

LEMON SAUCE 2

Prep time: 5 minutes

Cook time: 1-2 hours

Ingredients

2 C chicken broth
1 C lemon juice
1 C white sugar
½ tsp paprika

½ tsp lemon pepper
Zest of 1 lemon
3 tbsp corn starch
3 tbsp water

Directions

Combine all ingredients except corn starch and water in slow cooker. Cook on low for 1-2 hours. Dissolve corn starch in water and add to mixture. Stir until thickened.

Snacks and Appetizers

ℙARTY MIX 1

Prep time: 10 minutes

Cook time: 3 hours

Ingredients
½ C butter, melted
¼ C Worcestershire sauce
2 tsp seasoned salt
2 tsp garlic powder
2 tsp onion powder
4 C corn square cereal

4 C rice square cereal
2 C wheat square cereal
2 C small salted pretzels
2 C small cheddar cheese crackers
2 C smoked nuts

Directions
Place all ingredients together in slow cooker. Cook on low for 3 hours.

ℙARTY MIX 2

Prep time: 10 minutes

Cook time: 3 hours

Ingredients
½ C butter, melted
¼ C Worcestershire sauce
2 tsp seasoned salt
2 tsp garlic powder
2 tsp onion powder
1 tsp chili powder

4 C corn Cheerios
4 C puffed rice cereal
2 C puffed wheat cereal
2 C small salted pretzels
2 C small cheddar cheese crackers

Directions
Place all ingredients together in slow cooker. Cook on low for 3 hours.

ℙARTY MIX 3

Prep time: 10 minutes

Cook time: 3 hours

Ingredients
½ C butter, melted
¼ C Worcestershire sauce
1 tbsp soya sauce
2 tsp seasoned salt
2 tsp garlic powder
2 tsp onion powder

2 tsp paprika
4 C unsalted peanuts
4 C Chex cereal
2 C Shreddies
2 C small salted pretzels

Directions
Place all ingredients together in slow cooker. Cook on low for 3 hours.

PARTY MIX 4

Prep time: 10 minutes

Cook time: 3 hours

Ingredients
½ C butter, melted
¼ C raw honey
2 tsp ground cinnamon
2 tsp seasoned salt

4 C corn square cereal
4 C rice square cereal
2 C wheat square cereal
2 C small salted pretzels

Directions
Place all ingredients together in slow cooker. Cook on low for 3 hours.

PARTY MIX 5

Prep time: 10 minutes

Cook time: 3 hours

Ingredients
½ C butter, melted
¼ C Worcestershire sauce
2 tsp salt
2 tsp garlic powder
2 tsp onion powder
½ tsp ground black pepper

4 C corn square cereal
4 C rice square cereal
2 C wheat square cereal
2 C Chinese noodles
2 C Cheerios

Directions
Place all ingredients together in slow cooker. Cook on low for 3 hours.

PARTY MIX 6

Prep time: 10 minutes

Cook time: 3 hours

Ingredients
½ C butter, melted
¼ C Worcestershire sauce
1 tbsp soya sauce
3 tsp garlic powder
2 tsp onion powder
1 tsp chili powder

1 tsp paprika
½ tsp cayenne pepper
4 C corn square cereal
4 C rice square cereal
2 C wheat square cereal
2 C small salted pretzel sticks

Directions
Place all ingredients together in slow cooker. Cook on low for 3 hours.

PARTY MIX 7

Prep time: 10 minutes

Cook time: 3 hours

Ingredients
½ C butter, melted
¼ C Worcestershire sauce
2 tsp seasoned salt
2 tsp garlic powder

4 C corn square cereal
4 C Chinese noodles
2 C Shreddies
2 C small salted pretzel sticks

Directions
Place all ingredients together in slow cooker. Cook on low for 3 hours.

PARTY MIX 8

Prep time: 10 minutes

Cook time: 3 hours

Ingredients
½ C butter, melted
¼ C Worcestershire sauce
2 tsp garlic powder
2 tsp onion powder

4 C corn square cereal
4 C rice square cereal
2 C corn chips
2 C small salted pretzels

Directions
Place all ingredients together in slow cooker. Cook on low for 3 hours.

PARTY MIX 9

Prep time: 10 minutes

Cook time: 3 hours

Ingredients
½ C butter, melted
¼ C Worcestershire sauce
2 tsp seasoned salt
2 tsp garlic powder
2 tsp onion powder
2 tsp paprika
1 tsp curry powder

4 C corn square cereal
4 C rice square cereal
2 C wheat square cereal
2 C small salted pretzels
2 C small cheddar cheese crackers
2 C corn chips
2 C cashews

Directions
Place all ingredients together in slow cooker. Cook on low for 3 hours.

Party Mix 10

Prep time: 10 minutes   Cook time: 3 hours

Ingredients
½ C butter, melted   4 C rice square cereal
¼ C Worcestershire sauce   2 C wheat square cereal
2 tsp onion powder   2 C corn chips
4 C corn square cereal   2 C Cheerios

Directions
Place all ingredients together in slow cooker. Cook on low for 3 hours.

Cocktail Meatballs 1

Prep time: 20 minutes   Cook time: 3-4 hours

Ingredients
1 pound lean ground beef   1 C grape jelly
1 C bread crumbs   1 C chili sauce
1 egg   1 tbsp brown sugar, packed
Salt and pepper to taste   1 tbsp lemon juice
3 tbsp minced onion

Directions
Mix ground beef, crumbs, salt, pepper, and egg together and form 2" meatballs. Place meatballs and remaining ingredients together in slow cooker. Cook on low for 3-4 hours.

Cocktail Meatballs 2

Prep time: 20 minutes   Cook time: 3-4 hours

Ingredients
1 pound lean ground beef   Salt and pepper to taste
1 C bread crumbs   3 tbsp minced onion
1 egg   1 C barbecue sauce

Directions
Mix ground beef, crumbs, salt, pepper, and egg together and form 2" meatballs. Place meatballs and sauce together in slow cooker. Cook on low for 3-4 hours.

COCKTAIL MEATBALLS 3

Prep time: 20 minutes

Cook time: 3-4 hours

Ingredients

1 pound lean ground beef
1 C bread crumbs
1 egg
Salt and pepper to taste
3 tbsp minced onion

1 C ketchup
1 C raw honey
½ C white vinegar
1 tbsp lemon juice

Directions

Mix ground beef, crumbs, salt, pepper, and egg together and form 2" meatballs. Place meatballs and remaining ingredients together in slow cooker. Cook on low for 3-4 hours.

COCKTAIL MEATBALLS 4

Prep time: 20 minutes

Cook time: 3-4 hours

Ingredients

1 pound lean ground beef
1 C bread crumbs
1 egg
Salt and pepper to taste

3 tbsp minced onion
1 C cranberry juice
1 C barbecue sauce

Directions

Mix ground beef, crumbs, salt, pepper, and egg together and form 2" meatballs. Place meatballs and remaining ingredients together in slow cooker. Cook on low for 3-4 hours.

COCKTAIL MEATBALLS 5

Prep time: 20 minutes

Cook time: 3-4 hours

Ingredients

1 pound lean ground beef
1 C bread crumbs
1 egg
Salt and pepper to taste
3 tbsp minced onion

1 C apple juice
1 C beef broth
1 tbsp brown sugar, packed
1 tbsp lemon juice

Directions

Mix ground beef, crumbs, salt, pepper, and egg together and form 2" meatballs. Place meatballs and remaining ingredients together in slow cooker. Cook on low for 3-4 hours.

COCKTAIL MEATBALLS 6

Prep time: 20 minutes

Cook time: 3-4 hours

Ingredients

1 pound lean ground beef
1 C bread crumbs
1 egg
Salt and pepper to taste

3 tbsp minced onion
1 C tomato juice
1 C beef broth
1 tbsp brown sugar, packed

Directions

Mix ground beef, crumbs, salt, pepper, and egg together and form 2" meatballs. Place meatballs and remaining ingredients together in slow cooker. Cook on low for 3-4 hours.

COCKTAIL MEATBALLS 7

Prep time: 20 minutes

Cook time: 3-4 hours

Ingredients

1 pound lean ground beef
1 C bread crumbs
1 egg
Salt and pepper to taste
3 tbsp minced onion

1 C orange juice
1 C beef broth
1 tbsp brown sugar, packed
1 tbsp lemon juice

Directions

Mix ground beef, crumbs, salt, pepper, and egg together and form 2" meatballs. Place meatballs and remaining ingredients together in slow cooker. Cook on low for 3-4 hours.

COCKTAIL MEATBALLS 8

Prep time: 20 minutes

Cook time: 3-4 hours

Ingredients

1 pound lean ground beef
1 C bread crumbs
1 egg
Salt and pepper to taste
3 tbsp minced onion

2 C sweet & sour sauce
1 C beef broth
1 tbsp brown sugar, packed
1 tbsp lemon juice

Directions

Mix ground beef, crumbs, salt, pepper, and egg together and form 2" meatballs. Place meatballs and remaining ingredients together in slow cooker. Cook on low for 3-4 hours.

COCKTAIL MEATBALLS 9

Prep time: 20 minutes

Cook time: 3-4 hours

Ingredients
1 pound lean ground beef
1 C bread crumbs
1 egg
Salt and pepper to taste
3 tbsp minced onion

1 C raw honey
1 C beef broth
¼ C soya sauce
¼ C white vinegar

Directions
Mix ground beef, crumbs, salt, pepper, and egg together and form 2" meatballs. Place meatballs and remaining ingredients together in slow cooker. Cook on low for 3-4 hours.

COCKTAIL MEATBALLS 10

Prep time: 20 minutes

Cook time: 3-4 hours

Ingredients
1 pound lean ground beef
1 C bread crumbs
1 egg
Salt and pepper to taste

3 tbsp minced onion
1 C beef broth
1 C pure maple syrup
¼ C soya sauce

Directions
Mix ground beef, crumbs, salt, pepper, and egg together and form 2" meatballs. Place meatballs and remaining ingredients together in slow cooker. Cook on low for 3-4 hours.

POPCORN SNACK MIX 1

Prep time: 10 minutes

Cook time: 3 hours

Ingredients
7 C popped popcorn
½ C butter
¾ C brown sugar

1/3 C raw honey
1 C small pretzels

Directions
Combine all ingredients together in slow cooker. Cook on low for 3 hours, stirring every half hour.

POPCORN SNACK MIX 2

Prep time: 10 minutes

Cook time: 3 hours

Ingredients
7 C popped popcorn
½ C butter
¾ C brown sugar

1/3 C pure maple syrup
1 C small pretzels

Directions
Combine all ingredients together in slow cooker. Cook on low for 3 hours, stirring every half hour.

POPCORN SNACK MIX 3

Prep time: 10 minutes

Cook time: 3 hours

Ingredients
7 C popped popcorn
½ C butter
¾ C brown sugar
1/3 C raw honey

2 tsp ground cinnamon
2 C peanuts
1 C cashews
1 C small pretzels

Directions
Combine all ingredients together in slow cooker. Cook on low for 3 hours, stirring every half hour.

POPCORN SNACK MIX 4

Prep time: 10 minutes

Cook time: 3 hours

Ingredients
7 C popped popcorn
½ C butter
¾ C brown sugar
1/3 C raw honey

3 C mixed nuts
1 tsp ground cinnamon
½ tsp ground cloves
½ tsp ground nutmeg

Directions
Combine all ingredients together in slow cooker. Cook on low for 3 hours, stirring every half hour.

POPCORN SNACK MIX 5

Prep time: 10 minutes

Cook time: 3 hours

Ingredients
7 C popped popcorn
½ C butter
¾ C brown sugar

1/3 C Worcestershire sauce
1 tsp garlic powder
1 tsp onion powder

Directions
Combine all ingredients together in slow cooker. Cook on low for 3 hours, stirring every half hour.

POPCORN SNACK MIX 6

Prep time: 10 minutes

Cook time: 3 hours

Ingredients
7 C popped popcorn
½ C butter
¾ C brown sugar
1/3 C Worcestershire sauce
1 tsp garlic powder

1 tsp onion powder
1 tsp paprika
1 tsp chili powder
3 C peanuts

Directions
Combine all ingredients together in slow cooker. Cook on low for 3 hours, stirring every half hour.

POPCORN SNACK MIX 7

Prep time: 10 minutes

Cook time: 3 hours

Ingredients
7 C popped popcorn
½ C butter
¾ C brown sugar
1/3 C Worcestershire sauce

1 tbsp soya sauce
1 tsp garlic powder
3 C peanuts

Directions
Combine all ingredients together in slow cooker. Cook on low for 3 hours, stirring every half hour.

POPCORN SNACK MIX 8

Prep time: 10 minutes

Cook time: 3 hours

Ingredients
7 C popped popcorn
½ C butter
¾ C brown sugar
1/3 C Worcestershire sauce

1 tbsp teriyaki sauce
1 tsp garlic powder
1 tsp onion powder

Directions
Combine all ingredients together in slow cooker. Cook on low for 3 hours, stirring every half hour.

POPCORN SNACK MIX 9

Prep time: 10 minutes   Cook time: 3 hours

Ingredients
7 C popped popcorn   1 tbsp soya sauce
½ C butter   1 tbsp teriyaki sauce
¾ C brown sugar   1 tsp garlic powder
1/3 C Worcestershire sauce   1 tsp paprika

Directions
Combine all ingredients together in slow cooker. Cook on low for 3 hours, stirring every half hour.

POPCORN SNACK MIX 10

Prep time: 10 minutes   Cook time: 3 hours

Ingredients
7 C popped popcorn   1 tsp garlic powder
½ C butter   1 tsp onion powder
1/3 C Worcestershire sauce

Directions
Combine all ingredients together in slow cooker. Cook on low for 3 hours, stirring every half hour.

CHOCOLATE CANDY 1

Prep time: 10 minutes   Cook time: 3 hours

Ingredients
2 pounds unsalted peanuts   2 C semisweet chocolate chips
4 squares sweet baker's chocolate   2 pounds dark almond bark

Directions
Place ingredients together in slow cooker. Cook on low for 3 hours. Stir until smooth. Line a baking sheet with waxed paper, and drop mixture by spoonfuls. Allow to cool completely.

CHOCOLATE CANDY 2

Prep time: 10 minutes   Cook time: 3 hours

Ingredients
2 pounds unsalted cashews   3 C milk chocolate chips
4 squares semi-sweet baker's chocolate   1 C Chinese noodles
2 C semisweet chocolate chips

Directions
Place ingredients except Chinese noodles together in slow cooker. Cook on low for 3 hours. Stir until smooth, adding noodles. Line a baking sheet with waxed paper, and drop mixture by spoonfuls. Allow to cool completely.

CHOCOLATE CANDY 3

Prep time: 10 minutes

Cook time: 3 hours

Ingredients
1 pound unsalted peanuts
1 pound mixed nuts
8 squares sweet baker's chocolate

1 C semisweet chocolate chips
2 pounds milk chocolate almond bark

Directions
Place ingredients together in slow cooker. Cook on low for 3 hours. Stir until smooth. Line a baking sheet with waxed paper, and drop mixture by spoonfuls. Allow to cool completely.

CHOCOLATE CANDY 4

Prep time: 10 minutes

Cook time: 3 hours

Ingredients
2 pounds unsalted peanuts
4 squares sweet baker's chocolate
2 C semisweet chocolate chips

2 pounds dark almond bark
2 C Thompson's raisins
1 C shredded coconut

Directions
Place ingredients together in slow cooker. Cook on low for 3 hours. Stir until smooth. Line a baking sheet with waxed paper, and drop mixture by spoonfuls. Allow to cool completely.

CHOCOLATE CANDY 5

Prep time: 10 minutes

Cook time: 3 hours

Ingredients
2 pounds mixed nuts
4 squares sweet baker's chocolate
2 C semisweet chocolate chips

2 pounds dark almond bark
2 C broken brittle candy

Directions
Place ingredients together in slow cooker. Cook on low for 3 hours. Stir until smooth. Line a baking sheet with waxed paper, and drop mixture by spoonfuls. Allow to cool completely.

White Chocolate Candy 1

Prep time: 10 minutes

Cook time: 3 hours

Ingredients

2 pounds unsalted peanuts
4 squares sweet baker's white chocolate

2 C white chocolate chips
2 pounds white almond bark

Directions

Place ingredients together in slow cooker. Cook on low for 3 hours. Stir until smooth. Line a baking sheet with waxed paper, and drop mixture by spoonfuls. Allow to cool completely.

White Chocolate Candy 2

Prep time: 10 minutes

Cook time: 3 hours

Ingredients

2 pounds unsalted peanuts
4 squares white baker's chocolate
2 C white chocolate chips

2 pounds white almond bark
1 C raisins
1 C dried cranberries

Directions

Place ingredients together in slow cooker. Cook on low for 3 hours. Stir until smooth. Line a baking sheet with waxed paper, and drop mixture by spoonfuls. Allow to cool completely.

White Chocolate Candy 3

Prep time: 10 minutes

Cook time: 3 hours

Ingredients

4 squares white baker's chocolate
2 C white chocolate chips
2 pounds white almond bark

25 crushed candy canes
1 tsp peppermint extract

Directions

Place ingredients together in slow cooker. Cook on low for 3 hours. Stir until smooth. Line a baking sheet with waxed paper, and drop mixture by spoonfuls. Allow to cool completely.

WHITE CHOCOLATE CANDY 4

Prep time: 10 minutes

Cook time: 3 hours

Ingredients
2 pounds unsalted cashews
4 squares white baker's chocolate
2 C white chocolate chips

2 pounds white almond bark
2 C miniature marshmallows

Directions
Place ingredients except marshmallows together in slow cooker. Cook on low for 3 hours. Stir until smooth, and add marshmallows. Line a baking sheet with waxed paper, and drop mixture by spoonfuls. Allow to cool completely.

WHITE CHOCOLATE CANDY 5

Prep time: 10 minutes

Cook time: 3 hours

Ingredients
2 pounds unsalted mixed nuts
4 squares white baker's chocolate
2 C white chocolate chips

2 pounds white almond bark
1 C Chinese noodles
1 C Skor bits

Directions
Place ingredients except Skor bits and Chinese noodles together in slow cooker. Cook on low for 3 hours. Stir until smooth, and add Skor bits and Chinese noodles. Line a baking sheet with waxed paper, and drop mixture by spoonfuls. Allow to cool completely.

CHICKEN BITES 1

Prep time: 10 minutes

Cook time: 3 hours

Ingredients
2 C cubed chicken breast, browned
2 C sweet & sour sauce

1 garlic clove, minced

Directions
Combine ingredients together in slow cooker. Cook on low for 3 hours.

CHICKEN BITES 2

Prep time: 10 minutes

Cook time: 3 hours

Ingredients
2 C cubed chicken breast, browned
2 C dry garlic sauce

1 garlic clove, minced

Directions
Combine ingredients together in slow cooker. Cook on low for 3 hours.

CHICKEN BITES 3

Prep time: 10 minutes

Cook time: 3 hours

Ingredients
2 C cubed chicken breast, browned
2 C spaghetti sauce

1 garlic clove, minced

Directions
Combine ingredients together in slow cooker. Cook on low for 3 hours.

CHICKEN BITES 4

Prep time: 10 minutes

Cook time: 3 hours

Ingredients
2 C cubed chicken breast, browned
2 C chicken gravy

1 garlic clove, minced
Salt and pepper to taste

Directions
Combine ingredients together in slow cooker. Cook on low for 3 hours.

CHICKEN BITES 5

Prep time: 10 minutes

Cook time: 3 hours

Ingredients
2 C cubed chicken breast, browned
2 C cream of chicken soup

1 garlic clove, minced
Salt and pepper to taste

Directions
Combine ingredients together in slow cooker. Cook on low for 3 hours.

CHICKEN BITES 6

Prep time: 10 minutes

Cook time: 3 hours

Ingredients
2 C cubed chicken breast, browned
1 can cream of celery soup
1 C water
1 celery stalk, chopped

1 garlic clove, minced
1 small onion, minced
Salt and pepper to taste

Directions
Combine ingredients together in slow cooker. Cook on low for 3 hours.

CHICKEN BITES 7

Prep time: 10 minutes

Cook time: 3 hours

Ingredients
2 C cubed chicken breast, browned
1 C spaghetti sauce

1 garlic clove, minced
Salt and pepper to taste

Directions
Combine ingredients together in slow cooker. Cook on low for 3 hours.

CHICKEN BITES 8

Prep time: 10 minutes

Cook time: 3 hours

Ingredients
2 C cubed chicken breast, browned
2 C teriyaki dipping sauce
1 C sliced carrots

1 garlic clove, minced
Salt and pepper to taste

Directions
Combine ingredients together in slow cooker. Cook on low for 3 hours.

CHICKEN BITES 9

Prep time: 10 minutes

Cook time: 3 hours

Ingredients
2 C cubed chicken breast, browned
1 large can stewed, diced tomatoes, not drained
1 C tomato juice

1 garlic clove, minced
1 small onion, minced
Salt and pepper to taste

Directions
Combine ingredients together in slow cooker. Cook on low for 3 hours.

CHICKEN BITES 10

Prep time: 10 minutes

Cook time: 3 hours

Ingredients
2 C cubed chicken breast, browned
1 can cranberry jelly
1 C barbecue sauce

1 tbsp soya sauce
1 garlic clove, minced

Directions
Combine ingredients together in slow cooker. Cook on low for 3 hours.

COCKTAIL WIENERS 1

Prep time: 10 minutes

Cook time: 3 hours

Ingredients

2 16-ounce packages miniature smoked sausage links

1 C grape jelly
1 C barbecue sauce

Directions

Combine all ingredients together in slow cooker. Cook on low for 3 hours.

COCKTAIL WIENERS 2

Prep time: 10 minutes

Cook time: 3 hours

Ingredients

2 16-ounce packages miniature smoked sausage links
1 can cranberry jelly

1 C barbecue sauce
1 tbsp yellow mustard

Directions

Combine all ingredients together in slow cooker. Cook on low for 3 hours.

COCKTAIL WIENERS 3

Prep time: 10 minutes

Cook time: 3 hours

Ingredients

2 16-ounce packages miniature smoked sausage links

2 C cream of mushroom soup

Directions

Combine all ingredients together in slow cooker. Cook on low for 3 hours.

COCKTAIL WIENERS 4

Prep time: 10 minutes

Cook time: 3 hours

Ingredients

2 16-ounce packages miniature smoked sausage links

1 C beef broth
1 C cream of beef soup

Directions

Combine all ingredients together in slow cooker. Cook on low for 3 hours.

COCKTAIL WIENERS 5

Prep time: 10 minutes

Cook time: 3 hours

Ingredients
2 16-ounce packages miniature smoked sausage links

2 C sweet & sour sauce

Directions
Combine all ingredients together in slow cooker. Cook on low for 3 hours.

COCKTAIL WIENERS 6

Prep time: 10 minutes

Cook time: 3 hours

Ingredients
2 16-ounce packages miniature smoked sausage links

2 C dry garlic sauce

Directions
Combine all ingredients together in slow cooker. Cook on low for 3 hours.

COCKTAIL WIENERS 7

Prep time: 10 minutes

Cook time: 3 hours

Ingredients
2 16-ounce packages miniature smoked sausage links

2 C teriyaki dipping sauce

Directions
Combine all ingredients together in slow cooker. Cook on low for 3 hours.

COCKTAIL WIENERS 8

Prep time: 10 minutes

Cook time: 3 hours

Ingredients
2 16-ounce packages miniature smoked sausage links
1 C raw honey

1 C apple cider
½ C barbecue sauce

Directions
Combine all ingredients together in slow cooker. Cook on low for 3 hours.

COCKTAIL WIENERS 9

Prep time: 10 minutes   Cook time: 3 hours

Ingredients

2 16-ounce packages miniature smoked   2 C barbecue sauce
sausage links

Directions

Combine all ingredients together in slow cooker. Cook on low for 3 hours.

COCKTAIL WIENERS 10

Prep time: 10 minutes   Cook time: 3 hours

Ingredients

2 16-ounce packages miniature smoked   2 C spaghetti sauce
sausage links

Directions

Combine all ingredients together in slow cooker. Cook on low for 3 hours.

Cakes

WHITE CAKE 1

Prep time: 10 minutes

Cook time: 3 hours

Ingredients
1 ½ C flour
1 C sugar
1 C milk
½ C butter

1 egg
1 tsp baking soda
1 tsp vanilla extract

Directions
Mix cake ingredients as usual. Line slow cooker with parchment paper. Pour cake batter into slow cooker. Cook on low for 3 hours, and allow to cool for ½ hour before cutting.

WHITE CAKE 2

Prep time: 10 minutes

Cook time: 3 hours

Ingredients
1 ½ C flour
1 C sugar
1 C milk
½ C butter

1 egg
1 tsp baking soda
1 tsp coconut extract
1 C shredded coconut

Directions
Mix cake ingredients as usual. Line slow cooker with parchment paper. Pour cake batter into slow cooker. Cook on low for 3 hours, and allow to cool for ½ hour before cutting.

WHITE CAKE 3

Prep time: 10 minutes

Cook time: 3 hours

Ingredients
1 ½ C flour
1 C sugar
1 C milk
½ C butter

1 egg
1 tsp baking soda
1 tsp strawberry extract
1 C dehydrated strawberries, dredged in flour

Directions
Mix cake ingredients as usual. Line slow cooker with parchment paper. Pour cake batter into slow cooker. Cook on low for 3 hours, and allow to cool for ½ hour before cutting.

WHITE CAKE 4

Prep time: 10 minutes

Cook time: 3 hours

Ingredients

1 ½ C flour
1 C sugar
1 C milk
½ C butter

1 egg
1 tsp baking soda
1 tsp vanilla extract
1 C mini M&M's

Directions

Mix cake ingredients as usual. Line slow cooker with parchment paper. Pour cake batter into slow cooker. Cook on low for 3 hours, and allow to cool for ½ hour before cutting.

WHITE CAKE 5

Prep time: 10 minutes

Cook time: 3 hours

Ingredients

1 ½ C flour
1 C sugar
1 C milk
½ C butter

1 egg
1 tsp baking soda
1 tsp vanilla extract
½ C peanut butter

Directions

Mix cake ingredients as usual. Line slow cooker with parchment paper. Pour cake batter into slow cooker. Cook on low for 3 hours, and allow to cool for ½ hour before cutting.

WHITE CAKE 6

Prep time: 10 minutes

Cook time: 3 hours

Ingredients

1 ½ C flour
1 C sugar
1 C milk
½ C butter

1 egg
1 tsp baking soda
1 tsp vanilla extract
1 C strawberry preserves

Directions

Mix cake ingredients as usual. Line slow cooker with parchment paper. Pour cake batter into slow cooker. Cook on low for 3 hours, and allow to cool for ½ hour before cutting.

WHITE CAKE 7

Prep time: 10 minutes   Cook time: 3 hours

Ingredients

1 ½ C flour   1 egg
1 C sugar   1 tsp baking soda
1 C milk   1 tsp vanilla extract
½ C butter   1 C chocolate chips

Directions

Mix cake ingredients as usual. Line slow cooker with parchment paper. Pour cake batter into slow cooker. Cook on low for 3 hours, and allow to cool for ½ hour before cutting.

WHITE CAKE 8

Prep time: 10 minutes   Cook time: 3 hours

Ingredients

1 ½ C flour   1 egg
1 C sugar   1 tsp baking soda
1 C milk   1 tsp vanilla extract
½ C butter   1 C blueberries dredged in flour

Directions

Mix cake ingredients as usual. Line slow cooker with parchment paper. Pour cake batter into slow cooker. Cook on low for 3 hours, and allow to cool for ½ hour before cutting.

WHITE CAKE 9

Prep time: 10 minutes   Cook time: 3 hours

Ingredients

1 ½ C flour   1 egg
1 C sugar   1 tsp baking soda
1 C milk   1 tsp vanilla extract
½ C butter   Red, purple, and pink food coloring

Directions

Mix cake ingredients as usual. Line slow cooker with parchment paper. Pour cake batter into slow cooker. Cook on low for 3 hours, and allow to cool for ½ hour before cutting.

White Cake 10

Prep time: 10 minutes

Cook time: 3 hours

Ingredients

1 ½ C flour
1 C sugar
1 C milk
½ C butter
1 egg

1 tsp baking soda
1 tsp lemon extract
2 tbsp lemon zest
2 tbsp lemon juice

Directions

Mix cake ingredients as usual. Line slow cooker with parchment paper. Pour cake batter into slow cooker. Cook on low for 3 hours, and allow to cool for ½ hour before cutting.

Chocolate Cake 1

Prep time: 10 minutes

Cook time: 3 hours

Ingredients

¾ C flour
¾ C cocoa
1 ½ C sugar
½ C butter

3 large eggs, separated
1 tsp vanilla extract
½ tsp baking powder

Directions

Mix cake ingredients as usual. Line slow cooker with parchment paper. Pour cake batter into slow cooker. Cook on low for 3 hours, and allow to cool for ½ hour before cutting.

Chocolate Cake 2

Prep time: 10 minutes

Cook time: 3 hours

Ingredients

¾ C flour
¾ C cocoa
1 ½ C sugar
½ C butter

3 large eggs, separated
1 tsp vanilla extract
½ tsp baking powder
1 C chocolate chips

Directions

Mix cake ingredients as usual. Line slow cooker with parchment paper. Pour cake batter into slow cooker. Cook on low for 3 hours, and allow to cool for ½ hour before cutting.

Chocolate Cake 3

Prep time: 10 minutes

Cook time: 3 hours

Ingredients

¾ C flour
¾ C cocoa
1 ½ C sugar
½ C butter
3 large eggs, separated

1 tsp vanilla extract
½ tsp baking powder
1 tbsp hot water
2 tsp instant coffee

Directions

Mix cake ingredients as usual. Line slow cooker with parchment paper. Pour cake batter into slow cooker. Cook on low for 3 hours, and allow to cool for ½ hour before cutting.

Chocolate Cake 4

Prep time: 10 minutes

Cook time: 3 hours

Ingredients

¾ C flour
¾ C cocoa
1 ½ C sugar
½ C butter

3 large eggs, separated
1 tsp vanilla extract
½ tsp baking powder
1 C hot fudge sauce

Directions

Mix cake ingredients as usual. Line slow cooker with parchment paper. Pour cake batter into slow cooker. Cook on low for 3 hours, and allow to cool for ½ hour before cutting.

Chocolate Cake 5

Prep time: 10 minutes

Cook time: 3 hours

Ingredients

¾ C flour
¾ C cocoa
1 ½ C sugar
½ C butter
3 large eggs, separated

1 tsp vanilla extract
½ tsp baking powder
1 large milk chocolate bar, chopped
½ C raisins

Directions

Mix cake ingredients as usual. Line slow cooker with parchment paper. Pour cake batter into slow cooker. Cook on low for 3 hours, and allow to cool for ½ hour before cutting.

CHOCOLATE CAKE 6

Prep time: 10 minutes

Cook time: 3 hours

Ingredients

¾ C flour
¾ C cocoa
1 ½ C sugar
½ C butter
3 large eggs, separated

1 tsp vanilla extract
½ tsp baking powder
1 C toasted shredded coconut
½ C finely chopped peanuts

Directions

Mix cake ingredients as usual. Line slow cooker with parchment paper. Pour cake batter into slow cooker. Cook on low for 3 hours, and allow to cool for ½ hour before cutting.

CHOCOLATE CAKE 7

Prep time: 10 minutes

Cook time: 3 hours

Ingredients

¾ C flour
¾ C cocoa
1 ½ C sugar
½ C butter
3 large eggs, separated

1 tsp vanilla extract
½ tsp baking powder
1 tbsp hot water
1 tbsp instant coffee
½ C chocolate covered coffee beans

Directions

Mix cake ingredients as usual. Line slow cooker with parchment paper. Pour cake batter into slow cooker. Cook on low for 3 hours, and allow to cool for ½ hour before cutting.

CHOCOLATE CAKE 8

Prep time: 10 minutes

Cook time: 3 hours

Ingredients

¾ C flour
¾ C cocoa
1 ½ C sugar
½ C butter

3 large eggs, separated
1 tsp vanilla extract
½ tsp baking powder
1 C caramel sauce

Directions

Mix cake ingredients as usual. Line slow cooker with parchment paper. Pour cake batter into slow cooker. Cook on low for 3 hours, and allow to cool for ½ hour before cutting.

CHOCOLATE CAKE 9

Prep time: 10 minutes

Cook time: 3 hours

Ingredients
¾ C flour
¾ C cocoa
1 ½ C sugar
½ C butter
3 large eggs, separated

1 tsp vanilla extract
½ tsp baking powder
½ C toffee bits
½ C chocolate chips
½ C fudge sauce

Directions
Mix cake ingredients as usual. Line slow cooker with parchment paper. Pour cake batter into slow cooker. Cook on low for 3 hours, and allow to cool for ½ hour before cutting.

CHOCOLATE CAKE 10

Prep time: 10 minutes

Cook time: 3 hours

Ingredients
¾ C flour
¾ C cocoa
1 ½ C sugar
½ C butter
3 large eggs, separated

1 tsp vanilla extract
½ tsp baking powder
1 C raspberry preserves
1 C raspberries dredged in flour

Directions
Mix cake ingredients as usual. Line slow cooker with parchment paper. Pour cake batter into slow cooker. Cook on low for 3 hours, and allow to cool for ½ hour before cutting.

BIRTHDAY CAKE 1

Prep time: 10 minutes

Cook time: 3 hours

Ingredients
3 C flour
2 C sugar
2 C milk
1 C butter

2 eggs
2 tsp baking soda
2 tsp vanilla extract

Directions
Mix cake ingredients as usual. Line slow cooker with parchment paper. Pour cake batter into slow cooker. Cook on low for 3 hours, and allow to cool for ½ hour before cutting.

BIRTHDAY CAKE 2

Prep time: 10 minutes

Cook time: 3 hours

Ingredients

3 C flour
2 C sugar
2 C milk
1 C butter

2 eggs
2 tsp baking soda
2 tsp vanilla extract
1 C birthday candy confetti

Directions

Mix cake ingredients as usual. Line slow cooker with parchment paper. Pour cake batter into slow cooker. Cook on low for 3 hours, and allow to cool for ½ hour before cutting.

BIRTHDAY CAKE 3

Prep time: 10 minutes

Cook time: 3 hours

Ingredients

3 C flour
2 C sugar
2 C milk
1 C butter

2 eggs
2 tsp baking soda
2 tsp strawberry extract

Directions

Mix cake ingredients as usual. Line slow cooker with parchment paper. Pour cake batter into slow cooker. Cook on low for 3 hours, and allow to cool for ½ hour before cutting.

BIRTHDAY CAKE 4

Prep time: 10 minutes

Cook time: 3 hours

Ingredients

3 C flour
2 C sugar
2 C milk
1 C butter
2 eggs

2 tsp baking soda
2 tsp vanilla extract
2 C toasted shredded coconut
1 C miniature marshmallows

Directions

Mix cake ingredients as usual. Line slow cooker with parchment paper. Pour cake batter into slow cooker. Cook on low for 3 hours, and allow to cool for ½ hour before cutting.

BIRTHDAY CAKE 5

Prep time: 10 minutes

Cook time: 3 hours

Ingredients
3 C flour
2 C sugar
2 C milk
1 C butter

2 eggs
2 tsp baking soda
2 tsp vanilla extract
2 C mini jelly beans dredged in flour

Directions
Mix cake ingredients as usual. Line slow cooker with parchment paper. Pour cake batter into slow cooker. Cook on low for 3 hours, and allow to cool for ½ hour before cutting.

BIRTHDAY CAKE 6

Prep time: 10 minutes

Cook time: 3 hours

Ingredients
3 C flour
2 C sugar
1 C milk
1 C applesauce

1 C butter
2 eggs
2 tsp baking soda
2 tsp vanilla extract

Directions
Mix cake ingredients as usual. Line slow cooker with parchment paper. Pour cake batter into slow cooker. Cook on low for 3 hours, and allow to cool for ½ hour before cutting.

BIRTHDAY CAKE 7

Prep time: 10 minutes

Cook time: 3 hours

Ingredients
3 C flour
2 C sugar
2 C milk
1 C butter

2 eggs
2 tsp baking soda
2 tsp vanilla extract
1 C dried red and green cherry pieces

Directions
Mix cake ingredients as usual. Line slow cooker with parchment paper. Pour cake batter into slow cooker. Cook on low for 3 hours, and allow to cool for ½ hour before cutting.

BIRTHDAY CAKE 8

Prep time: 10 minutes

Cook time: 3 hours

Ingredients
3 C flour
2 C sugar
2 C milk
1 C butter
2 eggs

2 tsp baking soda
2 tsp coconut extract
2 C shredded coconut
Red food coloring

Directions
Mix cake ingredients as usual. Line slow cooker with parchment paper. Pour cake batter into slow cooker. Cook on low for 3 hours, and allow to cool for ½ hour before cutting.

BIRTHDAY CAKE 9

Prep time: 10 minutes

Cook time: 3 hours

Ingredients
3 C flour
2 C sugar
2 C milk
1 C butter
2 eggs

2 tsp baking soda
2 tsp vanilla extract
½ C mini M&M's
½ C chocolate covered sunflower seeds
½ C chopped, unsalted cashews

Directions
Mix cake ingredients as usual. Line slow cooker with parchment paper. Pour cake batter into slow cooker. Cook on low for 3 hours, and allow to cool for ½ hour before cutting.

BIRTHDAY CAKE 10

Prep time: 10 minutes

Cook time: 3 hours

Ingredients
3 C flour
2 C sugar
2 C milk
1 C butter

2 eggs
2 tsp baking soda
2 tsp lemon extract
1 C mini gumdrops, dredged in flour

Directions
Mix cake ingredients as usual. Line slow cooker with parchment paper. Pour cake batter into slow cooker. Cook on low for 3 hours, and allow to cool for ½ hour before cutting.

Drinks

SIMPLE APPLE CIDER

Prep time: 5 minutes

Cook time: 2-3 hours

Ingredients
5 C apple cider
¼ C lemon juice
3 cinnamon sticks

2 tbsp ground cloves
1/3 C sugar

Directions
Combine cloves and cinnamon stick and place in a cheesecloth bag. Combine remaining ingredients in slow cooker and stir until sugar dissolves. Place spice bag in the liquid. Cook on low for 2-3 hours.

APPLE CIDER

Prep time: 5 minutes

Cook time: 2-3 hours

Ingredients
1 quart apple cider
1 cinnamon stick
½ tsp whole cloves

½ tsp ground allspice
¼ C brown sugar, packed

Directions
Combine cloves, cinnamon stick, and allspice, and place in a cheesecloth bag. Place cider and brown sugar in slow cooker and stir until sugar dissolves. Place spice bag in the liquid. Cook on low for 2-3 hours.

CARAMEL APPLE CIDER

Prep time: 5 minutes

Cook time: 2-3 hours

Ingredients
4 C apple cider or apple juice
2/3 C caramel sundae topping
2 tbsp lemon juice

1 cinnamon stick
1 tsp allspice

Directions
Combine allspice and cinnamon and place in a cheesecloth bag. Combine remaining ingredients in slow cooker, and add spice bag. Cook on low for 2-3 hours.

CHERRY CIDER

Prep time: Cook time:

Ingredients
1 gallon apple cider
2 packages cherry Jell-O

                                         1 cinnamon stick

Directions
Combine cider and cinnamon stick in slow cooker. Cook on high for 3 hours. Stir in Jell-O and cook on high for 1 hour.

ORANGE CIDER

Prep time: 5 minutes   Cook time: 2-3 hours

Ingredients
6 C orange juice
2 C water
3 C sugar

                                         5 cinnamon sticks
¼ C whole cloves

Directions
Combine cloves and cinnamon sticks and place in a cheesecloth bag. Place remaining ingredients in slow cooker and stir until sugar dissolves. Place spice bag in the liquid. Cook on low for 2-3 hours.

PEACH CIDER

Prep time: 5 minutes   Cook time: 5-6 hours

Ingredients
4 5.5-ounce cans peach nectar
2 C apple cider
½ tsp ground ginger

                                         ½ tsp ground cinnamon
½ tsp ground nutmeg

Directions
Combine all ingredients in slow cooker. Cook on low for 5-6 hours.

SPICED CIDER

Prep time: 5 minutes   Cook time: 2-3 hours

Ingredients
3 C apple juice
1 C orange juice
½ C sugar
3 tbsp lemon juice

                                         ½ tsp ground nutmeg
1 tsp ground cinnamon
1 tsp ground cloves

Directions
Combine all ingredients in slow cooker. Cook on low for 2-3 hours.

HOLIDAY CIDER

Prep time: 5 minutes

Cook time: 3-4 hours

Ingredients
8 C apple cider
4 C cranberry juice
2 C orange juice
½ C pineapple juice

½ C sugar
3 cinnamon sticks
1 tsp whole allspice
1 tsp whole cloves

Directions
Combine cinnamon, cloves, and allspice, and place in a cheesecloth bag. Combine remaining ingredients in slow cooker, stirring until sugar dissolves. Add spice bag. Cook on low for 3-4 hours.

PINEAPPLE/ORANGE CIDER

Prep time: 5 minutes

Cook time: 3-4 hours

Ingredients
2 quarts apple juice
1 C pineapple juice
1 C orange juice
2 tbsp brown sugar

1 tbsp lemon juice
5 whole cloves
5 orange slices, not peeled
5 cinnamon sticks

Directions
Combine all ingredients together in slow cooker. Cook for 3-4 hours. Strain out cinnamon, cloves, and orange slices before serving.

GRAPE CIDER

Prep time: 30 minutes

Cook time: 3 hours

Ingredients
5 pounds Concord grapes
8 C water
1 ½ C white sugar

5 cinnamon sticks
5 whole cloves

Directions
Combine grapes and 2 C water in a large saucepan. Bring to a boil, press through a strainer and cheesecloth, and put juice in the slow cooker. Add remaining ingredients. Cook on low for 3 hours. Strain to remove cinnamon sticks and cloves before serving.

APPLE CRANBERRY CIDER

Prep time: 5 minutes

Cook time: 2-3 hours

Ingredients
2 quarts apple cider
3 C cranberry juice
2 tbsp brown sugar

3 cinnamon sticks
5 whole cloves

Directions
Place cinnamon sticks and cloves in a cheesecloth bag. Combine remaining ingredients in slow cooker, and add spice bag. Cook on low for 2-3 hours.

PEAR CIDER

Prep time: 5 minutes

Cook time: 3-4 hours

Ingredients
10 C apple juice
5 C pear nectar

10 cinnamon sticks

Directions
Place cinnamon sticks in a cheesecloth bag. Combine juices in slow cooker, and add spice bag. Cook on low for 3-4 hours.

LEMONADE CIDER

Prep time: 5 minutes

Cook time: 2-3 hours

Ingredients
8 C apple cider
4 C lemonade

2 tbsp brown sugar, packed
10 cinnamon sticks

Directions
Place cinnamon sticks in a cheesecloth bag. Combine remaining ingredients in slow cooker, and add spice bag. Cook for 2-3 hours.

CITRUS CIDER

Prep time: 5 minutes

Cook time: 2-3 hours

Ingredients
2 quarts apple cider
1 C orange juice
2/3 C lemon juice

¼ C raw honey
6 cinnamon sticks
6 whole cloves

Directions
Place cinnamon sticks and cloves in a cheesecloth bag. Combine remaining ingredients in slow cooker, and add spice bag. Cook for 2-3 hours.

CIDER PUNCH

Prep time: 5 minutes

Cook time: 4-5 hours

Ingredients
4 C apple cider
2 ½ C water
1 C orange juice concentrate
1 tsp ground nutmeg

1 tsp ground ginger
2 tsp ground cinnamon
4-5 whole cloves

Directions
Place cloves in a cheesecloth bag. Place remaining ingredients in slow cooker and stir until sugar dissolves. Place spice bag in the liquid. Cook on low for 4-5 hours.

CINNAMON PUNCH

Prep time: 5 minutes

Cook time: 3-4 hours

Ingredients
1 quart apple cider
1 quart brewed tea
1 quart orange juice

1 quart pineapple juice
10 ounces Red Hots candies

Directions
Combine all ingredients together in slow cooker. Cook on low for 3-4 hours.

HOLIDAY PUNCH

Prep time: 5 minutes

Cook time: 3-4 hours

Ingredients
4 C cranberry juice
4 ½ C pineapple juice

1/3 C Red Hots candies

Directions
Combine all ingredients in slow cooker. Cook on low for 3-4 hours.

Spicy Punch

Prep time: 10 minutes   Cook time: 1 hour

Ingredients
4 C hot tea   1 ¼ C white sugar
4 C cranberry juice   1 C lemon juice
4 C apple juice, unsweetened   4 cinnamon sticks
2 C orange juice (no pulp)   15 whole cloves

Directions
Combine first 6 ingredients in slow cooker. Combine cloves and cinnamon sticks and place in a cheesecloth bag, and place in liquid. Cook on high for 1 hour.

Hot Pomegranate Punch

Prep time: 5 minutes   Cook time: 2-3 hours

Ingredients
5 C pomegranate juice   ½ C lemon juice
5 C apple juice   4 cinnamon sticks
2 C tea   15 whole cloves
½ C white sugar

Directions
Combine cloves and cinnamon sticks, and place in a cheesecloth bag. Place remaining ingredients in slow cooker and stir until sugar dissolves. Place spice bag in the liquid. Cook on low for 2-3 hours.

Ambrosia Punch

Prep time: 5 minutes   Cook time: 3-4 hours

Ingredients
4 C apple cider   3 cinnamon sticks
3 C apricot nectar   1 tsp gingerroot, finely minced
1 C peach nectar   1 tsp grated orange peel
½ C water   10 whole cloves
¼ C lemon juice

Directions
Combine cloves, cinnamon stick, gingerroot, and orange peel, and place in a cheesecloth bag. Place remaining ingredients in slow cooker and stir until sugar dissolves. Place spice bag in the liquid. Cook on low for 3-4 hours.

CRANBERRY PUNCH

Prep time: 5 minutes

Cook time: 2-3 hours

Ingredients
1 32-ounce bottle cranberry juice
1 11.5-ounce can frozen white grape/raspberry concentrate

4 C water
5 whole cloves
5 cinnamon sticks

Directions
Combine cloves and cinnamon sticks in a cheesecloth bag. Combine remaining ingredients in slow cooker and add spice bag. Cook on low for 2-3 hours.

TROPICAL PUNCH

Prep time: 5 minutes

Cook time: 2 hours, 15 minutes

Ingredients
5 C pineapple/orange/banana juice
2 C mango nectar
1 1/3 C water
¼ C raw honey

2 dashes aromatic bitters
2 tsp lime zest
2 12-ounce bottles ginger ale
2 tbsp lime juice

Directions
Combine all ingredients except ginger ale and lime juice together in slow cooker. Cook on low for 2 hours. Add ginger ale and lime juice, and cook on low for an additional 15 minutes.

VIENNESE COFFEE

Prep time: 10 minutes

Cook time: 3 hours

Ingredients
3 C coffee, strong and black
3 tbsp fudge syrup
1 tsp white sugar

1/3 C heavy cream
¼ C Irish cream liqueur

Directions
Combine coffee, syrup, and sugar in the slow cooker, and cook on low for 2 ½ hours. Add cream and Irish cream, and cook for another 30 minutes on low. Garnish with whipped cream.

SPICED COFFEE

Prep time: 5 minutes

Cook time: 2-3 hours

Ingredients
8 C coffee, black
1/3 C white sugar
1/3 C fudge syrup

4 cinnamon sticks
2 tsp whole cloves

Directions
Combine cloves, cinnamon stick, and allspice, and place in a cheesecloth bag. Place remaining ingredients in slow cooker and stir until sugar dissolves. Place spice bag in the liquid. Cook on low for 2-3 hours.

KAHLUA COFFEE

Prep time: 5 minutes

Cook time: 3-4 hours

Ingredients
2 quarts hot water
½ C Kahlua
¼ C crème de cacao
4 tbsp instant coffee

2 C heavy cream
1/3 C sugar
1 tsp vanilla

Directions
Combine Kahlua, crème de cacao, water, and instant coffee granules. Cook on low for 3-4 hours. Whip cream with sugar and vanilla, and serve with coffee.

CHAI TEA

Prep time: 10 minutes

Cook time: 8 hours

Ingredients
9 black tea bags
1 can sweetened condensed milk
3 ounces gingerroot, sliced thinly and peeled
25-30 whole cloves

15 crushed cardamom pods
4 cinnamon sticks
4 quarts water

Directions
Combine cloves, cardamom pods, cinnamon sticks, and gingerroot and place in a cheesecloth bag. Place bag and water in slow cooker. Cook on low for 8 hours. Add teabags, and steep for 5-10 minutes.

GINGER TEA

Prep time: 10 minutes

Cook time: 2-3 hours

Ingredients
4 C water, boiling
15 green tea bags
5 C white grape juice

2 tbsp raw honey
1 tbsp gingerroot, minced

Directions
Combine water and tea bags in slow cooker. Cover and steep for 10 minutes, and remove tea bags. Add remaining ingredients and cook on low for 2-3 hours.

SPICED GREEN TEA

Prep time: 15 minutes

Cook time: 5-6 hours

Ingredients
4 C brewed green tea
4 C orange juice

5 cinnamon sticks
1 tbsp crystallized ginger

Directions
Place cinnamon and ginger in a cheesecloth bag. Combine remaining ingredients in slow cooker, and add spice bag. Cook on low for 5-6 hours.

GINGER POMEGRANATE TEA

Prep time:

Cook time:

Ingredients
3 C pomegranate juice
3 C water
2 C apple cider
1 ½ C dry red wine

½ C sugar
1 cinnamon stick
3 tea bags

Directions
Combine all ingredients except tea bags in slow cooker. Cook on low for 5 hours. Add tea bags and let steep for 2 minutes. Remove tea bags before serving.

SPICED HOT CRANBERRY JUICE

Prep time: 5 minutes

Cook time: 2-3 hours

Ingredients
7 C water
5 C cranberry juice
1 C orange juice

¼ C lemon juice
10 whole cloves
1/3 C Red Hots candies

Directions
Place cloves in a cheesecloth bag. Place remaining ingredients in slow cooker and stir until sugar dissolves. Place spice bag in the liquid. Cook on low for 2-3 hours.

SPICED HOT WINE

Prep time: 5 minutes

Cook time: 4-5 hours

Ingredients
2 750-ml bottles red wine
½ C sugar
3 cinnamon sticks

4 whole cloves
1 tbsp lemon juice

Directions
Combine cloves and cinnamon sticks, and place in a cheesecloth bag. Place remaining ingredients in slow cooker and stir until sugar dissolves. Place spice bag in the liquid. Cook on low for 4-5 hours.

MULLED WINE

Prep time: 5 minutes

Cook time: 1 hour

Ingredients
2 750-ml bottles Merlot
½ C sugar
½ C brandy

½ C orange juice
5 cinnamon sticks
5 whole cloves

Directions
Combine cinnamon sticks and cloves, and place in a cheesecloth bag. Combine remaining ingredients in slow cooker, stirring until sugar dissolves. Cook on low for 1 hour.

WINE PUNCH

Prep time: 5 minutes

Cook time: 1 ½ hours

Ingredients
4 C cranberry juice
1 750-ml bottle dry white wine
1/3 C brown sugar, packed

5 whole cloves
3 cinnamon sticks

Directions
Combine cinnamon sticks and cloves, and place in a cheesecloth bag. Combine remaining ingredients except wine in slow cooker, stirring until sugar dissolves. Cook on low for 1 hour. Remove spice bag. Add wine, and cook for another 30 minutes on low.

HOT LEMON DRINK

Prep time: 5 minutes

Cook time: 2-3 hours

Ingredients
3 quarts water
3 C sugar
2 C orange juice
2/3 C lemon juice

¼ C pineapple juice
1 cinnamon stick
5 whole cloves

Directions
Combine cloves and cinnamon stick, and place in a cheesecloth bag. Place remaining ingredients in slow cooker and stir until sugar dissolves. Place spice bag in the liquid. Cook on low for 2-3 hours.

HOT DR. PEPPER

Prep time: 5 minutes

Cook time: 2-3 hours

Ingredients
8 C Dr. Pepper
¼ C brown sugar, packed
¼ C lemon juice

½ tsp ground allspice
½ tsp ground cloves
1 tsp ground cinnamon

Directions
Combine all ingredients in slow cooker. Cook on low for 2-3 hours.

Hot Coca Cola

Prep time: 5 minutes

Cook time: 2-3 hours

Ingredients

8 C Coca Cola
¼ C brown sugar, packed
¼ C lemon juice

½ tsp ground cloves
1 tsp ground cinnamon

Directions

Combine all ingredients in slow cooker. Cook on low for 2-3 hours.

Hot Root Beer

Prep time: 5 minutes

Cook time: 2-3 hours

Ingredients

8 C root beer
¼ C brown sugar, packed
¼ C lemon juice

½ tsp ground allspice
½ tsp ground cloves
1 tsp ground cinnamon

Directions

Combine all ingredients in slow cooker. Cook on low for 2-3 hours.

Hot Cream Soda

Prep time: 5 minutes

Cook time: 2-3 hours

Ingredients

8 C cream soda
¼ C brown sugar, packed

¼ C lemon juice
1 tsp ground cinnamon

Directions

Combine all ingredients in slow cooker. Cook on low for 2-3 hours.

Bourbon Citrus Drink

Prep time: 10 minutes

Cook time: 2.5 hours

Ingredients

6 C apple cider
½ C bourbon
¼ C sugar
8 cinnamon sticks

5 whole cloves
½ tsp anise seeds
1 large Naval orange, sliced
1 lemon, sliced

Directions

Combine all ingredients except orange and lemon slices together in slow cooker. Cook on low for 2 hours. Add lemon and orange slices, and cook for 30 minutes on low. Strain out spices before serving.

HOT CHOCOLATE 1

Prep time: 10 minutes

Cook time: 3 hours

Ingredients
2/3 C hot water
½ C unsweetened cocoa
1 cans sweetened condensed milk

1 ½ C heavy cream
6 C milk
2 tsp vanilla extract

Directions
Combine water and cocoa in slow cooker, stirring until smooth. Add remaining ingredients. Cook on low for 3 hours, stirring occasionally.

HOT CHOCOLATE 2

Prep time: 10 minutes

Cook time: 3 hours

Ingredients
2/3 C hot water
½ C unsweetened cocoa
1 cans sweetened condensed milk
1 ½ C heavy cream

6 C milk
2 tsp vanilla extract
2 tsp ground cinnamon

Directions
Combine water and cocoa in slow cooker, stirring until smooth. Add remaining ingredients. Cook on low for 3 hours, stirring occasionally.

HOT CHOCOLATE 3

Prep time: 10 minutes

Cook time: 3 hours

Ingredients
2/3 C hot water
½ C unsweetened cocoa
1 cans sweetened condensed milk

1 ½ C heavy cream
6 C milk
2 tsp raspberry extract

Directions
Combine water and cocoa in slow cooker, stirring until smooth. Add remaining ingredients. Cook on low for 3 hours, stirring occasionally.

HOT CHOCOLATE 4

Prep time: 10 minutes

Cook time: 3 hours

Ingredients
2/3 C hot water
½ C unsweetened cocoa
1 cans sweetened condensed milk

1 ½ C heavy cream
6 C milk
2 tsp coconut extract

Directions
Combine water and cocoa in slow cooker, stirring until smooth. Add remaining ingredients. Cook on low for 3 hours, stirring occasionally.

HOT CHOCOLATE 5

Prep time: 10 minutes

Cook time: 3 hours

Ingredients
2/3 C hot water
½ C unsweetened cocoa
1 cans sweetened condensed milk
1 ½ C heavy cream

6 C milk
2 tsp vanilla extract
1 C marshmallow fluff

Directions
Combine water and cocoa in slow cooker, stirring until smooth. Add remaining ingredients. Cook on low for 3 hours, stirring occasionally. Stir in fluff and serve.

HOT CHOCOLATE 6

Prep time: 10 minutes

Cook time: 3 hours

Ingredients
2/3 C hot water
½ C unsweetened cocoa
1 cans sweetened condensed milk

1 ½ C heavy cream
6 C milk
2 tsp orange extract

Directions
Combine water and cocoa in slow cooker, stirring until smooth. Add remaining ingredients. Cook on low for 3 hours, stirring occasionally.

Hot Chocolate 7

Prep time: 10 minutes

Cook time: 3 hours

Ingredients
2/3 C hot water
½ C unsweetened cocoa
1 cans sweetened condensed milk

1 ½ C heavy cream
6 C milk
2 tsp peppermint extract

Directions
Combine water and cocoa in slow cooker, stirring until smooth. Add remaining ingredients. Cook on low for 3 hours, stirring occasionally.

Hot Chocolate 8

Prep time: 10 minutes

Cook time: 3 hours

Ingredients
2/3 C hot water
½ C unsweetened cocoa
1 cans sweetened condensed milk

1 ½ C heavy cream
6 C milk
½ tsp anise

Directions
Combine water and cocoa in slow cooker, stirring until smooth. Add remaining ingredients. Cook on low for 3 hours, stirring occasionally.

Hot Chocolate 9

Prep time: 10 minutes

Cook time: 3 hours

Ingredients
2/3 C hot water
½ C unsweetened cocoa
1 cans sweetened condensed milk

1 ½ C heavy cream
6 C milk
2 tsp strawberry extract

Directions
Combine water and cocoa in slow cooker, stirring until smooth. Add remaining ingredients. Cook on low for 3 hours, stirring occasionally.

HOT CHOCOLATE 10

Prep time: 10 minutes

Cook time: 3 hours

Ingredients

2/3 C hot water
½ C unsweetened cocoa
1 cans sweetened condensed milk
1 ½ C heavy cream

6 C milk
2 tsp vanilla extract
2 tbsp Kahlua

Directions

Combine water and cocoa in slow cooker, stirring until smooth. Add remaining ingredients. Cook on low for 3 hours, stirring occasionally.

HOT CHOCOLATE 11

Prep time: 10 minutes

Cook time: 3 hours

Ingredients

2/3 C hot water
½ C unsweetened cocoa
1 cans sweetened condensed milk
1 ½ C heavy cream

6 C milk
2 tsp vanilla extract
1 ounce whiskey

Directions

Combine water and cocoa in slow cooker, stirring until smooth. Add remaining ingredients. Cook on low for 3 hours, stirring occasionally.

HOT CHOCOLATE 12

Prep time: 10 minutes

Cook time: 3 hours

Ingredients

2/3 C hot water
½ C unsweetened cocoa
1 cans sweetened condensed milk
1 ½ C heavy cream

6 C milk
2 tsp vanilla extract
1 ounce chocolate liqueur

Directions

Combine water and cocoa in slow cooker, stirring until smooth. Add remaining ingredients. Cook on low for 3 hours, stirring occasionally.

HOT CHOCOLATE 13

Prep time: 10 minutes

Cook time: 3 hours

Ingredients
2/3 C hot water
½ C unsweetened cocoa
1 cans sweetened condensed milk
1 ½ C heavy cream

6 C milk
2 tsp vanilla extract
1 ounce crème de menthe liqueur

Directions
Combine water and cocoa in slow cooker, stirring until smooth. Add remaining ingredients. Cook on low for 3 hours, stirring occasionally.

HOT CHOCOLATE 14

Prep time: 10 minutes

Cook time: 3 hours

Ingredients
2/3 C hot water
½ C unsweetened cocoa
1 cans sweetened condensed milk
1 ½ C heavy cream

6 C milk
2 tsp vanilla extract
1 ounce Irish cream

Directions
Combine water and cocoa in slow cooker, stirring until smooth. Add remaining ingredients. Cook on low for 3 hours, stirring occasionally.

HOT CHOCOLATE 15

Prep time: 10 minutes

Cook time: 3 hours

Ingredients
2/3 C hot water
½ C unsweetened cocoa
1 cans sweetened condensed milk
1 ½ C heavy cream

6 C milk
2 tsp vanilla extract
1 ounce cherry brandy

Directions
Combine water and cocoa in slow cooker, stirring until smooth. Add remaining ingredients. Cook on low for 3 hours, stirring occasionally.

HOT CHOCOLATE 16

Prep time: 10 minutes

Cook time: 2 hours

Ingredients
1 1/3 C hot water
4 tbsp cocoa
2 C semi-sweet chocolate chips
2 cans sweetened condensed milk

2 tsp ground cinnamon
2 tsp chili powder
4 C milk

Directions
Combine cocoa and hot water in slow cooker and stir until cocoa is dissolved. Add remaining ingredients and stir well. Cook on low for 2 hours, stirring every half hour.

HOT CHOCOLATE 17

Prep time: 10 minutes

Cook time: 4 hours

Ingredients
5 C milk
½ C cocoa
½ C Nutella

½ C sugar
1 C hot water

Directions
Combine cocoa and hot water in slow cooker and stir until cocoa is dissolved. Add remaining ingredients and stir well. Cook on low for 4 hours, stirring every half hour.

HOT CHOCOLATE 18

Prep time: 10 minutes

Cook time: 4 hours

Ingredients
5 C French roast brewed coffee
2 ½ C milk

2 C chocolate syrup
½ C peppermint syrup

Directions
Combine all ingredients together in slow cooker. Cook on low for 4 hours, stirring occasionally.

HOT CHOCOLATE 19

Prep time: 5 minutes

Cook time: 4 hours

Ingredients
5 C milk
½ C cocoa
½ C sugar

1 C hot water
¼ C caramel syrup
½ tsp coarse sea salt

Directions
Combine all ingredients together in slow cooker. Cook on low for 4 hours.

Hot Chocolate 20

Prep time: 5 minutes

Cook time: 3-4 hours

Ingredients
6 C dry powdered milk
2 C sugar
1 C French vanilla powdered coffee creamer

2 C Nesquick
1 box French vanilla pudding mix
6 C water

Directions
Combine all ingredients in slow cooker. Cook on low for 3-4 hours.

Hot Chocolate 21

Prep time: 5 minutes

Cook time: 3-4 hours

Ingredients
6 C dry powdered milk
2 C sugar
1 C hazelnut powdered coffee creamer

2 C Nesquick
1 box chocolate pudding mix
6 C water

Directions
Combine all ingredients in slow cooker. Cook on low for 3-4 hours.

Pumpkin Cinnamon Hot Toddy

Prep time: 5 minutes

Cook time: 3-4 hours

Ingredients
5 C water
½ C apple-cinnamon schnapps
½ C pure maple syrup

1 C rye whiskey
1/3 C canned pumpkin

Directions
Combine water, maple syrup, and pumpkin in the slow cooker. Cook on low for 3-4 hours. Stir in whiskey and schnapps and serve.

Chamomile Hot Toddy

Prep time:

Cook time:

Ingredients
1 750-ml bottle Riesling
2 C water
½ C brandy
8 chamomile tea bags

¼ C raw honey
5 whole cloves
1 lemon

Directions
Juice the lemon. Combine lemon juice, wine, water, lemon juice, honey, and cloves in the slow cooker. Cook on low for 2 hours. Add brandy and tea bags, cook for an additional 5 minutes, and remove tea bags.

CONCLUSION

We hope you have enjoyed browsing through all of the 1001 Slow Cooker Recipes. You now have meals for every day of the year, and then some, not to mention loads of great snack and drink recipes. Now, all you have to do is start playing with your slow cooker, and recreate these delicious meals on your own. Don't be afraid to experiment and change things around either. You never know what kind of delicious creations you will come up with.